American Indians:

A Select Catalog

of

National Archives

Microfilm Publications

WITHDRAWN

National Archives Trust Fund Board
U.S. General Services Administration
Washington, D.C.
1984

Library of Congress Cataloging in Publication Data

United States. National Archives and Records
    Service American Indians.

    Rev. ed. of: The American Indian. 1972.
    Includes index.
    1. Indians of North America—Government
relations—Sources—Bibliography—Microforms
catalogs. 2. Indians of North America—Government relations—Manuscripts—Microform catalogs. 3. United States. National Archives and
Research Service—Microform catalogs. 4. Documents on microfilm—Catalogs. I. United States.
National Archives and Records Service. American Indian. II. Title.
Z1209.053 1983 [E93] 016.3058'97'073 83-13412

ISBN 0-911333-09-6

Foreword

The National Archives and Records Service, a part of the General Services Administration, is responsible for administering the permanently valuable noncurrent records of the Federal Government. The holdings of the National Archives now amount to more than 1.3 million cubic feet. They date from the First Continental Congress and consist of the basic records of the legislative, judicial, and executive branches of Government. The Presidential libraries of Herbert Hoover, Franklin D. Roosevelt, Harry S. Truman, Dwight D. Eisenhower, John F. Kennedy, Lyndon B. Johnson, and Gerald R. Ford contain the papers of those Presidents and many of their associates in office. These research resources document significant events in our Nation's history, but most of them are preserved for continuing practical use in the ordinary processes of Government; for the protection of individual rights; and for the research use of scholars, students, and other individual researchers.

The National Archives Microfilm Publication Program

Since 1940, the National Archives has been microfilming selected groups of Federal records that have high research value. Under this program, negative microfilm is retained by the National Archives and positive prints are made from these master negatives and sold at moderate prices. The chief purposes of the program are to make archival sources more easily accessible to libraries, research centers, and individuals and to insure against loss of valuable information should the original records be destroyed. In this way, microfilm publications are a partial answer to the researcher's need for more extensive publication of archival materials, because they provide a relatively inexpensive method by which he or she can obtain facsimile reproductions of entire series of documents.

Although the microfilm publication program is one of the oldest continuing programs of the National Archives, it was not firmly established financially until 1948, when a grant of $20,000 from the Rockefeller Foundation provided for accelerated production of microfilm and insured the continuation of the program through the establishment of a revolving fund. By 1982, more than 175,000 rolls of master negative microfilm had been produced.

National Archives microfilm publications now provide basic documentation for research in the fields of American, European, Far Eastern, African, and Latin American history as well as in local history and genealogy. They are also valuable for work in other fields, such as economics, public administration, political science, law, and ethnology. As the program has developed, more emphasis has been placed on microfilming groups of records that are directly related to one another, as in the case of records relating to the same general subject or to a specific geographic area. In this way researchers can obtain reasonably complete documentation in many fields of interest. For example, a number of microfilm publications document diplomatic, consular, and naval relations between the United States and the Far Eastern countries of China, Japan, and Korea from the late 18th century. Similarly, almost complete coverage of relations between the United States and other countries throughout the world is provided. Microfilm publications have also been produced concerning the administration of affairs in individual territories of the United States.

Types of Microfilm Publications

National Archives microfilm publications are divided into two series, identified by "M" numbers and "T" numbers. In general, records selected for filming as "M" publications have high research value for a variety of studies, and the ratio of research value to volume is high. Usually each publication reproduces an entire series of records. Most "M" publications include explanatory material prepared by archivists to help researchers glean information from the filmed records more easily. "M" publications usually have an introduction that describes the origin, content, and arrangement of the filmed records and lists related records. Some introductions also include special aids, such as indexes and registers.

Descriptive pamphlets (DPs) are available for many "M" publications. Each pamphlet contains the publication's introduction (including special lists or indexes prepared to simplify the use of the microfilm publication) and a table of contents that identifies the material contained on each roll. "M" publications that have descriptive pamphlets are indicated in this catalog by the symbol DP at the end of a publication title. The pamphlets are made available on request to prospective purchasers so they can evaluate more thoroughly the value of the publication's contents for their research.

"T" publications, unlike "M" publications, do not usually reproduce a complete series of records; that is, they may contain only segments, by date or subject, of a larger series. In many cases, "T" publications were produced in response to specific reference requests. Also, over the years the National Archives has accessioned as record material microfilm produced by other Federal agencies. Some of this film, when it is not defense classified and is deemed of sufficient research value, is reproduced and made available for sale as "T" publications. These publications are reproduced and sold exactly as they were filmed; they contain no introductions, nor are descriptive pamphlets available for them. All of the Immigration and Naturalization Service (INS) records described in this catalog are "T" publications that were filmed by and accessioned from the INS.

Catalogs of Microfilm Publications

This catalog is one in a series describing National Archives microfilm publications related to subjects of high research interest. Each catalog is being compiled through an extensive review of all microfilmed records to locate publications relevant to each topic. The catalogs contain both detailed descriptions of the records and roll-by-roll listings for each publication.

The initial six catalogs in the series cover the following topics:

American Indians
Black Studies
Diplomatic Records
Genealogical and Biographical Research
Immigrant and Passenger Arrivals
Military Service Records

These catalogs are part of a larger effort undertaken by the National Archives Trust Fund to increase public awareness of the availability of the records in the National Archives and to improve access to them. If you have suggestions of new catalog topics, new types of products based on the holdings, or new ways in which the Trust Fund can help you with your research, please contact the National Archives Trust Fund Board (NJ), National Archives, Washington, D.C 20408.

Microfilm Pricing Policy

The price of each roll of microfilm in this catalog is $17. Prices are subject to change without advance public notice. Film can be bought as either individual rolls or a complete publication.

The microfilm price includes the cost of film stock, chemicals, boxes and reels, postage, and salaries. A fixed price per roll has been established because most of the costs of reproducing and selling microfilm are the same for all rolls of film, regardless of length. The establishment of such a price permits a substantial savings in order processing costs.

The National Archives microfilm publications program is financed from a trust fund established by the National Archives Trust Fund Board Act (44 U.S.C. 2307). Revenue received through the sale of microfilm publications is returned to the Trust Fund for use in financing additional publications and other products designed both to facilitate access to Federal records held by the National Archives and to make them more widely available to a larger portion of the public.

Microfilm Specifications

All microfilm sold through the National Archives Microfilm Publications program is silver-halide positive microfilm. Unless otherwise specified, it is 35mm reel microfilm, with plastic reels. Reduction ratios used range from 12:1 to 20:1. The number of frames on each reel varies.

In some instances, it is possible to obtain either microfilm in a different form (e.g., duplicate negative rather than positive) or paper copies. If you desire such services, please contact the Publications Sales Branch (NEPS), National Archives, Washington, DC 20408 (phone: 202-523-3181), for a price quotation.

Contents

Civilian Agency Records

Military Establishment Records

Introduction

This select catalog lists the records published on microfilm by the National Archives and Records Service (NARS) that relate directly to American Indians, to the formation of Federal Indian policy, and to the personnel who created or enforced that policy. The catalog is divided into civilian agency records and military establishment records. In each section, the publications containing the most information about Indians are listed first.

Brief narratives give the history of the office that created or accumulated the records, as well as the type, scope, and organization of the records themselves. In several cases, the narrative has been omitted because the publication titles are self-explanatory and the publication consists of only a single roll of microfilm. In other cases, narratives are used sparingly because the records on microfilm cover a broad range of subjects, only a few of which relate directly to American Indians. For such microfilm publications, only the rolls dealing primarily with Indian subjects are listed. However, when a microfilm publication relating to Indians and other subjects contains only a few rolls, all the rolls are listed. Rolls of microfilm may be purchased individually.

The narratives in this catalog are necessarily less detailed than the information contained in the descriptive pamphlets (DPs). Descriptive pamphlets contain explanations of the origin, content, and arrangement of records for most microfilm publications. Researchers wanting more information on individual publications that have DPs may want to consult them before ordering the publication. Because this select catalog lists only records published by NARS on microfilm, it reflects only a portion of manuscript material relating to Indians in the National Archives.

For more complete information on the subject, see *Guide to Records in the National Archives Relating to American Indians*, compiled by Edward E. Hill (1981), which is for sale from the National Archives Publications Sales Branch, NEPS, Washington, DC 20408. The *Guide* provides a comprehensive review and description of NARS records, including those on microfilm, that are concerned with American Indians and their relations to the American Government and the people of the United States. Indians who lived along the international boundaries of Canada and Mexico and in former colonies of European nations and who had direct contacts with, and were a matter of domestic concern to the United States, are within the scope of the *Guide*. The *Guide* does not include information about Indians in other parts of the Americas with whom the United States may have had more remote concern in the conduct of foreign affairs or who were the subject of a survey or study.

The records listed in this catalog are from the following record groups:

Record Group	Title
11	General Records of the United States Government
22	Records of the Fish and Wildlife Service
45	Naval Records Collection of the Office of Naval Records and Library
48	Records of the Office of the Secretary of the Interior
56	General Records of the Department of the Treasury
57	Records of the Geological Survey
59	General Records of the Department of State
75	Records of the Bureau of Indian Affairs
93	War Department Collection of Revolutionary War Records
94	Records of the Adjutant General's Office, 1780's–1917
107	Records of the Office of the Secretary of War
108	Records of the Headquarters of the Army
109	War Department Collection of Confederate Records
123	Records of the United States Court of Claims
153	Records of the Office of the Judge Advocate General (Army)
267	Records of the United States Supreme Court
360	Records of the Continental and Confederation Congresses and the Constitutional Convention
393	Records of United States Army Continental Commands, 1821–1920

This catalog revision was compiled by Cynthia G. Fox, with assistance from Robert H. Gruber, Robert M. Kvasnicka, Geraldine N. Phillips, Carmelita S. Ryan, and Edward E. Hill. The principal editor was Constance Potter.

CIVILIAN AGENCY RECORDS

Records of the Bureau of Indian Affairs (Record Group 75)

The Bureau of Indian Affairs, usually known as the Office of Indian Affairs, was established as a separate agency within the War Department in 1824. Congress established the position of Commissioner of Indian Affairs in 1832. The Office of Indian Affairs was transferred in 1849 to the newly created Department of the Interior, where it has remained. In 1947, the Office of Indian Affairs was renamed the Bureau of Indian Affairs.

Predecessors

Records of the Superintendent of Indian Trade

By 1795 the United States Government had begun operating factories, or posts, to trade with the Indians, and in 1806, the Office of Indian Trade was formally established.

Letters Sent, 1807–1823. M16. 6 rolls.

This publication includes handwritten copies of the outgoing correspondence of the Superintendents of Indian Trade with the Secretary of War, factors and other representatives of the Office of Indian Trade, Indian agents, the Secretary of the Treasury and other Treasury officials, the President, merchants, manufacturers, bankers, and others. The letters relate to the purchase of goods for the factories, the disposal of furs and other commodities received from the factories, the operation of the factories, annuity payments, accounts, and appointments, as well as to Indian trade and Indian affairs in general. Each volume is arranged chronologically, but there is some overlapping between volumes. Each volume is indexed by name of addressee.

Roll	Contents
1	Oct. 31, 1807–May 27, 1809
2	June 1, 1809–June 26, 1812
3	June 26, 1812–Apr. 18, 1816
4	Apr. 12, 1816–Apr. 11, 1818
5	Mar. 31, 1818–July 20, 1820

Roll	Contents
6	July 11, 1820–Apr. 18, 1823

Letters Received, 1806–1824. T58. 1 roll.

This series consists mainly of correspondence received by the Superintendents of Indian Trade. Included are incoming correspondence of the transportation agent and, after the closing of the Office of Indian Trade, of the principal agent for the liquidation of the factories. There are letters from factors, purchasing and transportation agents, the Secretary of War, the Secretary of the Treasury, merchants, members of missionary societies, and others interested in Indian trade or Indians generally. Also included are some drafts of outgoing correspondence, memorandums, and accounting records. For the most part, the letters are arranged chronologically, although sometimes letters received from one person during a calendar year are grouped together.

Trading Posts

Letterbook, Arkansas Trading House, 1805–1810. M142. 1 roll.

Records of the Creek Trading House, 1795–1816. M4. 1 roll.

Records of the Choctaw Trading House, 1803–1824. T500. 6 rolls.

Roll	Contents	Dates
1	Indent Book, 1805–20; miscellaneous accounts	1803–10
2	Miscellaneous accounts	1811–15
3	Miscellaneous accounts	1816–24
4	Daybooks	1808–13
5	Daybooks	1814–16
6	Daybooks	1817–19

Letterbook of the Natchitoches-Sulphur Fork Factory, 1809–1821. T1029. 1 roll.

Office of the Secretary of War

The two publications described below contain letters received and sent by the Office of the Secretary of War before the establishment of the Office of Indian Affairs in 1824. During this period, Indian affairs were handled directly by the Office of the Secretary of War. These records were transferred to the Office of Indian Affairs when it was established in 1824.

Letters Received by the Secretary of War Relating to Indian Affairs, 1800–1823. M271. 4 rolls.

This series primarily concerns Indians in the southern United States and the Seneca in New York. It represents only a small part of the original incoming correspondence relating to Indian affairs. The series contains correspondence from Indian superintendents and agents, factors of trading posts, Territorial and State governors, military commanders, Indians, and missionaries. Some drafts of letters sent, vouchers, receipts, requisitions, abstracts and statements, certificates of deposit, depositions, and newspapers are included. The records relate to the negotiation of Indian treaties, land reserves of individual Indians, mission schools, Government trading posts, issuance of licenses to private traders, distribution of annuities, slaves in Indian country, liquor control, investment of Indian moneys, accounts, and other subjects. The correspondence is arranged by year, thereunder alphabetically by the name of the writer, and thereunder chronologically by the date of the letter.

Roll	Dates
1	1800–16
2	1817–19
3	1820–21
4	1822–23

Letters Sent by the Secretary of War Relating to Indian Affairs, 1800–1824. M15. 6 rolls.

This series includes handwritten copies of letters to Territorial governors, Indian superintendents, Indian agents and subagents, the Superintendent of Indian Trade, factors of trading posts, military commanders, private traders, bankers, persons having commercial dealings with the Department, missionaries, Indians, and others. Some of the letters are noted as signed by clerks in the Department rather than by the Secretary, and a few are noted as signed by the President. Included are copies of addresses to Indian delegations, appointments, passports issued for travel in Indian country, and instructions to treaty commissioners. This series is arranged chronologically. Each volume is indexed alphabetically, primarily by name of addressee but sometimes by name of tribe or other principal subject.

Roll	Dates
1	Nov. 17, 1800–Apr. 20, 1804
2	Apr. 23, 1804–July 5, 1809
3	July 8, 1809–Dec. 31, 1816
4	Jan. 8, 1818–July 31, 1820
5	Aug. 3, 1820–Oct. 5, 1823
6	Oct. 28, 1823–Apr. 26, 1824

Correspondence of the Office of Indian Affairs (Central Office) and Related Records

Registers of Letters Received, 1824–1880. M18. 126 rolls.

These are registers for the records filmed as microfilm publication M234. Each letter includes the name of the writer; the date the letter was written; the date it was received, beginning in April 1834; the place where it was written; a summary of its contents; the jurisdiction or other heading under which the letter was filed; and, beginning in July 1836, the file number assigned to each letter upon its receipt.

Each volume is divided into alphabetical sections; the letters "i" and "j" were combined for registering and filing purposes. The registers contain some cross-references to enclosures and to letters registered under a name different from the expected one.

Roll	Dates
1	Jan. 1, 1824–Dec. 31, 1826
2	Jan. 1, 1827–Dec. 31, 1830
3	Jan. 1, 1831–Dec. 31, 1832
4	Jan. 1, 1833–Mar. 31, 1834
5	Apr. 1, 1834–Jan. 31, 1835
6	Feb. 1, 1835–Mar. 28, 1836
7	Mar. 29–Dec. 8, 1836
8	Dec. 9, 1836–June 2, 1837
9	June 3–Sept. 19, 1837
10	Sept. 20–Dec. 31, 1837
11	Jan. 1–Mar. 31, 1838
12	Apr. 1–June 12, 1838
13	June 12–Sept. 24, 1838
14	Sept. 25–Dec. 31, 1838
15	Jan. 1–Mar. 12, 1839
16	Mar. 13–July 31, 1839
17	Aug. 1, 1839–Jan. 31, 1840
18	Feb. 1–July 2, 1840
19	July 3, 1840–Feb. 27, 1841
20	Mar. 1–July 31, 1841
21	Aug. 1, 1841–Jan. 31, 1842
22	Feb. 1–June 30, 1842
23	July 1–Dec. 31, 1842
24	Jan. 1–May 31, 1843
25	June 1–Oct. 31, 1843
26	Nov. 1, 1843–Mar. 3, 1844
27	Mar. 4–June 26, 1844
28	June 25–Oct. 31, 1844
29	Nov. 1, 1844–Apr. 1, 1845
30	Apr. 1–Sept. 1, 1845
31	Sept. 1, 1845–Feb. 1, 1846
32	Feb. 1–Dec. 1, 1846
33	Dec. 1, 1846–June 30, 1847
34	July 1, 1847–Mar. 31, 1848
35	Apr. 1–Dec. 31, 1848
36	Jan. 1–Dec. 31, 1849
37	Jan. 1–Oct. 11, 1850
38	Oct. 12, 1850–Apr. 30, 1851
39	May 1–Dec. 31, 1851
40	Jan. 1–Dec. 31, 1852
41	Jan. 1–Oct. 4, 1853
42	Oct. 5, 1853–May 14, 1854
43	May 15, 1854–Jan. 3, 1855
44	Jan. 4–July 31, 1855

Roll	Dates
45	Aug. 1–Dec. 31, 1855
46	Jan. 1–June 30, 1856
47	July 1–Dec. 31, 1856
48	Jan. 1–June 30, 1857
49	July 1–Dec. 31, 1857
50	Jan. 1–June 30, 1858
51	July 1–Dec. 31, 1858
52	Jan. 1–June 30, 1859
53	July 1–Dec. 31, 1859
54	Jan. 1–May 31, 1860
55	June 1–Dec. 31, 1860
56	Jan. 1–June 30, 1861
57	July 1–Dec. 31, 1861
58	Jan. 1–June 30, 1862
59	July 1–Dec. 31, 1862
60	Jan. 1–June 30, 1863
61	July 1–Dec. 31, 1863
62	Jan. 1–May 31, 1864
63	June 1–Dec. 31, 1864
64	Jan. 1–June 30, 1865
65	July 1–Dec. 31, 1865
66	Jan. 1–Apr. 30, 1866
67	May 1–Aug. 31, 1866
68	Sept. 1–Dec. 31, 1866
69	Jan. 2–Mar. 31, 1867
70	Apr. 1–June 30, 1867
71	July 1–Sept. 30, 1867
72	Oct. 1–Dec. 31, 1867
73	Jan. 1–Mar. 31, 1868
74	Apr. 1–June 30, 1868
75	July 1–Sept. 30, 1868
76	Oct. 1–Dec. 31, 1868
77	Jan. 1–Mar. 31, 1869
78	Apr. 1–June 30, 1869
79	July 1–Sept. 20, 1869
80	Sept. 22–Dec. 31, 1869
81	Jan. 1–Mar. 30, 1870
82	Apr. 1–June 30, 1870
83	July 1–Sept. 3, 1870
84	Oct. 1–Dec. 31, 1870
85	Jan. 1–Mar. 31, 1871
86	Apr. 1–June 30, 1871
87	July 1–Sept. 30, 1871
88	Oct. 1–Dec. 31, 1871
89	Jan. 1–Mar. 31, 1872
90	Apr. 1–June 30, 1872
91	July 1–Sept. 30, 1872
92	Oct. 1–Dec. 31, 1872
93	Jan. 1–Mar. 31, 1873
94	Apr. 1–June 30, 1873
95	July 1–Sept 30, 1873
96	Oct. 1–Dec. 31, 1873
97	Jan. 1–Mar 31, 1874
98	Feb. 26–June 30, 1874
99	July 1–Sept. 30, 1874
100	Oct. 1–Dec. 31, 1874
101	Jan. 1–Mar. 31, 1875
102	Apr. 1–June 30, 1875
103	July 1–Sept. 30, 1875
104	Oct. 1–Dec. 31, 1875
105	Jan. 1–Mar. 31, 1876
106	Apr. 1–June 30, 1876
107	July 1–Sept. 30, 1876
108	Oct. 1–Dec. 31, 1876

Roll	Dates
109	Jan. 1–Mar. 31, 1877
110	Apr. 1–June 30, 1877
111	July 1–Sept. 30, 1877
112	Oct. 1–Dec. 31, 1877
113	Jan. 1–Mar. 31, 1878
114	Apr. 1–June 30, 1878
115	July 1–Sept. 30, 1878
116	Oct. 1–Dec. 31, 1878
117	Jan. 1–Apr. 30, 1879, A–M
118	Jan. 1–June 30, 1879, N–Z
119	May 1–Aug. 31, 1879, A–M
120	Sept. 1–Dec. 31, 1879, A–M
121	July 1–Dec. 31, 1879, N–Z
122	Jan. 1–May 31, 1880, A–M
123	June 1–Oct. 31, 1880, A–M
124	Nov. 1–Dec. 31, 1880, A–M
125	Jan. 1–May 31, 1880, N–Z
126	June 1–Dec. 31, 1880, N–Z

Letters Received, 1824–1881. M234. 962 rolls. DP.

This series contains incoming correspondence from all sources concerning Indian lands, emigration, treaty negotiations, subsistence, annuity payments, conflicts, depredations, claims, traders and licenses, population, education, progress in agriculture, health, employees, buildings, supplies, accounts, other administrative matters, and many other subjects relating to Indians and to the operations of the Bureau. The letters are arranged alphabetically by name of field jurisdiction (superintendency or agency) or other subject heading, thereunder by year, and thereunder in registry order (alphabetically by initial letter of surname or other designation of writer and thereunder chronologically by date of receipt). Letters relating to an agency for all or part of its existence may be filed under the agency's own name or under the name of the superintendency to which it was or had been responsible. The registers for these records have been filmed as microfilm publication M18.

Roll	Subject and Inclusive Dates
1	Alaska Agency, 1873–74
	Annuity goods, 1858–69
2	Annuity goods, 1870–78
	Apalachicola Agency, 1826–42
	Apalachicola Agency Reserves, 1841–42
	Arizona Superintendency, 1863–80
3	1863–69
4	1870–71
5	1872 (A747–H532)
6	1872 (I1117–W648)
7	1873 (A375–B1065)
8	1873 (C354–R515)
9	1873 (S391–W1764)
10	1874 (A45–I958)
11	1874 (I959–T205)
12	1874 (T215–W2061)
13	1875 (A49–H1624)
14	1875 (I5–S1786)
15	1875 (T26–W1803)
16	1876 (A11–L420)
17	1876 (M24–Z1)
18	1877 (A128–S1047)
19	1877 (S1048–Z4)
20	1878 (A4–I1568)

Roll	*Subject and Inclusive Dates*	Roll	*Subject and Inclusive Dates*
135	1824–29	191	1841–42
136	1830–35	192	1843
137	1836–39	193	1844
138	1840–43	194	1845
139	1844–49	195	1846–50
140	1850–52	196	1851–60
141	1853–55		Colorado Superintendency, 1861–80
142	1856–61, 1867–70	197	1861–64
	(Chickasaw Agency Emigration)	198	1865–66
143	1837–38	199	1867–68
144	1839–50	200	1869–70
	(Chickasaw Agency Reserves)	201	1871
145	1836–37	202	1872
146	1838–39	203	1873
147	1840–42	204	1874
148	1843–50	205	1875
	Chippewa Agency, 1851–80	206	1876
149	1851–53	207	1877
150	1854–55	208	1878 (A20–L861)
151	1856–57	209	1878 (M19–Y201)
152	1858–61	210	1879 (A2–M572)
153	1862–63	211	1879 (M602–S1094)
154	1864–65	212	1879 (S1131–W2608)
155	1866–67	213	1880 (A100–S1159)
156	1868–69	214	1880 (S1205–W2762)
157	1870		Council Bluffs Agency, 1836–57
158	1871	215	1836–43
159	1872	216	1844–46
160	1873	217	1847–51
161	1874	218	1852–57
162	1875		Creek Agency, 1824–76
163	1876	219	1824–25 (O)
164	1877	220	1825–(P)–1826
165	1878 (A239–K186)	221	1827–28
166	1878 (K207–Z3)	222	1829–31
167	1879	223	1832–33
168	1880; Chippewa Agency Emigration, 1850–59; and Chippewa Agency Reserves, 1853–55	224	1834–35
	Choctaw Agency, 1824–76	225	1836–38
169	1824–31	226	1839–42
170	1832–38	227	1843–47
171	1839–51	228	1848–52
172	1852–53	229	1853–56
173	1854	230	1857–63
174	1855–56	231	1864–68
175	1857–59	232	1869–70
176	1860–66	233	1871–72
177	1867–68	234	1873
178	1869	235	1874–76
179	1870–71		(Creek Agency, West)
180	1872–73	236	1826–36
181	1874		(Creek Agency Emigration)
182	1875	237	1826–36
183	1876	238	1837
	(Choctaw Agency, West)	239	1838–39
184	1825–38	240	1840–49
	(Choctaw Agency Emigration)		(Creek Agency Reserves)
185	1826–45	241	1832–34
186	1846–49	242	1835
187	1850–59	243	1836
	(Choctaw Agency Reserve)	244	1837
188	1833–35	245	1838
189	1836–37	246	1839
190	1838–40	247	1840–41
		248	1842–50

Roll	*Subject and Inclusive Dates*	Roll	*Subject and Inclusive Dates*
249	Crow Creek Agency, 1871–76; Crow Wing Agency, 1835–40		Grand River Agency, 1871–75
	Dakota Superintendency, 1861–80	305	1871–72
250	1861–67	306	1873–75
251	1868–70		Great Nemaha Agency, 1837–76
252	1871–73	307	1837–47
253	1874	308	1848–56
254	1875 (A47–I856)	309	1857–59
255	1875 (I865–W18421/2)	310	1860–62
256	1876 (A4–H893)	311	1863–64
257	1876 (H919–R310)	312	1865–68
258	1876 (R357–Y3)	313	1869–72
259	1877 (A6–D392)	314	1873–76
260	1877 (D395–L338)		Great Nemaha Agency Emigration, 1837–38
261	1877 (L358–W92)		Green Bay Agency, 1824–80
262	1877 (W94–Y159)	315	1824–32
263	1878 (A10–D541)	316	1833–37
264	1878 (D543–H853)	317	1838–39
265	1878 (H858–M1460)	318	1840–43
266	1878 (M1495–Y165)	319	1844–47
267	1879 (A4–D252)	320	1848–50
268	1879 (D264–G333)	321	1851–52
269	1879 (G341–O353)	322	1853–55
270	1879 (O354–Y151)	323	1856–60
271	1880 (A2–D141)	324	1861–64
272	1880 (D143–H1465)	325	1865–67
273	1880 (H1505–Y82)	326	1868–69
	Delaware Agency, 1855–73	327	1870–71
274	1855–57	328	1872
275	1858–61	329	1873
276	1862–64	330	1874
277	1865–66	331	1875
278	1867	332	1876
279	1868	333	1877
280	1869–73	334	1878
	Devils Lake Agency, 1871–80	335	1879
281	1871–73	336	1880
282	1874–76 (M889)		Idaho Superintendency, 1863–80
283	1876 (M930)–1878 (M452)	337	1863–67
284	1878 (M471)–1880	338	1868–69
285	Flandreau Agency, 1873–76	339	1870–71
	Florida Superintendency, 1824–53	340	1872
286	1824–26	341	1873
287	1827–31	342	1874
288	1832–37	343	1875
289	1838–50	344	1876
290	Florida Superintendency Emigration, 1828–38	345	1877 (A71–N692)
291	Florida Superintendency Emigration, 1839–53	346	1877 (N702–W1284)
	Florida Superintendency Reserves, 1839–47	347	1878 (A91–I2488)
	Fort Berthold Agency, 1867–80	348	1878 (K26–W691)
292	1867–70	349	1878 (W979–Y177)
293	1871–72	350	1879 (A231–N313)
294	1873–74	351	1879 (P104–W2625)
295	1875–76	352	1880 (A338–W40)
296	1877–78 (A908)	353	1880 (W56–W2658)
297	1878 (A910)–1879 (E361)		Indiana Agency, 1824–50
298	1879 (E362–W2331)	354	1824–34
299	1880	355	1835–37
	Fort Leavenworth Agency, 1824–51	356	1838–39
300	1824–36	357	1840
301	1837–42	358	1841
302	1843–48	359	1842
303	1849–51	360	1843–50
304	Fort Wayne Agency, 1824–30	361	Indiana Agency Emigration, 1833–49
			Indiana Agency Reserves, 1836–50

Roll	Subject and Inclusive Dates
362	Ioway Agency, 1825–37
363	Iowa Superintendency, 1838–49
	Kansas Agency, 1851–76
364	1851–55
365	1856–61
366	1862–64
367	1865–68
368	1869–71
369	1872–73
370	1874–76
	Kickapoo Agency, 1855–76
371	1855–63
372	1864–66
373	1867–71
374	1872–76
	Kiowa Agency, 1864–80
375	1864–68
376	1869–70
377	1871–72
378	1873
379	1874
380	1875
381	1876
382	1877
383	1878 (A263–H1917)
384	1878 (H1959)–1879 (H309)
385	1879 (H324–Y114)
386	1880
	La Pointe Agency, 1831–80
387	1831–39
388	1840–43
389	1844–47
390	1848–50
391	1855–59
392	1860–62
393	1863–66
394	1867–72
395	1873–74
396	1875–76
397	1877
398	1878
399	1879
400	1880
401	Lower Brule Agency, 1875–76
	Mackinac Agency, 1828–80
402	1828–38
403	1839–52
404	1853–55
405	1856–57
406	1858–61
407	1862–66
408	1867–69
409	1870–71
410	1872–73
411	1874–76
412	1877
413	1878
414	1879
415	1880
	Mackinac Agency Emigration, 1838–39
	Miami Agency, 1824–53
416	1824–41; 1846–50
417	Miami Agency Reserves, 1838–50
418	Miami Agency Emigration, 1842–53

Roll	Subject and Inclusive Dates
	Michigan Superintendency, 1824–51
419	1824–27
420	1828–31
421	1832–35
422	1836–37
423	1838–39
424	1840–41
425	1842–45
426	1846–51
427	Michigan Superintendency Emigration, 1830–48, and Michigan Superintendency Reserves, 1837–48
428	Minnesota Superintendency, 1849–56
	Miscellaneous, 1824–80
429	1824–26
430	1827
431	1828
432	1829
433	1830
434	1831–32
435	1833–35
436	1836
437	1837
438	1838
439	1839
440	1840
441	1841
442	1842–43
443	1844–45
444	1846
445	1847
446	1848–49
447	1850
448	1851
449	1852
450	1853
451	1854
452	1855
453	1856
454	1857
455	1858–59
456	1860–61
457	1862–63
458	1864–65
459	1866
460	1867
461	1868
462	1869
463	1870
464	1871
465	1872
466	1873 (A365–I1004)
467	1873 (K5–Y16)
468	1874 (A39–I1529)
469	1874 (I1536–W2009)
470	1875 (A5–P534)
471	1875 (P538–Y15)
472	1876 (A21–P265)
473	1876 (P266–W1530)
474	1877 (A16–R548)
475	1877 (S68–Y146)
476	1878 (A2–H1350)
477	1878 (H1375–O112)

Roll	Subject and Inclusive Dates	Roll	Subject and Inclusive Dates
478	1878 (P28–T91)		Nevada Superintendency, 1861–80
479	1878 (T112–Z31;2)	538	1861–69
480	1879 (A5–F221)	539	1870–71
481	1879 (F222–I2537)	540	1872–73
482	1879 (K72–S1632)	541	1874–75
483	1879 (S1655–Y88)	542	1876–77
484	1880 (A22–I551)	543	1878
485	1880 (I561–P1126)	544	1879
486	1880 (P1144–Z6)	545	1880
487	Miscellaneous Emigration, 1824–48		New Mexico Superintendency, 1849–80
	Montana Superintendency, 1864–80	546	1849–53
488	1864–68	547	1854–55
489	1869	548	1856–57
490	1870	549	1858–59
491	1871	550	1860–61
492	1872 (A88–V297)	551	1862–63
493	1872 (V298–W512)	552	1864–65
494	1873 (A386–E124)	553	1866
495	1873 (F34–S323)	554	1867
496	1873 (S324–W327)	555	1868
497	1873 (W328–W1757)	556	1869
498	1874 (A2–I231)	557	1870
499	1874 (I232–M1469)	558	1871
500	1874 (N93–W2048)	559	1872 (A667–P256)
501	1875 (A10–F546)	560	1872 (P257)–1873 (D315)
502	1875 (G20–R514)	561	1873 (D317–W1742)
503	1875 (S45–Y7)	562	1874 (A1–L334)
504	1876 (A7–I1174)	563	1874 (L336–Y11)
505	1876 (K5–Y17)	564	1875 (A8–S105)
506	1877 (A43–C1921)	565	1875 (S114–W1823)
507	1877 (D72–I861)	566	1876 (A5–G385)
508	1877 (K6–Y281;2)	567	1876 (G386–R92)
509	1878 (A47–E145)	568	1876 (R95–S663)
510	1878 (F1–I2484)	569	1876 (S676–W1374)
511	1878 (K25–V9)	570	1877 (A2–M931)
512	1878 (W101–Y176)	571	1877 (N44–P427)
513	1879 (A68–K345)	572	1877 (P431–W1238)
514	1879 (K362–P1344)	573	1878 (A8–I2047)
515	1879 (Q1–Y147)	574	1878 (I2064–T187)
516	1880 (A16–L1844)	575	1878 (T192–W2487)
517	1880 (M44–T1654)	576	1879 (A120–R383)
518	1880 (W15–Y279)	577	1879 (R384–T470)
	Nebraska Agencies, 1876–80	578	1879 (T471–Y11)
519	1876	579	1880 (A27–M1998)
520	1877 (A28–L100)	580	1880 (M2276–T9)
521	1877 (L108–W109)	581	1880 (T11–W240)
522	1877 (W121)–1878 (I1260)	582	1880 (W247–Y70)
523	1878 (I1306–O2)		New York Agency, 1829–80
524	1878 (O32–W2614)	583	1835–39
525	1879 (A15–K530)	584	1840–42
526	1879 (K531–V16)	585	1843–44
527	1879 (V22)–1880 (G94)	586	1845–47
528	1880 (G106–L532)	587	1848–51
529	1880 (L568–Y19)	588	1852–57
	Neosho Agency, 1831–75	589	1858–61
530	1831–47	590	1862–68
531	1848–58	591	1869–73
532	1859–61	592	1874–75
533	1862–65	593	1876
534	1866–67	594	1877
535	1868–69	595	1878
536	1870–71	596	1879–80
537	1872–75	597	New York Agency Emigration, 1829–51

Roll	Subject and Inclusive Dates
710	1879 (K911)–1880 (D335)
711	1880 (D353–H106)
712	1880 (H133–L1304)
713	1880 (L1313–Z11)
714	Raccoon River Agency, 1843–45
	Red Cloud Agency, 1871–80
715	1871
716	1872
717	1873
718	1874
719	1875
720	1876
721	1877
722	1878 (A5–I1975)
723	1878 (I1976–W2582)
724	1879 (A6–M2227)
725	1879 (M2228–W2595)
726	1880
727	Red River Agency, 1824–30
	Sac and Fox Agency, 1824–80
728	1824–33
729	1834–37
730	1838–40
731	1841–42
732	1843–50
733	1851–58
734	1859–61
735	1862–64
736	1865–66
737	1867–68
738	1869–70
739	1871–73
740	1874–75
741	1876
742	1877–78
743	1879
744	1880
	Sac and Fox Emigration, 1845–47, and Sac and Fox Agency Reserves, 1837–50
	Saginaw Agency, 1824–50
745	1824–39
746	1840–50
	St. Louis Superintendency, 1824–51
747	1824–26
748	1827–28
749	1829–31
750	1832–35
751	1836–38
752	1839–41
753	1842–45
754	1846–47
755	1848–49
756	1850–51, and St. Louis Superintendency Emigration, 1837–41
	St. Peter's Agency, 1824–70
757	1824–36
758	1837–39
759	1840–44
760	1845–50
761	1851–54
762	1855–58
763	1859–61
764	1862–65
765	1866–67

Roll	Subject and Inclusive Dates
766	1868–70, and St. Peter's Agency Reserves, 1839–49
767	Sandy Lake Agency, 1850–51, and Santa Fe Agency, 1849–51
	Santee Sioux Agency, 1871–76
768	1871–73
769	1874–76
	Sault Ste. Marie Agency, 1824–52
770	1824–41
771	1842–52
	Schools, 1824–73
772	1824–25
773	1826–28
774	1829–30
775	1831–32
776	1833–34
777	1835–36
778	1837–38
779	1839–40
780	1841–42
781	1843
782	1844–45
783	1846–47
784	1848–49
785	1850–51
786	1852–53
787	1854
788	1855
789	1856
790	1857
791	1858–59
792	1860–61
793	1862–63
794	1864–65
795	1866
796	1867–68
797	1869–70
798	1871
799	1872–73, and Schools Reserves, 1837–39
	Seminole Agency, 1824–76
800	1824–45
801	1846–55
802	1856–58
803	1859–67
804	1868–71
805	1872–76
	Seminole Agency Emigration, 1827–59
806	1827–46
807	1848–59
808	Seneca Agency in New York, 1824–32
	Shawnee Agency, 1855–76
809	1855–57
810	1858–59
811	1860
812	1861–62
813	1863–64
814	1865–66
815	1867
816	1868
817	1869
818	1870 (A637–G375)
819	1870 (G395–W1629)
820	1871

Roll	Subject and Inclusive Dates
821	1872–73
822	1874
823	1875–76
	Sisseton Agency, 1867–80
824	1867–71
825	1872–73
826	1874
827	1875
828	1876
829	1877–78
830	1879
831	1880
832	Six Nations Agency, 1824–34
	Southern Superintendency, 1851–71
833	1851–56
834	1857–62
835	1863–64
836	1865
837	1866–67
838	1868–69
839	1870–71
	Spotted Tail Agency, 1875–80
840	1875–76 (H338)
841	1876 (H345)–1877
842	1878 (A183–L394)
843	1878 (L395)–1879 (H400)
844	1879 (H606–W1923)
845	1880
	Standing Rock Agency, 1875–80
846	1875–76 (B829)
847	1876 (B835)–1877 (H181)
848	1877 (H182–W1124)
849	1878 (A295–W42)
850	1878 (W116)–1879
851	1880 (A81–S1874)
852	1880 (S1885–W2575)
	Stocks, 1836–73
853	1836–39
854	1840–45
855	1846–52
856	1853–63
857	1864–73
	Texas Agency, 1847–59
858	1847–52
859	1853–54
860	1855–57
861	1858–59
	Turkey River Agency, 1842–46
862	1842–43
863	1844–45
864	1846
	Union Agency, 1875–80
865	1875–76 (M1008)
866	1876 (M1025–W1364)
867	1877 (A54–P557)
868	1877 (R6–W1268)
869	1878 (A13–M168)
870	1878 (M196–Z1)
871	1879 (A7–L377)
872	1879 (L419–W1381)
873	1879 (W1415)–1880 (H647)
874	1880 (H665–L956)
875	1880 (L1113–S3875)

Roll	Subject and Inclusive Dates
876	1880 (T5–899)
877	1880 (T902–Y62)
	Upper Arkansas Agency, 1855–74
878	1855–64
879	1865–67
880	1868–70
881	1871–73
882	1874
	Upper Missouri Agency, 1824–74
883	1824–35
884	1836–51
885	1852–64
886	1865–66
887	1867–69
888	1870–74, and Upper Missouri Agency Reserve, 1837–49
	Upper Platte Agency, 1846–70
889	1846–56
890	1857–62
891	1863–66
892	1867
893	1868
894	1869
895	1870 (A628–D1020)
896	1870 (D1024–W1625)
	Utah Superintendency, 1849–80
897	1849–55
898	1856–58
899	1859–60
900	1861–62
901	1863–65
902	1866–69
903	1870–72
904	1873–74
905	1875–77
906	1878–80
	Washington Superintendency, 1853–80
907	1853–57, 1861–62
908	1863–64
909	1865–67
910	1868–69
911	1870–71
912	1872–73
913	1874
914	1875 (A18)–1876 (H716)
915	1876 (H722)–1877 (N848)
916	1877 (N886)–1878 (I1895)
917	1878 (I1912–W1910)
918	1878 (W1917)–1879 (S2604)
919	1879 (S2605)–1880 (M2502)
920	1880 (M2507–W2765)
	Western Superintendency, 1832–51
921	1832–36
922	1837–39
923	1840–46
924	1847–51, and Western Superintendency Emigration, 1836–42
	Whetstone Agency, 1871–74
925	1871–72
926	1873
927	1874
	Wichita Agency, 1857–78
928	1857–66

Roll	Subject and Inclusive Dates
929	1867–75
930	1876–78

Winnebago Agency, 1826–75

931	1826–47
932	1848–50
933	1851–53
934	1854–59
935	1860–62
936	1863
937	1864
938	1865
939	1866
940	1867
941	1868
942	1869–70
943	1871–72
944	1873
945	1874
946	1875
947	Winnebago Agency Emigration, 1833–52, and Winnebago Agency Reserves, 1836–47

Wisconsin Superintendency, 1836–48

948	1836–40
949	1841–48

Wyandot Agency, 1843–63, 1870–72

950	1843–49
951	1850–51, 1870–72
952	Wyandot Agency Emigration, 1839–51, and Wyandot Agency Reserves, 1845–63

Wyoming Superintendency, 1869–80

953	1869–71
954	1872–74
955	1875–77
956	1878
957	1879
958	1880

Yankton Agency, 1859–76

959	1859–63
960	1864–69
961	1870–72
962	1873–76

Historical Sketches for Jurisdictional and Subject Headings Used for the Letters Received by the Office of Indian Affairs. 1824–1880. T1105. 1 roll.

The historical sketches are brief histories of the Office's many major field units including information on the dates of establishment and discontinuance; tribes and geographical areas of responsibility; locations of headquarters, related units, and names and dates of appointment of superintendents and agents. A detailed analysis of the letters received is part of the descriptive pamphlet for M234.

Special Files, 1807–1904. M574. 85 rolls. DP.

The Special Files consist of correspondence, reports, accounts, affidavits, and other records that were brought together for easier reference. The records relate principally to claims and investigations, but include some other subjects. The claims were those of traders for goods furnished to Indians or to the Government, transportation contractors furnished to Indians or to the Government,

transportation contractors for shipping services, attorneys for legal fees, other persons for services to Indians or to the Government, both Indians and whites for losses from depredations, Indians for losses resulting from their removal from the East, and persons claiming the right to share in tribal benefits. Many of the claims were submitted in conformance with provisions of treaties between Indian tribes and the United States. The investigations, other than those of claims, related principally to the conduct of employees of the Office. The descriptive pamphlet contains an index of names and subjects and a list of file numbers, subjects, and date spans.

Most of the records in the series were withdrawn from the general incoming correspondence of the Office. But some records of special commissions, transmitted to the Office when their work was completed, also are included. Most of the files relate to a single subject. The inclusive dates of the series are those of the records in the files, usually the date of receipt in the Office or by a commission. The actual dates of individual documents, especially those submitted as evidence for claims, may be much earlier. Researchers should consult the descriptive pamphlet for a list of the subjects covered on each roll.

Letters Sent, 1824–1881. M21. 166 rolls. DP.

This series consists of handwritten copies of the general outgoing correspondence of the Office of Indian Affairs. Included are instructions to superintendents, agents, and other employees; and acknowledgments of and replies to incoming correspondence. Reports to the Secretary of War (or to the Secretary of the Interior after 1849) and to certain other officials, including chairmen of congressional committees, were copied in a separate series of volumes called "Report Books" (see M348).

Until 1869, the letters were copied in chronological order. Beginning in that year, two or more books were used simultaneously. Letters relating to certain broad subjects (such as land, finance, and civilization) were copied into separate books, but within each book the arrangement continued to be chronological. Most of the volumes are indexed by name of addressee and, to some extent, by subject. There are also marginal notations of the page numbers for other letters to the same person.

Roll	Dates
1	Mar. 18, 1824–May 3, 1825
2	May 4, 1825–May 31, 1826
3	June 1, 1826–Mar. 31, 1827
4	Apr. 1, 1827–June 5, 1828
5	June 5, 1828–June 7, 1829
6	June 8, 1829–July 30, 1830
7	Aug. 1, 1830–Dec. 31, 1831
8	Jan. 1–July 4, 1832
9	July 5, 1832–Jan. 27, 1833
10	Jan. 28–June 18, 1833
11	June 19–Dec. 31, 1833
12	Jan. 1–May 31, 1834
13	June 1–Sept. 30, 1834
14	Oct. 1, 1834–Jan. 31, 1835
15	Feb. 1–Apr. 28, 1835
16	Apr. 28–Aug. 23, 1835
17	Aug. 24, 1835–Jan. 31, 1836
18	Feb. 1–May 31, 1836
19	June 1–Sept. 30, 1836
20	Oct. 1, 1836–Jan. 27, 1837
21	Jan. 28–June 20, 1837

Roll	Dates
22	June 21–Nov. 27, 1837
23	Nov. 28, 1837–Mar. 31, 1838
24	Apr. 1–July 26, 1838
25	July 27, 1838–Jan. 30, 1839
26	Jan. 31–June 30, 1839
27	July 1–Dec. 31, 1839
28	Jan. 1–June 30, 1840
29	July 1–Dec. 31, 1840
30	Jan. 1–Aug. 1, 1841
31	Aug. 2, 1841–Feb. 23, 1842
32	Feb. 24–Oct. 2, 1842
33	Oct. 3, 1842–May 15, 1843
34	May 16, 1843–Feb. 25, 1844
35	Feb. 26–Oct. 15, 1844
36	Oct. 15, 1844–July 22, 1845
37	July 23, 1845–Mar. 20, 1846
38	Mar. 21–Oct. 31, 1846
39	Nov. 2, 1846–July 31, 1847
40	Aug. 2, 1847–May 31, 1848
41	June 1, 1848–Mar. 31, 1849
42	Apr. 1, 1849–Jan. 31, 1850
43	Feb. 1–Oct. 31, 1850
44	Nov. 1, 1850–July 20, 1851
45	July 21, 1851–Mar. 31, 1852
46	Apr. 1, 1852–Jan. 20, 1853
47	Jan. 21–Aug. 24, 1853
48	Aug. 25, 1853–Mar. 27, 1854
49	Mar. 28–Aug. 26, 1854
50	Aug. 27, 1854–Feb. 20, 1855
51	Feb. 21–June 12, 1855
52	June 13–Oct. 27, 1855
53	Oct. 28, 1855–Mar. 19, 1856
54	Mar. 20–July 31, 1856
55	July 31–Dec. 31, 1856
56	Jan. 1–May 25, 1857
57	May 26–Oct. 31, 1857
58	Nov. 1, 1857–Apr. 30, 1858
59	May 1–Oct. 23, 1858
60	Oct. 25, 1858–Apr. 29, 1859
61	Apr. 30–Aug. 23, 1859
62	Aug. 24, 1859–Feb. 9, 1860
63	Feb. 10–June 26, 1860
64	June 27–Dec. 7, 1860
65	Dec. 8, 1860–June 1, 1861
66	June 3–Oct. 23, 1861
67	Oct. 24, 1861–Mar. 25, 1862
68	Mar. 26–Aug. 7, 1862
69	Aug. 8, 1862–Jan. 20, 1863
70	Jan. 20–June 5, 1863
71	June 5–Oct. 14, 1863
72	Oct. 15, 1863–Jan. 8, 1864
73	Jan. 9–Apr. 23, 1864
74	Apr. 25–July 28, 1864
75	July 28–Dec. 7, 1864
76	Dec. 8, 1864–Apr. 4, 1865
77	Apr. 4–Aug. 3, 1865
78	Aug. 3–Dec. 8, 1865
79	Dec. 9, 1865–Apr. 6, 1866
80	Apr. 6–July 17, 1866
81	July 18–Oct. 26, 1866
82	Oct. 27, 1866–Apr. 18, 1867
83	Apr. 19–Aug. 2, 1867
84	Aug. 3–Nov. 14, 1867
85	Nov. 15, 1867–Feb. 25, 1868

Roll	Dates
86	Feb. 26–June 9, 1868
87	June 10–Sept. 24, 1868
88	Sept. 25, 1868–Jan. 13, 1869
89	Jan. 14–Apr. 30, 1869
90	Apr. 30–July 8, 1869
91	July 8–Oct. 14, 1869
92	Land and civilization, Aug. 2–Dec. 14, 1869
93	Finance and miscellaneous, Oct. 14, 1869–Mar. 12, 1870
94	Land and civilization, Dec. 15, 1869–Apr. 14, 1870
95	Finance and miscellaneous, Mar. 14–Aug. 3, 1870
96	Land and civilization, Apr. 15–Aug. 25, 1870
97	Finance and miscellaneous, Aug. 4–Dec. 30, 1870
98	Land and miscellaneous, Aug. 26–Dec. 21, 1870
99	Finance and miscellaneous, Jan. 3–May 23, 1871
100	Land and civilization, Dec. 22, 1870–Apr. 19, 1871
101	Finance and miscellaneous, May 24–Aug. 26, 1871
102	Land and civilization, Apr. 20–Aug. 24, 1871
103	Land and civilization, Aug. 25, 1871–Jan. 25, 1872
104	Finance and miscellaneous, Aug. 28–Dec. 18, 1871
105	Finance and miscellaneous, Dec. 19, 1871–Apr. 23, 1872
106	Land and civilization, Jan. 26–May 21, 1872
107	Finance and miscellaneous, Apr. 24–Oct. 16, 1872
108	Land and civilization, May 22–Oct. 8, 1872
109	Finance and miscellaneous, Oct. 17, 1872–Apr. 16, 1873
110	Land and civilization, Oct. 9, 1872–Mar. 21, 1873
111	Finance, Apr. 17–July 30, 1873
112	Land and civilization, Mar. 21–July 26, 1873
113	Finance, July 31–Nov. 15, 1873
114	Land and civilization, July 28–Dec. 20, 1873
115	Finance, Nov. 17, 1873–Mar. 17, 1874
116	Land and civilization, Dec. 20, 1873–Apr. 7, 1874
117	Finance, Mar. 18–July 15, 1874
118	Land and civilization, Apr. 7–Aug. 4, 1874
119	Finance, July 13–Sept. 21, 1874
120	Land and civilization, Aug. 5–Nov. 23, 1874
121	Finance, Sept. 22–Dec. 22, 1874
122	Land and civilization, Nov. 24, 1874–Mar. 20, 1875
123	Finance, Dec. 22, 1874–Apr. 3, 1875
124	Miscellaneous, Mar. 22–July 7, 1875
125	Finance, Apr. 3–June 24, 1875
126	Miscellaneous, July 8–Nov. 6, 1875
127	Finance, June 25–Sept. 25, 1875
128	Miscellaneous, Nov. 6, 1875–Mar. 18, 1876
129	Finance, Sept. 25, 1875–Jan. 19, 1876
130	Miscellaneous, Mar. 18–Aug. 28, 1876
131	Finance, Jan. 20–Apr. 20, 1876
132	Miscellaneous, Aug. 28, 1876–Mar. 22, 1877
133	Finance, Apr. 20–Aug. 21, 1876
134	Accounts, Nov. 17, 1876–Sept. 8, 1877
135	Finance, Aug. 21–Dec. 14, 1876
136	Miscellaneous, Mar. 22–Sept. 3, 1877
137	Finance, Dec. 14, 1876–Apr. 21, 1877

Roll	Dates
138	Miscellaneous, Sept. 3, 1877–Mar. 13, 1878
139	Finance, Apr. 20–Aug. 25, 1877
140	Accounts, Sept. 10, 1877–Apr. 10, 1878
141	Finance, Aug. 25–Dec. 15, 1877
142	Miscellaneous, Mar. 14–July 31, 1878
143	Accounts, Apr. 10–Sept. 23, 1878
144	Miscellaneous, July 31, 1878–Jan. 20, 1879
145	Finance, Dec. 17, 1877–Mar. 27, 1878
146	Accounts, Sept. 23, 1878–Feb. 1, 1879
147	Land, Jan. 2–Aug. 2, 1879
148	Accounts, Feb. 3–June 13, 1879
149	Accounts, June 13–Sept. 29, 1879
150	Miscellaneous, Jan. 21–Sept. 25, 1879
151	Accounts, Sept. 30, 1879–Jan. 26, 1880
152	Land, Aug. 2, 1879–Apr. 5, 1880
153	Finance, Mar. 27–July 10, 1878
154	Miscellaneous, Sept. 25, 1879–Oct. 15, 1880
155	Accounts, Jan. 26–June 15, 1880
156	Finance, July 11–Oct. 13, 1878
157	Accounts, June 15–Oct. 9, 1880
158	Land, Apr. 6, 1880–May 6, 1881
159	Miscellaneous, Oct. 16, 1880–Jan. 5, 1882
160	Finance, Oct. 16, 1878–Mar. 31, 1879
161	Finance, Apr. 1–July 31, 1879
162	Accounts, Oct. 11, 1880–Feb. 7, 1881
163	Finance, Aug. 1–Dec. 13, 1879
164	Finance, Dec. 15, 1879–May 4, 1880
165	Finance, May 4–Aug. 31, 1880
166	Finance, Sept. 1, 1880–Jan. 10, 1881

Report Books, 1838–1885. M348. 53 rolls. DP.

These Report Books contain manuscript copies of communications sent by the Office to members of the President's cabinet having supervisory responsibility for Indian affairs. The Report Books also contain some copies of letters to the President, Members of Congress, and other Government officials. During the early years of the Office, the letters to the President and the Members of Congress were often signed by the Secretary of War rather than by the Commissioner of Indian Affairs. The use of the Report Books to record letters to officials other than the supervising Secretary was gradually discontinued, and by 1870 Report Books contained only copies of letters to the Secretary of the Interior.

All communications to the Secretary were considered "reports." They range from extensive narratives, such as annual reports, to brief letters transmitting documents or recommending appointments. They relate to almost every aspect of the administration of Indian affairs, including the negotiation and enforcement of treaties; estimates and appropriations; legislation; investigations; claims (particularly for depredations); maintenance of order and military operations; liquor control; establishment of reservations, trust funds, and schools; the field organization of the Indian service; location of agencies; appointments; and employees, buildings, supplies, and accounts.

The letters were transcribed in chronological order, with some exceptions. Frequently, at the end of a volume there are some letters that were omitted from their proper date order in the book. Report Book 33 (reproduced on roll 33) contains many letters erroneously omitted from other volumes.

The earlier volumes have indexes to both subjects and addresses. There are also notations in the margin, opposite the copied document, that indicate the page number of the last preceding and the next succeeding letters to the same correspondent.

The original Report Books are on M825, *Selected Classes of Letters Received by the Indian Division of the Office of the Secretary of the Interior, 1849–1880.*

Roll	Dates
1	Nov. 25, 1838–Mar. 21, 1840
2	Mar. 21, 1840–Aug. 31, 1841
3	Sept. 1, 1841–Aug. 17, 1843
4	Aug. 18, 1843–Feb. 26, 1846
5	Feb. 27, 1846–July 25, 1848
6	July 25, 1848–June 23, 1851
7	June 28, 1851–Apr. 29, 1854
8	May 1, 1854–Aug. 9, 1855
9	Aug. 10, 1855–Dec. 31, 1856
10	Jan. 2, 1857–May 31, 1858
11	June 1, 1858–Aug. 29, 1860
12	Sept. 3, 1860–Dec. 11, 1862
13	Dec. 12, 1862–Aug. 19, 1864
14	Aug. 19, 1864–Dec. 11, 1865
15	Dec. 13, 1865–Sept. 29, 1866
16	Oct. 1, 1866–Oct. 25, 1867
17	Oct. 26, 1867–Oct. 31, 1868
18	Nov. 2, 1868–Aug. 23, 1869
19	Aug. 24, 1869–Sept. 9, 1870
20	Sept. 10, 1870–Sept. 6, 1871
21	Sept. 7, 1871–June 21, 1872
22	June 24, 1872–May 13, 1873
23	May 13, 1873–Jan. 17, 1874
24	Jan. 19–Aug. 7, 1874
25	Aug. 8, 1874–Mar. 13, 1875
26	Mar. 15–Sept. 28, 1875
27	Sept. 27, 1875–Apr. 4, 1876
28	Apr. 4, 1876–Mar. 13, 1877
29	Mar. 13–Dec. 29, 1877
30	Jan. 2–June 1, 1878
31	July 1–Dec. 19, 1878
32	Jan. 2–Apr. 12, 1879
33	Mar. 30, 1878–Oct. 19, 1882
34	Apr. 14–July 26, 1879
35	July 26–Dec. 31, 1879
36	Jan. 2–May 20, 1880
37	July 1–Nov. 30, 1880
38	Dec. 1, 1880–Mar. 31, 1881
39	Apr. 1–July 23, 1881
40	July 25–Dec. 31, 1881
41	Jan. 3–Apr. 12, 1882
42	Apr. 13–July 24, 1882
43	July 24–Dec. 19, 1882
44	Dec. 19, 1882–Apr. 30, 1883
45	May 1–Sept. 13, 1883
46	Sept. 14, 1883–Jan. 10, 1884
47	Jan. 10–Mar. 28, 1884
48	Mar. 28–June 30, 1884
49	July 1–Oct. 8, 1884
50	Oct. 9, 1884–Jan. 28, 1885
51	Jan. 28–Apr. 30, 1885
52	May 1–Aug. 17, 1885
53	Aug. 18–Nov. 12, 1885

Selected Letters Received by the Office of Indian Affairs Relating to the Cherokees of North Carolina, 1851–1905. M1059. 7 rolls. DP.

This microfilm publication reproduces selected letters received by the Office of Indian Affairs, 1851–1905, relating to the Cherokee of North Carolina, the establishment of their reserves, and related litigation. This file reflects the Office's somewhat sporadic involvement in matters concerning the North Carolina Cherokee. For this reason, for some years, the file contains few or no records.

The Office used two filing systems to arrange the records reproduced here. Letters received during 1851–75 are arranged by year, thereunder alphabetically by the correspondent's surname or the name of the organization, and thereunder numerically by register number. Letters received after 1875 are arranged by year, thereunder alphabetically by the writer's surname or by subject, and thereunder chronologically by the date received.

Roll	Dates
1	1851 and 1853–56
2	1857, 1859, 1868–69, 1872–75, and 1881–83
3	1884–85
4	1886–88
5	1889–93
6	1894–97
7	1898–1905 and undated

Superintendents' Annual Narrative and Statistical Reports from Field Jurisdictions of the Bureau of Indian Affairs, 1907–1938. M1011. 174 rolls. DP.

The annual narrative reports, 1910–38, and the annual statistical reports, 1920–35, reproduced in this publication are a continuation of the annual reports of the agents and superintendents that, prior to 1907, had been published as part of the *Annual Report of the Commissioner of Indian Affairs.* Between 1907 and 1909, the reports were printed in pamphlet form at Indian schools where printing was taught. No complete set of reports for these years is available in the National Archives, but a few scattered reports that were filed in the central correspondence of the Bureau of Indian Affairs are reproduced on roll 1.

In 1910, the narrative and statistical data were submitted as one report. Beginning in 1911, however, the annual reports had two separate parts, narrative and statistical. The statistical reports (not including the 1907–9 statistical reports in the central correspondence files) begin with 1920 because those for 1911–19 were destroyed with congressional authorization in 1932. The narrative report was not required after 1934, but certain jurisdictions, fewer in number each year, continued to submit them voluntarily. Most of the statistical reports submitted after 1935, along with selected sections of narrative reports, constitute another series of records that has not been included in this publication, and is not available on microfilm.

The annual narrative reports, 1910–38, document the operations and accomplishments at the agencies, schools, hospitals, and other field jurisdictions. The reports relate to law and order, health, land ownership, population, industries, forestry, allotments, land sales, and other subjects.

For the most part, the reports for 1907–9 that are reproduced on roll 1 are arranged chronologically and by type of report, thereunder alphabetically by the name of agency or other jurisdiction. No attempt has been made to interfile the narrative and statistical reports. The reports for Indian Territory (Five Civilized Tribes) are arranged chronologically, but their format does not permit an alphabetical arrangement by jurisdiction. The reports for 1910–38 are arranged alphabetically by name of agency or other jurisdiction and thereunder by year. For 1920–35, the narrative and statistical reports for each jurisdiction are interfiled. The arrangement of the sections of individual statistical reports varies from jurisdiction to jurisdiction and sometimes from year to year within a jurisdiction. Although the sections are numbered, the arrangement usually does not follow the numerical sequence. In some cases, all sections within a report relating to a single tribe under a particular jurisdiction are grouped together; in other instances, similarly numbered sections are grouped together regardless of the tribe involved.

The descriptive pamphlet that accompanies this publication includes a guide to frequent jurisdictional changes and other pertinent facts mentioned in the reports. It also shows the period covered by the reports for each jurisdiction.

Roll	Contents
1	Central Classified Files: 70945–07–031 General Services, Part I Narrative Reports
	Central Classified Files: 70945–07–031 General Services, Part II Statistical Reports
	Central Classified Files: 80012–08–032 Indian Territory Narrative Reports
	Central Classified Files: 13460–08–032 Indian Territory Narrative Reports
	Central Classified Files: 50536–08–031 General Services Statistical Reports
	Central Classified Files: 71848–09–031 Indian Territory Statistical Reports
2	Albuquerque School
3	Armstrong Academy
	Bay Mills School
	Bena School
	Bishop School
4	Bismarck School
5	Blackfeet
6	Blackfeet
	Bloomfield Seminary
	Cahuilla School
	Camp McDowell School
	Campo School
7	Camp Verde School
	Canton Insane Asylum
8	Canton Insane Asylum
	Cantonment School
9	Capitan Grande School
	Carlisle School
	Carson School
10	Carson School
11	Carson School
	Carter
	Carter Seminary
	Cass Lake School
	Charles H. Burke School
12	Cherokee Orphan Training School
	Cherokee School

Roll	Contents	Roll	Contents
13	Cherokee School		Greenville School
14	Cheyenne and Arapahoe	59	Greenville School
15	Cheyenne and Arapahoe		Haskell Institute
16	Cheyenne River	60	Haskell Institute
17	Cheyenne River	61	Haskell Institute
18	Chilocco School	62	Havasupai School
19	Chilocco School	63	Hayward School
20	Choctaw (Mississippi)	64	Hoopa Valley School
21	Choctaw and Chickasaw Hospital	65	Hoopa Valley School
	Claremore Hospital		Hope School
	Coeur d'Alene		Hopi
22	Coeur d'Alene	66	Hopi
23	Collins Institute		Independence School
	Colorado River		Jicarilla School
24	Colorado River	67	Jicarilla School
25	Colville		Jones Male Academy
26	Colville	68	Kaibab School
27	Consolidated Chippewa		Kaw School
28	Consolidated Chippewa		Kayenta Sanatorium
29	Consolidated Ute	69	Keshena
30	Crow	70	Keshena
31	Crow		Kickapoo School
	Crow Creek		Kiowa
32	Crow Creek	71	Kiowa
33	Cushman School	72	Kiowa
	Digger	73	Klamath
	Eastern Navajo	74	Klamath
34	Eastern Navajo	75	Klamath
	Euchee School		Lac du Flambeau
35	Eufaula School	76	Lac du Flambeau
36	Fallon School		Laguna Sanatorium
	Five Civilized Tribes	77	La Jolla School
37	Five Civilized Tribes		Laona
38	Five Civilized Tribes		La Pointe
39	Five Civilized Tribes	78	La Pointe
40	Five Civilized Tribes		Leech Lake
41	Flandreau School	79	Leupp
42	Flandreau School	80	Liquor Traffic, Suppression of
	Flathead		Lovelocks School
43	Flathead		Lower Brule
	Fond du Lac	81	Lower Brule
	Fort Apache		Mackinac
44	Fort Apache		Malki
45	Fort Belknap		Martinez School
46	Fort Belknap		Mekuskey Academy
	Fort Berthold	82	Mekuskey Academy
47	Fort Berthold		Menominee Mills
48	Fort Bidwell		Mesa Grande School
	Fort Hall		Mescalero
49	Fort Hall	83	Mescalero
50	Fort Hall		Mission
51	Fort Lapwai Sanatorium	84	Mission
	Fort Lapwai School	85	Mission
	Fort McDermitt School	86	Mission
52	Fort Mojave	87	Mission
	Fort Peck		Moapa River School
53	Fort Peck	88	Moapa River School
	Fort Shaw School		Moqui
54	Fort Totten School	89	Mount Pleasant School
55	Fort Totten School		Navajo
	Fort Yuma	90	Navajo
56	Fort Yuma		Navajo Springs School
57	Genoa School		Neah Bay School
	Goshute	91	Neah Bay School
	Grand Junction School	92	Nett Lake School
	Grand Portage School		Nevada School
58	Grand Rapids		New York
		93	New York

Roll	Contents
168	Western Shoshoni
	Wheelock Female Orphan Academy
169	Wheelock Female Orphan Academy
	White Earth
	Wind River
	Winnebago
170	Winnebago
	Winslow Sanatorium
	Wittenberg School
171	Yakima
172	Yakima
	Yankton
173	Yankton
174	Zuni

Procedural Issuances: Orders and Circulars, 1854-1955. M1121. 17 rolls.

This publication reproduces two types of procedural issuances used by the Bureau of Indian Affairs to disseminate instructions for the operation of the central office and field offices. Six series of records are reproduced. Unnumbered orders, 1884–1925, relate chiefly to organization, office procedure, the handling of correspondence, and personnel matters, intended primarily for the employees of the central office of the bureau, known before 1947 as the Office of Indian Affairs. The numbered orders, 1916–55, were directed to field officials and relate mainly to financial matters. Prior to 1916, directives of this nature were issued as circulars. Miscellaneous circulars, 1854–85, were usually intended for superintendents and agents in the field and they relate to procedural matters. Unnumbered circulars, 1926–50, and numbered circulars, 1907–50, were sent to field officials and were designed to issue instructions, explain policy, and request or provide information. The publication includes an index to circulars, orders, and other directives either issued or received by the Office of Indian Affairs that contains entries listed under 34 separate headings and classifications. Because this index was compiled in 1936, it does not cover all of the documents included in the publication, but separate indexes and document lists are included with most of the series.

Roll	Contents	Dates
1	Index to the circulars, orders, etc.	Compiled in 1936
	Unnumbered orders	Oct. 18, 1884–Nov. 13, 1913
2	Unnumbered orders	Nov. 14, 1913–Aug. 11, 1925
3	Numbered orders, 1–356	Jan. 29, 1916–June 5, 1930
4	Numbered orders, 357–568	July 23, 1930–Aug. 31, 1955
5	Miscellaneous circulars	1854–85
6	Unnumbered circulars	Oct. 12, 1926–Dec. 29, 1938
7	Unnumbered circulars	Jan. 3, 1939–Dec. 31, 1943
8	Unnumbered circulars	Jan. 4, 1944–Dec. 27, 1950
9	Numbered circulars, 160–599	July 8, 1907–Jan. 18, 1912
10	Numbered circulars, 600–1000	Jan. 23, 1912–June 25, 1915
11	Numbered circulars, 1001–1400	July 8, 1915–Mar. 5, 1918
12	Numbered circulars, 1401–1900	Mar. 5, 1918–June 30, 1923
13	Numbered circulars, 1901–2500	July 5, 1923–Oct. 3, 1928
14	Numbered circulars, 2501–3000	Oct. 6, 1927–ca. June 20, 1934
15	Numbered circulars, 3001–3399	June 22, 1934–Apr. 7, 1941
16	Numbered circulars, 3400–3576	Mar. 14, 1941–Feb. 13, 1945
17	Numbered circulars, 3577–3715	Feb. 15, 1945–Nov. 10, 1950

Letters of Tench Coxe, Commissioner of the Revenue, Relating to the Procurement of Military, Naval, and Indian Supplies, 1794–1796. M74. 1 roll.

Records Relating to Investigations of the Fort Phil Kearny ("Fetterman") Massacre, 1866–1867. M740. 1 roll. DP.

Records of the Superintendencies and Agencies of the Office of Indian Affairs

By the time the Office of Indian Affairs was established in 1824, the system of superintendencies and agencies was well organized. Superintendents had general responsibility for Indian affairs in a geographical area, usually a Territory, but sometimes a larger area. Their duties included the supervision of intertribal relationships in their jurisdiction and between the tribes and citizens of the United States or other persons, and the supervision of the conduct and accounts of agents responsible to them. Agents were immediately responsible for the affairs of one or more tribes. They attempted to preserve or restore peace and often tried to induce Indians to cede their lands and to move to areas less threatened by white encroachment. They also distributed money and goods and carried out other provisions of treaties with the Indians. Gradually, as the Indians were confined on reservations, the agents became more concerned with educating and "civilizing" them.

The records maintained by field offices relate to almost all aspects of Indian administration in the field. Records of a superintendency include those of the agencies over which it had jurisdiction. Sometimes records of reservation schools and other field units are included with the agency records. The kinds of records maintained did not vary much from jurisdiction to jurisdiction, although there are great differences in the quantities that have survived. Most of the correspondence of superintendents and independent agents was conducted with the central office of the Bureau, but considerable correspondence was exchanged between superintendents and agents within the superintendency. Also found is correspondence with other field officials and employees, Army officers, businessmen, and Indians.

Records of the Central Superintendency of Indian Affairs, 1813–1878. M856. 108 rolls. DP.

Roll	Description	Dates
1	Registers of correspondence with the Commissioner of Indian Affairs, vols. 1 and 2	1847–66
	Registers of letters received from the Commissioner of Indian Affairs, vols. 1 and 2	1866–78
2	Records of the St. Louis Superintendency	1813–50
3	Contracts, records concerning accounts, letters received from the Commissioner of Indian Affairs, records relating to agencies, and miscellaneous records	1851–57
4	Letters received from the Commissioner of Indian Affairs	1858
5	Records relating to agencies, miscellaneous letters received, contract bids, contracts, and records concerning accounts	1858
6	Letters received from the Commissioner of Indian Affairs	1859
7	Records relating to agencies, miscellaneous letters received, contracts, and records concerning accounts	1859
8	Letters received from the Commissioner of Indian Affairs	1860
9	Records relating to agencies, miscellaneous letters received, and letters received relating to surveys of lands in Kansas	1860
10	Contract bids, contracts, and records concerning accounts	1860
11	Letters received from the Commissioner of Indian Affairs	1861
12	Letters received relating to agencies	1861
13	Miscellaneous letters received, letters received relating to surveys of lands in Kansas, contract bids, and records concerning accounts	1861
14	Letters received from the Commissioner of Indian Affairs	1862
15	Letters received relating to agencies, miscellaneous letters received, and records concerning accounts	1862
16	Letters received from the Commissioner of Indian Affairs, letters received relating to agencies, miscellaneous letters	1863
17	Letters received from the Commissioner of Indian Affairs, letters received relating to agencies, miscellaneous letters received, and records concerning accounts	1864
18	Letters received from the Commissioner of Indian Affairs, letters received relating to agencies, miscellaneous letters received, and correspondence relating to councils with the Upper Arkansas Indians	1865
19	Records concerning accounts	1866
20	Letters received from the Commissioner of Indian Affairs	1866
21	Letters received relating to agencies and from special agents, miscellaneous letters received, contract bids, and records concerning accounts	1866
22	Letters received from the Commissioner of Indian Affairs and letters received relating to agencies	1867
23	Miscellaneous letters received, statistics, contract bids, and records concerning accounts	1867
24	Letters received from the Commissioner of Indian Affairs	1868
25	Letters received relating to agencies, miscellaneous letters received, and records concerning accounts	1868
26	Letters received from the Commissioner of Indian Affairs	1869
27	Letters received relating to agencies, miscellaneous letters received, and records concerning accounts	1869
28	Letters received from the Commissioner of Indian Affairs	1870
29	Letters received relating to the Cherokee, Creek, Delaware, Kansas (Kaw), Kickapoo, Kiowa, and Neosho (Indian Territory and Kansas) Agencies	1870
30	Letters received relating to the Osage River, Pawnee, Potawatomi, Sac and Fox, Seminole, Shawnee, Upper Arkansas, and Wichita Agencies, and records relating to an investigation of the Ottawa University	1870
31	Miscellaneous letters received, records of the General Council of the Indian Territory, letters received from Army field commands,	1870

Roll	Description	Dates
	contracts, and records concerning accounts	
32	Letters received from the Commissioner of Indian Affairs (Jan.–June)	1871
33	Letters received from the Commissioner of Indian Affairs (July–Dec.)	1871
34	Letters received relating to the Cherokee, Choctaw and Chickasaw, Creek, Kansas (Kaw), Kickapoo, Kiowa, and Neosho (Indian Territory and Kansas) Agencies	1871
35	Letters received relating to the Osage River, Potawatomi, Quapaw, Sac and Fox, Shawnee, Upper Arkansas, and Wichita Agencies	1871
36	Miscellaneous letters received (Jan.–June)	1871
37	Miscellaneous letters received (July–Dec.), letters received relating to the General Council of the Indian Territory, and letters received from Army field commands	1871
38	Contracts and records concerning accounts	1871
39	Letters received from the Commissioner of Indian Affairs (Jan.–June)	1872
40	Letters received from the Commissioner of Indian Affairs (July–Dec.)	1872
41	Letters received relating to the Cherokee, Choctaw and Chickasaw, Creek, Kansas (Kaw), Kickapoo, Kiowa, Neosho (Osage), and Potawatomi Agencies	1872
42	Letters received relating to the Quapaw, Sac and Fox, Seminole, Shawnee, Upper Arkansas, and Wichita Agencies	1872
43	Miscellaneous letters received (Jan.–June)	1872
44	Miscellaneous letters received (July–Dec.), letters received from Army field commands, contract bids, and records concerning accounts	1872
45	Letters received from the Commissioner of Indian Affairs (Jan.–June)	1873
46	Letters received from the Commissioner of Indian Affairs (July–Dec.)	1873
47	Letters received relating to the Cherokee, Choctaw and Chickasaw, Creek, Kansas (Kaw), Kickapoo, and Kiowa Agencies	1873
48	Letters received relating to the Neosho (Osage), Potawatomi, Quapaw, and Sac and Fox Agencies	1873
49	Letters received relating to the Seminole, Upper Arkansas, and Wichita Agencies	1873
50	Miscellaneous letters received (Jan.–June)	1873
51	Miscellaneous letters received (July–Dec.), telegrams received and sent, and letters received from Army field commands	1873
52	Contract bids, contracts, and records concerning accounts	1873
53	Letters received from the Commissioner of Indian Affairs (Jan.–June)	1874
54	Letters received from the Commissioner of Indian Affairs (July–Dec.)	1874
55	Letters received relating to the Cherokee, Consolidated Five Civilized Tribes, Kaw, Kickapoo, Kiowa, and Mexican Kickapoo Agencies	1874
56	Letters received relating to the Neosho (Osage), Potawatomi, and Quapaw Agencies; and records relating to Osage Indians killed by the Kansas State Militia on Aug. 7, 1874	1874
57	Letters received relating to the Sac and Fox, Seminole, Upper Arkansas, and Wichita Agencies	1874
58	Miscellaneous letters received (Jan.–June)	1874
59	Miscellaneous letters received (July–Dec.), letters received from Army field commands, contracts, and records concerning accounts	1874
60	Letters received from the Commissioner of Indian Affairs	1875
61	Letters received relating to the "Agency of the Captive Indians of the Indian Territory" and to the Cheyenne and Arapahoe Agency	1875
62	Letters received relating to the Agency for Indians in Kansas (Potawatomi Agency) and the Kiowa Agency	1875
63	Letters received relating to the Osage Agency	1875
64	Letters received relating to the Quapaw and the Sac and Fox Agencies	1875
65	Letters received relating to the Union and the Wichita Agencies	1875
66	Miscellaneous letters received (Jan.–June)	1875

Roll	Description	Dates
67	Miscellaneous letters received (July–Dec.), letters received from Army field commands, contract bids, and contracts	1875
68	Letters received from the Commissioner of Indian Affairs (Jan.–June)	1876
69	Letters received from the Commissioner of Indian Affairs (July–Dec.)	1876
70	Letters received relating to the "Agency of the Captive Indians of the Indian Territory" and to the Cheyenne and Arapahoe Agency	1876
71	Letters received relating to the Agency for Indians in Kansas (Potawatomi Agency) and the Kiowa Agency	1876
72	Letters received relating to the Osage and Kaw Agencies	1876
73	Letters received relating to the Pawnee and the Quapaw Agencies	1876
74	Letters received relating to the Sac and Fox and the Union Agencies	1876
75	Letters received relating to the Wichita Agency	1876
76	Miscellaneous letters received, letters received from Army field commands, contract bids, contracts, and records concerning accounts	1876
77	Letters received from the Commissioner of Indian Affairs (Jan.–June)	1877
78	Letters received from the Commissioner of Indian Affairs (July–Dec.)	1877
79	Letters received relating to the Cheyenne and Arapahoe Agency and the Agency for Indians in Kansas (Potawatomi Agency)	1877
80	Letters received relating to the Kiowa Agency	1877
81	Letters received relating to the Osage and Kaw Agencies	1877
82	Letters received relating to the Pawnee and the Ponca Agencies	1877
83	Letters received relating to the Quapaw and the Sac and Fox Agencies	1877
84	Letters received relating to the Union and the Wichita Agencies	1877
85	Miscellaneous letters received (Jan.–June)	1877
86	Miscellaneous letters received (July–Dec.), and letters received from Army field commands	1877

Roll	Description	Dates
87	Contract bids, contracts, and records concerning accounts	1877
88	Vouchers and receipts	1877
89	Supply Reports	1877
	Letters received and related records	1878
	Miscellaneous records relating to Indian lands in Kansas	ca. 1866–75
90	Registers of letters and endorsements sent to the Commissioner of Indian Affairs, vols. 1–3	Feb. 1, 1866–Jan. 12, 1878
91	Letters sent to the Commissioner of Indian Affairs (handwritten copies), vols. 1 and 2	May 23, 1855–Feb. 5, 1863
92	Letters sent to the Commissioner of Indian Affairs (handwritten copies), vols. 3 and 4	Feb. 14, 1863–Apr. 10, 1871
93	Letters sent to the Commissioner of Indian Affairs (handwritten copies), vol. 5	Apr. 12, 1871–Feb. 21, 1874
94	Letters sent to the Commissioner of Indian Affairs (handwritten copies), vols. 6 and 7	Feb. 21, 1874–Jan. 31, 1876
95	Letters sent to the Commissioner of Indian Affairs (press copies), vols. 1 and 2	Sept. 25, 1875–June 30, 1876
96	Letters sent to the Commissioner of Indian Affairs (press copies), vols. 3 and 4	July 3, 1876–Apr. 17, 1877
97	Letters sent to the Commissioner of Indian Affairs (press copies), vols. 5 and 6	Apr. 17, 1877–Jan. 15, 1878
98	Letters sent to agents (handwritten copies), vols. 1 and 2	Oct. 4, 1858–Aug. 22, 1871
99	Letters sent to agents (press copies), vols. 1 and 2	June 28, 1873–Dec. 25, 1873; Sept. 4, 1875–Jan. 31, 1876
	Registers of letters sent to agents, vols. 1–3	Feb. 1, 1876–Jan. 8, 1878
100	Letters sent to agents (press copies), vols. 3 and 4	Feb. 1, 1876–Mar. 3, 1877
101	Letters sent to agents (press copies), vols. 5–7	Mar. 3, 1877–Jan. 8, 1878
102	Miscellaneous letters sent (handwritten copies), vols. 1 and 2	July 25, 1853–July 11, 1871
103	Miscellaneous letters sent (press copies), vol. 1	Feb. 1, 1876–Mar. 16, 1877
104	Miscellaneous letters sent (press copies), vols. 2 and 3	Mar. 16, 1877–Jan. 12, 1878
	Unbound drafts and copies of letters sent	1866, 1868, and 1875
	Superintendent's reports	1874–78
105	Statements of funds received and other statements	1868–78
	Tabular statements of funds remitted	1876–77

Roll	Description	Dates
	Statements of receipts and disbursements, vols. 1 and 2	1872–78
	Ledger for receipts and disbursements	1874–78
106	Abstracts of disbursements, vols. 1–3	1849–76
107	Statements of account current	1849–67
	Statements of account current and property returns, vols. 1 and 2	1853–65
	Property returns	1865–76
108	Letters sent by the disbursing agent at St. Louis, vols. 1–3	Aug. 1, 1834–May 5, 1840

Records of the Cherokee Indian Agency in Tennessee, 1801–1835. M208. 14 rolls. DP.

Roll	Description
1	Correspondence and miscellaneous records, 1801–2
2	Correspondence and miscellaneous records, 1803–4
3	Correspondence and miscellaneous records, 1805–7
4	Correspondence and miscellaneous records, 1808–9
5	Correspondence and miscellaneous records, 1810–12
6	Correspondence and miscellaneous records, 1813–15
7	Correspondence and miscellaneous records, 1816–18
8	Correspondence and miscellaneous records, 1819–20
9	Correspondence and miscellaneous records, 1821–23
10	Agency letter books, Dec. 30, 1822–Dec. 27, 1827, and Feb. 6, 1832–Dec. 2, 1835
11	Fiscal records, 1801–20, comprising (1) copies of accounts, receipts, and disbursements, 1801–20; (2) Cherokee journals, 1801–11
12	Fiscal records, 1801–34, comprising Cherokee day books
13	Fiscal records, 1801–17, comprising (1) receipt book, 1801–2; (2) journal and account book, 1801–17; (3) ledger, 1801–9; and (4) a passbook, 1801–4
14	Records of the Agent for the Department of War in Tennessee, 1800–15; and records of Joseph McMinn, Agent for Cherokee Removal, 1817–21

Miscellaneous Letters Sent by the Pueblo Indian Agency, 1874–1891. M941. 10 rolls. DP.

The records microfilmed here are at the Archives Branch of the National Archives and Record Center, Denver, Colorado.

Roll	Dates
1	Dec. 1, 1874–June 18, 1877
2	June 18, 1877–Dec. 21, 1878
3	Dec. 24, 1878–June 3, 1880
4	June 3, 1880–Apr. 2, 1881
5	Apr. 30, 1881–June 29, 1882
6	July 3, 1882–Aug. 10, 1883
7	Aug. 10, 1883–Nov. 22, 1884
8	Nov. 22, 1884–Aug. 17, 1886

Roll	Dates
9	Aug. 17, 1886–May 10, 1890
10	May 12, 1890–Oct. 9, 1891

Records of the Arizona Superintendency, 1863–1873. M734. 8 rolls. DP.

Roll	Description
1	Registers of letters received, 1868–72; letters received, 1863–66
2	1867–68
3	1869
4	1870
5	1871
6	1872
7	1873
8	Letter book of Charles D. Poston, 1863–64; letters sent, 1865–73

Records of the Dakota Superintendency, 1861–1870 and 1877–1878, and the Wyoming Superintendency, 1870. M1016. 13 rolls. DP.

Roll	Description	Dates
Dakota Superintendency:		
1	Letters received and accounts	1861–63
2	Letters received and accounts	1864–65
3	Letters received and accounts	1866
4	Letters received and accounts	1867
5	Letters received	1868
6	Letters received from the Commissioner of Indian Affairs and from the Cheyenne River, Crow Creek (Upper Missouri), Fort Berthold, and Grand River Agents	1869
7	Letters received from the Ponca, Whetstone, and Yankton Agents; miscellaneous letters received; monthly statements of letters received; tabular statements of funds remitted to the Superintendent	1869
8	Letters received from the Commissioner of Indian Affairs and from the Cheyenne River, Crow Creek (Upper Missouri), Fort Berthold, and Grand River Agents	1870
9	Letters received from the Ponca, Whetstone, and Yankton Agents; miscellaneous letters received; tabular statements of funds remitted to the Superintendent	1870
10	Miscellaneous records relating to Indian matters in Dakota	1873 and 1876
	Letters received from the Commissioner of Indian Affairs	1877–78
	Accounts	1877–78
11	Unbound copies of letters sent	1861–66
12	Letters sent	1865–70
13	Letters sent	1877–78
Wyoming Superintendency:		
	Letters sent and endorsements	1870

Records of the Idaho Superintendency, 1863–1870. M832. 3 rolls.

Roll	Description
1	Register of letters received, 1867–70; letters received from the Commissioner, 1863–70

Roll	Description
2	Letters received from: the Nez Perce Agency, 1863–70, special agents, 1866–69, the Fort Hall Agency, 1869–70, and miscellaneous sources, 1863 and 1866–69
3	Letters sent and miscellaneous records, 1863–70

Records of the Michigan Superintendency, 1814–1851. M1. 71 rolls.

Roll	Dates
Letters received and sent by the Superintendent, 1814–18:	
2	May 31, 1814–Apr. 17, 1817
3	Apr. 24, 1817–June 3, 1818
Letters sent by the Superintendent, 1818–23:	
4	June 6, 1818–Apr. 25, 1822
5	May 2, 1822–June 17, 1823
Letters received by the Superintendent, 1819–35:	
6	1819
7	1820
8	Jan.–June 1821
9	July–Dec. 1821
10	Jan.–June 1822
11	July–Dec. 1822
12	Jan.–June 1823; July–Aug. 16, 1824
13	July–Dec. 1823
14	Jan.–June 1824
15	Aug. 17–Dec. 1824
16	Jan.–June 1825
17	July–Dec. 1825
18	Jan.–June 1826
19	July–Dec. 1826
20	Jan.–June 1827
21	July–Dec. 1827
22	Jan.–May 1828
23	June–Dec. 1828
24	Jan.–June 1829
25	July–Dec. 1829
26	Jan.–July 1830
27	Aug.–Dec. 1830
28	Jan.–Aug. 1831; 1814–25
29	Aug.–Dec. 1831
30	Jan.–June 1832
31	July–Dec. 1832
32	Jan.–May 1833
33	June–Dec. 1833
34	Jan.–July 1834
35	Aug.–Dec. 1834
36	Jan.–Dec. 1835
Letters sent by the Superintendent and the Agent at Mackinac, 1836–51:	
37	July 18, 1836–June 26, 1839
38	July 1, 1839–Aug. 20, 1842
39	Aug. 20, 1842–May 2, 1845
40	May 2, 1845–Apr. 14, 1851
Letters received by the Superintendent and the Agent at Mackinac, 1836–51:	
41	July–Dec. 1836
42	Jan.–July 1837
43	Aug.–Dec. 1837
44	Jan.–June 1838
45	July–Dec. 1838
46	Dec. 1838–July 1839
47	July–Dec. 1839

Roll	Dates
48	Jan.–Aug. 1840
49	Aug.–Dec. 1840
50	Jan.–June 1841
51	July–Dec. 1841
52	Jan.–June 1842
53	July–Dec. 1842
54	Dec. 1842–June 1843
55	July–Dec. 1843
56	Dec. 1843–June 1844
57	June–Dec. 1844
58	Jan.–June 1845
59	July 1845–Jan. 1846
60	Dec. 1845–Dec. 1846
61	Jan.–Dec. 1847
62	Jan. 1848–Apr. 1849
63	Apr.–Dec. 1849
64	Jan.–Dec. 1850
Letters sent by the Agent at Sault Ste. Marie, 1822–33:	
65	July 22, 1822–May 2, 1833
Letters received by the Agent at Sault Ste. Marie, 1822–33:	
66	Apr. 7, 1822–Nov. 23, 1826
67	Jan. 21, 1827–Dec. 29, 1828
68	Jan. 1, 1829–Apr. 30, 1833
Letters sent by the Agent at Mackinac, 1833–36:	
69	May 31, 1833–July 1, 1836
Letters received by the Agent at Mackinac, 1816–36:	
70	May 7, 1816–Nov. 1, 1831
71	May 1, 1833–Dec. 29, 1834
72	Jan. 3, 1835–June 29, 1936

Records of the Minnesota Superintendency, 1849–1856. M842. 9 rolls.

Roll	Dates
Letters received:	
1	1849
2	1850
3	1851
4	1852
5	1853
6	1854
7	1855
8	1856
Letters sent:	
	June 18, 1849–May 17, 1853
9	May 20, 1853–Apr. 11, 1856

Records of the Montana Superintendency, 1867–1873. M833. 3 rolls.

Roll	Description
1	Letters received from the Commissioner, 1867 and 1869–73; the Blackfeet Agency, 1867 and 1869–73; and the Crow Agency, 1869–73
2	The Flathead Agency, 1869–70 and 1872–73; the Mills River Agency, 1869–73; the Lemhi Agency, 1873; and miscellaneous sources, 1867–73
3	Letters sent, 1867 and 1869–73; and miscellaneous records, 1867, 1869, 1871–73

Records of the Nevada Superintendency, 1869–1870. M837. 1 roll.

Records of the New Mexico Superintendency, 1849–1880. T21. 30 rolls.

Roll	Dates
1	1849–60
2	1854–56
3	1857–58
4	1859–60
5	1861–63
6	1864–65
7	1866–67
8	1867–69
9	1869
10	1869
11	1870
12	1870
13	1870–71
14	1871
15	1871–72
16	1872
17	1872
18	1873
19	1873
20	1873
21	1873
22	1874
23	1874
24	1875–80
25	Apr. 4, 1852–Jan. 8, 1856
26	Mar. 29, 1856–Dec. 11, 1859
27	Sept. 8–Nov. 30, 1851, and Jan. 7, 1860–Jan. 26, 1869
28	Nov. 2, 1868–June 30, 1870
29	July 1, 1870–July 7, 1872
30	July 16, 1872–July 24, 1873

Records of the Northern Superintendency, 1851–1876. M1166. 35 rolls.

Roll	Description	Dates
Correspondence:		
1	Vol. 1	1851–Dec. 24, 1854
2	Vols. 2 and 3	Dec. 26, 1854–1856
3	Statements of letters received from and letters sent to the Commissioner of Indian Affairs	1865–66
Letters received, 1852–56:		
4		1857
5		1858–59
6		1860
7		1861–66
8		1867
9		1868–69
10		1870–71
11		1871–72
12	F	1873–74
13	G–W	1874
14	A–G	1875
15	H–W	1875
16	B–W	1876

Roll	Description	Dates
Letters sent, 1857–61:		
17	Registers of letters sent, vols. 1–5	1869–75
18	Letters sent to the Commissioner of Indian Affairs,	
	Vol. 1	1865–May 25, 1869
	Vol. 2	May 27, 1869–Jan. 31, 1872
19	Vol. 3	Jan. 31, 1872–Aug. 2, 1875
	Vol. 4	Aug. 14, 1875–June 30, 1876
Letters sent to agents and various persons:		
20	Vol. 1	1865–May 25, 1869
	Vol. 2	May 27, 1869–Jan. 18, 1872
21	Vol. 3	Jan. 18, 1872–Oct. 28, 1874
22	Vol. 1	Nov. 2, 1874–Dec. 1, 1875
23	Vol. 2	Dec. 4, 1875–76
Administrative records, 1849–55:		
24		1856
25		1857
26		1858
27		1858–61
28		1862–66
29		1867–69
20		1870
31		1871
32		1872
33		1873–74
34		1875–76
	Miscellaneous accounting records	1851–55
	Statements of receipts and disbursements, and abstracts of disbursements	1866–68
35	Correspondence and related records concerning the pursuit of Ink-pa-duta and his band	1857–59
	Letters sent by the Winnebago Agency	1846, 1848, 1851, 1856–62, 1865–66, 1873

Records of the Oregon Superintendency, 1848–1873. M2. 29 rolls.

Roll	Description
2	Register of letters sent, 1849–72; copies of letters received, 1848–50; and copies of letters sent, 1849–50 and 1852–53
3	Copies of letters received and sent, July 1850–Dec. 1853
4	Copies of letters received and sent, Nov. 1853–Aug. 1854
5	Copies of letters received and sent, Mar. 1854–Jan. 1856

Roll	Description
6	Copies of letters sent, Jan. 1856–Sept. 1857
7	Annual reports, 1853–54; reports of subordinates, 1853–55; and copies of letters sent, Sept. 1857–Sept. 1859
8	Copies of letters sent, Sept. 1859–July 1861
9	Copies of letters sent, Aug. 1861–Mar. 1866
10	Register of letters sent, Apr. 1866–Dec. 1872; and copies of letters sent, Apr. 1866–Dec. 1872
11	Copies of instructions and reports, 1850–55
12	Register of letters received, Sept. 30, 1848–Jan. 14, 1873; and letters received, Sept. 30, 1848–Dec. 25, 1852

Letters received:

Roll	
13	Jan. 15, 1853–Dec. 31, 1855
14	Jan. 1–Dec. 31, 1856
15	Jan. 4–Dec. 31, 1857
16	Jan. 1–Dec. 30, 1858
17	Jan. 3–Dec. 30, 1859
18	Jan. 1–Dec. 31, 1860
19	Jan. 4–Dec. 27, 1861
20	Jan. 7, 1862–June 28, 1863
21	July 1, 1863–Aug. 10, 1865
22	Aug. 12, 1865–May 31, 1866
23	June 1, 1866–June 14, 1867
24	June 15, 1867–Mar. 31, 1868
25	Apr. 1, 1868–Mar. 8, 1870
26	Mar. 31–Dec. 1, 1870
27	Dec. 17, 1870–June 21, 1873

Other records:

28	Copies of treaty proceedings and depredation claims, 1851–56
29	Financial records, 1850–55 and 1861–73
30	Miscellaneous records, 1850–73

Records of the Southern Superintendency, 1832–1870, and Western Superintendency, 1832–1851. M640. 22 rolls.

Roll	Dates

Western Superintendency, letters received:

1	1832, 1834–37
2	1838–39
3	1840–41
4	1842–43
5	1844–45
6	1846–48
7	1849–51

Southern Superintendency, letters received:

8	1851–52
9	1853
10	1854
11	1855
12	1856
13	1857
14	1858
15	1859
16	1860–61

Letters sent:

17	June 1, 1853–June 1, 1854
18	June 3, 1854–May 7, 1855
19	May 26, 1855–Dec. 31, 1856
20	Jan. 5, 1857–May 3, 1860
21	June 27, 1860–June 12, 1861; correspondence, Oct. 12, 1869–Aug. 18, 1870

Roll	Dates
22	Agency records, 1860–70; Confederate records, 1861–62

Records of the Utah Superintendency, 1853–1870. M834. 2 rolls.

Roll	Description
1	Letters received 1858–70; letters sent, 1857, 1859–64, and 1866–67
2	Miscellaneous records, 1853 and 1855–70

Records of the Washington Superintendency, 1853–1874. M5. 26 rolls.

Roll	Dates

Copies and drafts of letters sent, 1853–74:

1	Mar. 21, 1853–Mar. 31, 1856
2	Apr. 2–Nov. 29, 1856
3	Dec. 1, 1856–June 2, 1857
4	June 2, 1857–Jan. 31, 1874
5	Jan. 11, 1867–Aug. 14, 1869
6	Aug. 4, 1869–Sept. 22, 1872

Letters from the Commissioner of Indian Affairs, 1853–74:

7	Apr. 18, 1853–Dec. 9, 1859
8	Mar. 2, 1861–June 30, 1874

Letters from agents and employees in local jurisdiction of the superintendency, 1853–74:

9	Letters from Agents assigned to the Puget Sound District as a whole, Dec. 4, 1853–Aug. 16, 1862
10	Letters from employees assigned to local Agencies of the Puget Sound District, Jan. 1, 1856–Nov. 29, 1858
11	Letters from employees assigned to the Puyallup Agency (Puyallup, Nisqualli, and Squaxon Reservations), serving Indians, parties to the Treaty of Medicine Creek, Dec. 31, 1856–Aug. 31, 1874
12	Letters from employees assigned to the Tulalip Agency, serving Indians, parties to the Treaty of Point Elliot, Apr. 24, 1861–July 1, 1874
13	Letters from employees assigned to the Sklallam Agency (Skokomish Reservation), serving tribes parties to the Treaty of Point No Point, Apr. 30, 1861–June 1, 1874
14	Letters from employees assigned to the Neah Bay Agency (Makah Reservation), serving Indians parties to the Treaty of Neah Bay, Sept. 24, 1861–July 1, 1874
15	Letters from employees assigned to the Quinaielt Agency (Quinaielt Reservation), serving Indians, parties to the Treaty of Olympia, Oct. 8, 1861–June 1, 1874
16	Letters from employees assigned to the Western, or Coast, District and the Chehalis Locality, serving Indians parties to no treaty, Mar. 11, 1856–Aug. 31, 1874
17	Letters from employees assigned to the Columbia River, or Southern, District and the Yakima Agency, May 1, 1854–July 20, 1861
18	Letters from employees assigned to the Yakima Agency, Aug. 16, 1861–Dec. 31, 1868
19	Letters from employees assigned to the Yakima Agency, Jan. 4, 1869–July 21, 1874
20	Letters from employees assigned to the Central, or Middle, District and the Colville Agency, Feb. 24, 1854–July 13, 1874

Roll	Dates
21	Letters from employees assigned to the Nez Perce and Umatilla Agencies, Jan. 24, 1856–May 15, 1864
22	Letters from employees assigned to the Eastern District, or Flathead Agency, and the Blackfeet Agency, Dec. 26, 1853–Jan. 30, 1863

Miscellaneous letters received, 1853–74:

23	Aug. 22, 1853–Apr. 9, 1861
24	May 17, 1861–June 24, 1868
25	July 2, 1868–July 14, 1874

Records relating to treaties:

26	Dec. 7, 1854–June 9, 1863

Records of the Wisconsin Superintendency, 1836–1848, and the Green Bay Subagency, 1850. M951. 4 rolls. DP.

Roll	Description

Wisconsin Superintendency, letters received:

1	1836–40
2	1841–45
3	1846–48
	Reports of Agents, Aug. 3, 1836–Nov. 14, 1846; Indian talks and communications, Sept. 28, 1836–June 25, 1845; contracts, 1838–41; estimates, 1836–46
4	Letters sent to Washington officials, July 12, 1836–May 13, 1848; Agents and others, Aug. 10, 1836–May 13, 1848

Green Bay Subagency:

Correspondence, 1850

Records of the Indian Division of the Office of the Secretary of the Interior (Record Group 48)

Selected Classes of Letters Received by the Indian Division of the Office of the Secretary of the Interior, 1849–1880. M825. 32 rolls. DP.

This publication consists chiefly of letters relating to the administration of Indian affairs received by the Secretary of the Interior from the President, the Secretary of State, the Secretary of War, the Attorney General and other Cabinet officers, Members of Congress, and some private individuals and organizations, including the Board of Indian Commissioners. Among the letters reproduced are a relatively small number from the Commissioner of Indian Affairs, primarily communications transmitting for approval deeds for land sold by Indians in Kansas, 1869–77. The bulk of the letters received from the Commissioner, 1849–80, are not included in this publication.

Letters received by the Indian Division relate to such subjects as contracts between Indians and claims agents; land allotments to Indians; surveys of Indian lands; Indian rights and Indian defense associations; annuity payments and trust funds; intruders on Indian reservations; negotiations with Indian tribes; contracts for Indian supplies, transportation, and buildings; deeds for Indian lands; depredation claims against Indians; employees in Indian service; Indian inspectors; and legislation.

Most of the letters are arranged by name of Government agency or office that sent them to the Department of the Interior, and thereunder chronologically. Letters from private individuals and non-Government organizations, filed in the "Miscellaneous" category, are arranged chronologically by the date of the letter. The date of a transmittal letter takes precedence over the dates of its enclosures. If the transmittal letter is missing, the date of the enclosure determines its placement in the files. If both the transmittal and the enclosures are missing, then the date on the wrapper, usually the date received in the Division, determines the location.

Manuscript copies of the Report Books are on M348, *Report Books, 1838–85.*

Roll	Contents

Executive Office:

1	May 25, 1852–Dec. 27, 1871
2	Jan. 1, 1872–Dec. 4, 1880

State Department:

3	Dec. 8, 1857–Nov. 10, 1880

Treasury Department:

4	Sept. 23, 1850–Dec. 6, 1873
5	Jan. 26, 1874–Dec. 16, 1880

War Department:

6	May 3, 1849–Dec. 22, 1869
7	Jan. 6, 1870–May 28, 1872
8	June 1, 1872–Mar. 26, 1874
9	Apr. 1, 1874–Dec. 22, 1875
10	Jan. 6, 1876–Jan. 29, 1878
11	Feb. 4, 1878–Dec. 20, 1880

Attorney General:

12	Aug. 30, 1852–Dec. 31, 1873
13	Jan. 3, 1874–Dec. 27, 1880

Commissioner of the General Land Office:

14	Sept. 10, 1862–Dec. 30, 1880

Board of Indian Commissioners:

15	Dec. 17, 1873–June 4, 1880

Commissioner of Indian Affairs:

16	Jan. 8–Dec. 16, 1869 Jan. 5, 1870–Apr. 24, 1871
17	May 1, 1871–Dec. 14, 1877

Miscellaneous:

18	Mar. 7, 1849–Dec. 21, 1854
19	Jan. 4, 1855–Dec. 27, 1858
20	Jan. 4, 1859–Dec. 22, 1862
21	Jan. 6, 1863–Dec. 31, 1864
22	Jan. 2–Dec. 27, 1865
23	Jan. 13, 1866–June 20, 1867
24	July 4, 1867–Dec. 22, 1868
25	Jan. 4, 1869–Aug. 31, 1870
26	Sept. 1, 1870–Dec. 27, 1871
27	Jan. 2–Dec. 31, 1872
28	Jan. 2–Sept. 30, 1873
29	Oct. 1, 1873–Mar. 31, 1874
30	Apr. 1, 1874–June 30, 1875
31	July 1, 1875–Dec. 21, 1876
32	Jan. 11, 1877–May 8, 1880

Letters Sent, 1849–1903. M606. 127 rolls. DP.

This microfilm publication reproduces handwritten transcripts of communications sent by the Indian Division of the Office of the Secretary of the Interior, 1849–1903, and accompanying indexes for 1849–97.

Letters were sent by the Indian Division to the Commissioner of Indian Affairs, the President, Cabinet members, Members of Congress, the Commissioner of the General Land Office, Treasury Department officials, inspectors, other Federal officials, State and local officials, businessmen, attorneys, Indians, religious leaders, and others. The letters relate to legislation, estimates and appropriations, negotiation and enforcement of treaties, investigations, depredation and other claims, education, health and sanitation, land sales and allotments, surveys, deeds, leases, mining, agriculture, irrigation, railroads, enrollments, annuity payments, trust funds, trade with Indians and the issuance of licenses to trade, liquor control, law and order, missionary work, attorneys, administration of the Indian field service, appointments and other personnel matters, contracts, authorizations for expenditures, buildings, supplies, and accounts.

For the most part, the letters were transcribed in chronological order. From 1868–82, letters to the Commissioner of Indian Affairs were copied in volumes separate from those containing letters to others. Sometimes letters were copied out of order, and this accounts for occasional overlapping of dates between volumes. The index volumes have been reproduced on the last seven rolls of this microfilm publication.

Some letters sent by the Indian Division were not copied in the volumes reproduced in this microfilm publication. These include letters relating to trust funds, 1857–80, letters to inspectors, 1880–82, some form letters, and letters after 1892 to the Commissioner of Indian Affairs authorizing expenditures. All of the records of the Indian Division of the Office of the Secretary of the Interior are to be found in the Records of the Office of the Secretary of the Interior, Record Group 48.

Roll	Contents
1	Mar. 10, 1849–July 28, 1854
2	July 28, 1854–July 18, 1857
3	July 21, 1857–Jan. 3, 1862
4	Jan. 3, 1862–June 30, 1864
5	July 1, 1864–Dec. 13, 1865
6	Dec. 14, 1865–Sept. 22, 1866
7	Sept. 24, 1866–Dec. 31, 1867
8	Miscellaneous, Jan. 3, 1868–Apr. 30, 1870
9	Commissioner of Indian Affairs, Jan. 3, 1868–Sept. 29, 1870
10	Miscellaneous, May 3, 1870–Apr. 8, 1872
11	Commissioner of Indian Affairs, Oct. 7, 1870–Oct. 19, 1873
12	Miscellaneous, Apr. 9, 1872–Sept. 29, 1873
13	Commissioner of Indian Affairs, Oct. 9, 1873–Nov. 30, 1875
14	Miscellaneous, Sept. 30, 1873–Feb. 2, 1875
15	Commissioner of Indian Affairs, Dec. 1, 1875–Oct. 24, 1877
16	Miscellaneous, Feb. 2, 1875–June 30, 1876
17	Commissioner of Indian Affairs, Oct. 25, 1877–Aug. 12, 1878
18	Miscellaneous, July 1, 1876–May 31, 1878
19	Commissioner of Indian Affairs, Aug. 12, 1878–Mar. 18, 1879

Roll	Contents
20	Miscellaneous, May 31, 1878–Dec. 5, 1879
21	Commissioner of Indian Affairs, Mar. 18–Oct. 22, 1879
22	Miscellaneous, Dec. 10, 1879–Dec. 30, 1880
23	Commissioner of Indian Affairs, Oct. 22, 1879–May 31, 1880
24	Commissioner of Indian Affairs, May 31–Dec. 30, 1880
25	Commissioner of Indian Affairs, Jan. 3–June 29, 1881
26	Miscellaneous, Jan. 5–Dec. 31, 1881
27	Commissioner of Indian Affairs, June 30–Dec. 30, 1881
28	Commissioner of Indian Affairs, Jan. 3–June 30, 1882
29	Miscellaneous, Jan. 3–Sept. 13, 1882
30	Commissioner of Indian Affairs, July 1–Dec. 30, 1882, and miscellaneous, Sept. 13–Dec. 30, 1882
31	Jan. 2–May 8, 1883
32	May 9–Sept. 4, 1883
33	Sept. 4, 1883–Jan. 10, 1884
34	Jan. 10–Mar. 14, 1884
35	Mar. 15–June 3, 1884
36	June 2–Aug. 22, 1884
37	Aug. 23–Nov. 18, 1884
38	Nov. 18, 1884–Jan. 31, 1885
39	Feb. 2–Apr. 16, 1885
40	Apr. 16–July 18, 1885
41	July 18–Oct. 20, 1885
42	Oct. 21, 1885–Jan. 2, 1886
43	Jan. 2–Feb. 8, 1886
44	Feb. 8–Apr. 13, 1886
45	Apr. 8–June 24, 1886
46	June 17–Sept. 11, 1886
47	Sept. 11–Nov. 15, 1886
48	Nov. 16, 1886–Jan. 26, 1887
49	Jan. 27–Mar. 30, 1887
50	Mar. 31–June 16, 1887
51	June 16–Aug. 30, 1887
52	Aug. 31–Nov. 10, 1887
53	Nov. 11, 1887–Feb. 4, 1888
54	Feb. 4–Apr. 24, 1888
55	Apr. 24–July 18, 1888
56	July 11–Sept. 19, 1888
57	Sept. 19–Dec. 4, 1888
58	Dec. 3, 1888–Feb. 19, 1889
59	Feb. 18–May 7, 1889
60	May 6–July 25, 1889
61	July 22–Oct. 10, 1889
62	Oct. 10–Dec. 17, 1889
63	Dec. 12, 1889–Feb. 27, 1890
64	Feb. 27–Apr. 25, 1890
65	Apr. 23–June 30, 1890
66	June 30–Aug. 30, 1890
67	Aug. 30–Nov. 3, 1890
68	Nov. 3–Dec. 22, 1890
69	Dec. 20, 1890–Feb. 4, 1891
70	Feb. 4–Mar. 20, 1891
71	Mar. 19–May 5, 1891
72	May 4–June 26, 1891
73	June 26–Oct. 17, 1891
74	Oct. 17, 1891–Mar. 4, 1892
75	Mar. 4–June 6, 1892
76	June 6–Aug. 22, 1892

Roll	Contents
77	Aug. 22, 1892–Jan. 14, 1893
78	Jan. 14–May 13, 1893
79	May 12–Oct. 7, 1893
80	Oct. 6, 1893–Mar. 15, 1894
81	Mar. 15–July 7, 1894
82	July 7–Oct. 11, 1894
83	Oct. 10, 1894–Jan. 5, 1895
84	Jan. 4–Mar. 20, 1895
85	Mar. 20–June 24, 1895
86	June 24–Oct. 25, 1895
87	Oct. 26, 1895–Feb. 21, 1896
88	Feb. 21–June 3, 1896
89	June 2–Oct. 13, 1896
90	Oct. 12, 1896–Feb. 12, 1897
91	Feb. 12–May 24, 1897
92	May 24–Oct. 5, 1897
93	Oct. 5, 1897–Jan. 15, 1898
94	Jan. 14–Apr. 1, 1898
95	Apr. 1–July 11, 1898
96	July 11–Oct. 11, 1898
97	Oct. 10, 1898–Jan. 14, 1899
98	Jan. 14–Apr. 14, 1899
99	Apr. 14–July 13, 1899
100	July 13–Nov. 7, 1899
101	Nov. 7, 1899–Feb. 14, 1900
102	Feb. 15–Apr. 27, 1900
103	Apr. 27–June 26, 1900
104	June 26–Sept. 20, 1900
105	Sept. 20–Dec. 20, 1900
106	Dec. 20, 1900–Feb. 28, 1901
107	Feb. 28–Apr. 26, 1901
108	Apr. 26–June 21, 1901
109	June 21–Aug. 16, 1901
110	Aug. 16–Nov. 19, 1901
111	Nov. 19, 1901–Feb. 7, 1902
112	Feb. 7–Apr. 1, 1902
113	Apr. 1–May 29, 1902
114	May 31–July 18, 1902
115	July 18–Sept. 13, 1902
116	Sept. 15–Nov. 24, 1902
117	Nov. 24, 1902–Feb. 5, 1903
118	Feb. 5–Apr. 6, 1903
119	Apr. 7–June 2, 1903
120	June 2–July 24, 1903
121	Index, 1849–Mar. 1858
122	Indexes, 1881–82
123	Index, 1883–85
124	Index, 1886–87
125	Index, 1888–90
126	Index, 1891–95
127	Index, 1896–June 1897

Reports of Inspection of the Field Jurisdictions of the Office of Indian Affairs, 1873–1900. M1070. 60 rolls. DP.

Inspectors for the Indian Service were first appointed July 1, 1873, under the provision of an act of February 14, 1873 (17 Stat. 463). Until March 25, 1880, inspectors were responsible to the Commissioner of Indian Affairs. After that date, inspectors came under the supervision of the Secretary of the Interior. This procedural change was necessary because the 1873 act required inspectors to report to the President. Reporting to the Secretary of the Interior was, in effect, the same as reporting to the President.

The 1873 act also provided for the appointment of five Indian inspectors, one for each of five geographical inspection divisions. The inspectors examined matters pertaining to the conditions of the Indians. They also examined the extent to which the Indians adopted white civilization, reservation boundaries, the use of reservation lands, the state of industry (usually the percentage of farming and cattle grazing by Government employees and Indians), the character and abilities of the agent and other employees, school conditions, the status of agency fiscal records, and enforcement or violation of the law.

During the 1890's, many inspection reports were submitted on printed forms showing the names and titles of employees at the agency; their residence, age, sex, and rate of compensation; the nature and extent of services performed; and comments on character, education, personal habits, and qualifications or fitness for the position. Other topics covered in the written reports include the health of the Indians; the receipt of rations; the removal and treatment of Indians by agents and other officials; traders' dealings with Indians; Indian courts; building repairs; conditions of dormitories, kitchens, and dining rooms; water supply; fire protection; and sanitation and drainage.

Special reports, responding to directives from the Secretary of the Interior were not uncommon. These reports concerned a wide variety of subjects but were generally related to charges or claims made by individuals against agents or employees, or changes in personnel at agencies. Inspectors could suspend superintendents, agents, or other employees and designate a temporary replacement subject to approval by the President. Inspectors also were authorized to examine all agency books, papers, and vouchers and to administer oaths for taking testimony from agency employees. Often the inspector wrote a separate report for an agency and for each of its day schools and mailed them as one unit to the Secretary. When the reports were received, clerks at the Interior Department registered each one as a separate item.

The Office of Indian Affairs maintained the reports for 1873–80 in a separate collection that is now part of Record Group 75, the Records of the Bureau of Indian Affairs. Reports from 1881–1900, however, were generally filed with letters received in the Indian division and are part of Record Group 48, Records of the Office of the Secretary of the Interior. To make this publication easier to use, these two groups of reports have been consolidated. They are arranged alphabetically by Indian agency, superintendency, or school and thereunder chronologically by the date of the document.

The descriptive pamphlet includes a list of inspectors and their periods of service and a list of inspection reports that gives the name of the field office in alphabetical order, the date and number of the report, and the name of the inspector.

Roll	Contents
1	Albuquerque School, Arizona Superintendency
2	Arizona Superintendency, Blackfeet Agency
3	Blackfeet Agency, California Superintendency, Carlisle School, Carson School, Central Superintendency, Cherokee Agency, Cheyenne Agency, Cheyenne and Arapahoe Agency
4	Cheyenne and Arapahoe Agency

Roll	Contents
5	Cheyenne River Agency
6	Chilocco School, Chippewa Agency, Colorado River Agency
7	Colorado Superintendency, Colville Agency
8	Crow Agency
9	Crow Agency, Crow Creek Agency
10	Dakota Superintendency, Devils Lake Agency
11	East Division, Eastern Cherokee Agency, Flandreau School, Flathead Agency
12	Forest Grove School, Fort Apache Agency, Fort Belknap Agency
13	Fort Berthold Agency, Fort Hall Agency
14	Fort Hall Agency, Fort Lapwai School, Fort Lewis School, Fort Mohave (Mojave) School, Fort Peck Agency
15	Fort Peck Agency
16	Fort Shaw School, Fort Stevenson School, Fort Totten School, Fort Yuma School, Genoa School
17	Genoa School, Grand Junction School, Grand River Agency, Grand Ronde Agency
18	Grand Ronde Agency, Great Nemaha Agency, Green Bay Agency
19	Green Bay Agency, Greenville School, Hampton Institute, Haskell Institute, Hoopa Valley School
20	Hope School, Hualapai School, Idaho Superintendency, Kickapoo School, Kiowa Agency, Kiowa, Comanche, and Wichita Agency
21	Kiowa, Comanche, and Wichita Agency, Klamath Agency
22	Klamath Agency, La Pointe Agency
23	La Pointe Agency
24	La Pointe Agency, Leech Lake Agency, Lemhi Agency Lincoln Institution, Lower Brule Agency, Mackinac Agency, Mdewakanton Sioux
25	Mescalero and Jicarilla Agency
26	Miscellaneous, Mission Agency, Montana Superintendency
27	Moqui Agency, Morris School, Mount Pleasant School, Navajo Agency
28	Navajo Agency, Neah Bay Agency
29	Nebraska Agencies, Nevada Superintendency, New Mexico Superintendency
30	New Mexico Superintendency, New York Agency, Nez Perce Agency
31	Nez Perce Agency, Nisqualli (Nisqually), Skokomish, and Puyallup Agency, North District, Omaha Agency, Omaha and Winnebago Agency
32	Omaha and Winnebago Agency
33	Oneida School, Oregon Superintendency, Osage Agency
34	Osage Agency, Oto (Otoe) Agency, Ouray Agency
35	Pacific District, Pawnee Agency, Perris School, Phoenix School, Pierre School, Pima, Maricopa, and Papago Agency
36	Pima, Maricopa, and Papago Agency, Pine Ridge Agency
37	Pine Ridge Agency, Pipestone School, Ponca Agency
38	Ponca, Pawnee, and Oto (Otoe) Agency
39	Ponca, Pawnee, and Oto (Otoe) Agency
40	Potawatomi Agency, Potawatomi and Great Nemaha Agency

Roll	Contents
41	Pueblo and Jicarilla Agency, Quapaw Agency
42	Quapaw Agency, Quinaielt Agency, Rapid City School, Red Cloud Agency
43	Rosebud Agency, Round Valley Agency
44	Round Valley Agency, Rushville Station, Sac and Fox Agency, Indian Territory
45	Sac and Fox Agency, Indian Territory, Sac and Fox Agency, Iowa, San Carlos Agency
46	San Carlos Agency, Santa Fe School
47	Santee Agency, Santee and Flandreau Agency
48	Seger Colony School, Seminole Agency, Seneca School, Shoshoni (Shoshone) Agency
49	Shoshoni (Shoshone) Agency, Siletz Agency, Sisseton Agency
50	Sisseton Agency
51	South District, Southern Ute Agency, Spotted Tail Agency
52	Standing Rock Agency
53	Standing Rock Agency, Tomah School, Tongue River Agency, Tonkawa Special Agency, Tulalip Agency, Tule River Agency
54	Uintah Agency, Uintah and Ouray Agency, Umatilla Agency
55	Umatilla Agency, Union Agency, Upper Missouri Agency, Utah Superintendency, Warm Springs Agency
56	Washington Superintendency, Western Shoshoni (Shoshone) Agency
57	Whetstone Agency, White Earth Agency
58	White Earth Agency, Wichita Agency, Winnebago Agency, Wittenberg School, Wyoming Superintendency, Yakima Agency
59	Yakima Agency, Yankton Agency
60	Yankton Agency

Records Relating to Census Rolls and Other Enrollments

Bureau of Indian Affairs (Record Group 75)

Because Indians on reservations were not citizens until 1924, nineteenth and early twentieth century census takers did not count Indians for congressional representation. Instead, the Government took special censuses in connection with Indian treaties. (The Government made its last treaty with the Indians in 1871.) The result of many treaties was to extinguish Indian titles to land. Typically, the Indians agreed to reduce their landholdings or to move to an area less desired for white settlement. Some treaties provided for the dissolution of the tribes and the allotment of land to individual Indians. The censuses determined who was eligible for the allotments.

Census of Creek Indians (Parsons and Abbott), 1832. T275. 1 roll.

By a treaty of March 24, 1832, the Creek Indians ceded to the United States all of their land east of the Mississippi River. Heads of families were entitled to tracts of land, which, if possible, were to include their improvements. In 1833 Benjamin S. Parsons and Thomas J. Abbott prepared a census of Creek Indian heads of families, which gave their names and the number of males, females, and slaves in each family. The entries were arranged by town and numbered; these numbers were used for identification in later records.

Census Roll, 1835, of Cherokee Indians East of the Mississippi. With Index. T496. 1 roll.

The first treaty by which Indians ceded land east of the Mississippi River in exchange for land to the west was that of July 8, 1817, with the Cherokee Nation. The major Cherokee removal, however, did not come until after the treaty of December 29, 1835. The census rolls for the Eastern Cherokee have been maintained with the removal records. The first, the Henderson Roll, 1835, is the roll customarily made before removal. It lists heads of families and gives information concerning each family and its property.

Old Settler Cherokee Census Roll, 1895, and Index to Payment Roll, 1895. T985. 2 rolls.

Roll	Contents
1	Index to Payment Roll for Old Settler Cherokee, 1896
2	Old Settler Cherokee Census Roll, 1895

Records Relating to Enrollment of the Eastern Cherokee by Guion Miller, 1908–1910. M685. 12 rolls. DP.

This publication includes Guion Miller's report and his supplemental report as well as the roll of Eastern Cherokee. In certifying the eligibility of the Cherokee, Miller used earlier census lists and rolls that had been made of the Cherokee between 1835 and 1884. Copies of the Chapman, Drennen, and Old Settler rolls of 1851 and the Hester roll of 1884, with the appropriate indexes, are reproduced as the final roll of this publication.

Roll	Contents
1	General Index to Eastern Cherokee Applications, vols. 1 and 2

Report submitted by Guion Miller, Special Commissioner, May 28, 1909:

2	Vols. 1 and 2, applications 1–6000
3	Vols. 3 and 4, applications 6001–16000
4	Vols. 5–7, applications 16001–31000
5	Vols. 8–10, applications 31001–45857
6	Roll of Eastern Cherokee, May 28, 1909, and report on exceptions, with supplemental roll, Jan. 5, 1910

Miscellaneous testimony taken before special commissioners, Feb. 1908–Mar. 1909:

7	Vols. 1 and 2
8	Vols. 3 and 4
9	Vols. 5 and 6
10	Vols. 7 and 8
11	Vols. 9 and 10

Roll	Contents
12	Indexes and rolls of Eastern Cherokee Indians, 1850, 1851, and 1884, and miscellaneous notes and drafts

Indian Census Rolls, 1885–1940. M595. 692 rolls. DP.

These census rolls were usually submitted each year by agents or superintendents in charge of Indian reservations, as required by an act of July 4, 1884 (23 Stat. 98). The data on the rolls vary to some extent, but usually given are the English and/or Indian name of the person, roll number, age or date of birth, sex, and relationship to head of family. Beginning in 1930, the rolls also show the degree of Indian blood, marital status, ward status, place of residence, and sometimes other information. For certain years—including 1935, 1936, 1938, and 1939—only supplemental rolls of additions and deletions were compiled. Most of the 1940 rolls have been retained by the Bureau of Indian Affairs and are not included in this publication.

There is not a census for every reservation or group of Indians for every year. Only persons who maintained a formal affiliation with a tribe under Federal supervision are listed on these census rolls.

Roll	Jurisdiction and Dates
1	Albuquerque School (Pueblo and Navajo Indians), 1904–7, 1910–11
2	Bay Mills School (Chippewa Indians), 1909–11, 1913–15
	Birch Cooley Agency (Mdewakanton Sioux Indians), 1891–93, 1895–98
	Bishop Agency (Paiute and other Indians), 1916–26
	Blackfeet Agency:
3	1890–96
4	1897–1906
5	1907–13
6	1914–19
7	1920–25
8	1926–30
9	1931–32
10	1933–35
11	1936–39
12	Bloomfield Seminary, 1924
	California Special:
	1907–11
13	1912–13
14	1914–15
15	Camp McDowell, 1905–9, 1911–12; Camp Verde (Apache-Mojave Indians), 1915–27; Campo (Mission Indians), 1916–20; Canton Asylum, 1910–11, 1921, 1924
	Cantonment (Cheyenne and Arapahoe Indians):
16	1903–16
17	1917–27
	Carlisle School, 1911
	Carson (chiefly Paiute, Shoshoni, and Washo Indians):
18	1909, 1925–30
19	1931–32
20	1933–36
21	1937–39
22	Carter (Potawatomi Indians), 1915
	Cherokee (North Carolina), 1898–99, 1904, 1906, 1909–12, 1914
23	1915–22
24	1923–29
25	1930–32

Roll	Jurisdiction and Dates
26	1933–39
	Cheyenne and Arapahoe:
27	1887–88, 1891–94
28	1895–1904
29	1905–20
30	1921–30
31	1931–33
32	1934–39
	Cheyenne River (Sioux Indians):
33	1886–87, 1890–91
34	1892, 1894–1900
35	1901–7, 1909
36	1910–14
37	1915–20
38	1921–29
39	1930–32
40	1933–42
	Choctaw (Mississippi):
41	1926–32
42	1933–39
	Coeur d'Alene:
43	(Coeur d'Alene, Kalispel, Kutenai, and Spokan Indians), 1906, 1910–25
44	(Coeur d'Alene, Kalispel, and Kutenai Indians), 1926–33
45	(Coeur d'Alene, Kalispel, Kutenai, and Nez Perce Indians), 1934–37
	Colorado River:
46	(Mohave, Chemehuevi, and Walapai Indians), 1885–93, 1895–1905
47	(Mohave, Chemehuevi, and other Indians), 1906–29
48	(Mohave, Chemehuevi, Cocopa, Yuma, and other Indians), 1930–40
	Colville:
49	(Colville, Spokan, Coeur d'Alene, Kalispel, Lake, Nespelem, Okanagon, Joseph's Band of Nez Perce, and Moses Band of Columbia Indians), 1885–88, 1890–93
	(Colville, Spokan, Coeur d'Alene, Lake, Nespelem, Okanagon, Sanpoil, Joseph's Band of Nez Perce, and Moses Band of Columbia Indians):
50	1894–98
51	1899–1905
52	(Colville, Spokan, Lake, Nespelem, Okanagon, Sanpoil, Kalispel, Wenatchee, Joseph's Band of Nez Perce, Moses Band of Columbia, and other Indians), 1906–16
53	(Colville Reservation), 1917–24
	(Colville and Spokane Reservations):
54	1925–29
55	1930–32
56	1933–39
	Consolidated Chippewa:
57	1923
58	1924
59	1925
60	1926
61	1927
62	1928
63	White Earth Subagency, 1929
64	Fond du Lac, Grand Portage, Leech Lake, and Nett Lake (Bois Forte) Subagencies, 1929
65	White Earth Reservation, 1930
66	Bois Forte (Nett Lake), Cass and Winnibigoshish, Fond du Lac, Grand Portage, Leech Lake, Mille Lac, and White Oak Point Reservations, 1930
67	White Earth Reservation, 1931
68	Bois Forte (Nett Lake), Cass and Winnibigoshish, Fond du Lac, Grand Portage, Leech Lake, and White Oak Point Reservations, 1931 (with supplemental rolls)
69	White Earth Reservation, 1932
70	Cass and Winnibigoshish, Fond du Lac, Grand Portage, Leech Lake, Nett Lake (Bois Forte), and White Oak Point Reservations, 1932 (with birth and death rolls)
71	White Earth Reservation, 1933
72	Cass and Winnibigoshish, Fond du Lac, Grand Portage, Leech Lake, Nett Lake (Bois Forte), Nonremoval Mille Lac, and White Oak Point Reservations, 1933 (with supplemental rolls)
73	White Earth Reservation, 1934
74	Cass and Winnibigoshish, Fond du Lac, Grand Portage, Leech Lake, Nett Lake (Bois Forte), Nonremoval Mille Lac, and White Oak Point Reservations, 1934, 1934–36 (supplemental rolls)
75	White Earth Reservation, 1937
76	Cass and Winnibigoshish, Fond du Lac, Grand Portage, Leech Lake, Nett Lake (Bois Forte), Nonremoval Mille Lac, and White Oak Point Reservations, 1937, 1937–39 (supplemental rolls)
	Consolidated Ute:
77	1923–24, 1926–31
78	1932–39
	Crow:
79	1891–95, 1897–98
80	1899–1905
81	1906–8, 1912–16
82	1917–24
83	1925–30
84	1931–33
85	1934–37
86	1938–40
	Crow Creek (Lower Yanktonai Sioux and Lower Brule Sioux Indians):
87	1886–92
88	1893–1905
89	(Lower Yanktonai Sioux Indians), 1906–20
	(Lower Yanktonai Sioux and Lower Brule Sioux Indians):
90	1921–29
91	1930–33
92	1934–39, 1942
93	Cushman (Skokomish, Clallam, Chehalis, Squaxin Island, Nisqualli, Muckleshoot, Quinaielt, Queet, and Georgetown Indians), 1910–13, 1915–20
	Devils Lake (Sioux and Chippewa Indians):
94	1885–90
95	1892–97
96	1898–1902
97	1903–5
	Digger, 1899–1904, 1915–20
	Eastern Navajo:
98	1929
99	1930
100	1931
101	1932

Roll	Jurisdiction and Dates
102	1933
103	1934–35
104	Fallon (Paiute Indians), 1909–24
	Flandreau:
105	1892–1921
106	1922–39
	Flathead:
107	(Flathead, Kutenai, Pend d'Oreille, and Kalispel Indians), 1886–93
108	(Flathead, Kutenai, Pend d'Oreille, Kalispel, and Spokan Indians), 1895–97, 1900–05
	Flathead:
109	1906–7, 1909–13
110	1914–18
111	1919–23
112	1924–28
113	1929–31
114	1932–34
115	1935–37
116	1938–39
117	Fond du Lac, 1910–20
	Fort Apache (White Mountain Apache Indians):
118	1898–1907
119	1908–13
120	1914–18
121	1919–23
122	1924–27
123	1929–31
124	1932–33
125	1934–39
	Fort Belknap (Grosventre and Assiniboin Indians):
126	1885–95
127	1896–1908
128	1909, 1911–20
129	1921–29
130	1930–35
131	1936–39
	Fort Berthold (Arikara, Grosventre, and Mandan Indians):
132	1889–93, 1895–1902
133	1903–15
134	1916–29
135	1930–35
136	1936–39
137	Fort Bidwell (Paiute, Pit River, and Digger Indians), 1915–30
	Fort Hall (Shoshoni and Bannock Indians):
138	1885–87, 1890–91, 1894–1901
139	1902–9
140	1910–18
141	1919–26
142	1927–31
143	1932–34
144	1935–39
	Fort Lapwai (Nez Perce Indians):
145	1902–10
146	1911–20
147	1921–29
148	1930–33
149	Fort Lewis (Southern Ute Indians), 1904–8; Fort McDermitt (Paiute Indians), 1910–23
150	Fort Mojave (Mohave and Chemehuevi Indians), 1892 (Hualapai or Walapai Indians—total only), 1905–7, 1909–15
	Fort Peck (Sioux and Assiniboin Indians):

Roll	Jurisdiction and Dates
151	1885–96
152	1897–1905
153	1906–12
154	1913–19
155	1920–25
156	1926–29
157	1930–31
158	1932–33
159	1934–36
160	1937–39
161	Fort Shaw School, 1910
	Fort Totten (Devils Lake Sioux and Turtle Mountain Chippewa Indians), 1906–9
	(Devils Lake Sioux Indians):
162	1910–20
163	1922–29
164	1930–39
	Fort Yuma (Yuma and Cocopa(h) Indians):
165	1905, 1915–29
166	1930–35
167	Goshute (Goshute, Shoshoni, Paiute, Kanosh, and Pahvant Indians), 1917–23 Grand Portage (Chippewa Indians), 1912, 1914–18, 1920–21
168	Grand Rapids (Winnebago Indians of Wisconsin), 1916–17, 1919–26
169	Grand Ronde, 1885–92, 1894–1914
	Great Lakes (Chippewa and Potawatomi Indians):
170	1936–37
171	1938–40
	Great Sioux Reservation, 1892 (totals only)
	Green Bay (Menominee, Oneida, and Stockbridge and Munsee Indians):
172	1885, 1888–89, 1891–94
173	1895–99
174	(Menominee and Stockbridge and Munsee Indians), 1900–8
175	Greenville (Digger and other Indians), 1916–23
	Haskell (Potawatomi, Kickapoo, Iowa, and Sauk and Fox Indians):
176	1927–31
177	1932–34
178	Havasupai, 1905–33
	Hayward (Lac Courte Oreilles Chippewa Indians):
179	1916–23
180	1924–26, 1928–29
181	1930–33
	Hoopa Valley:
182	(Hupa or Hoopa and Klamath Indians), 1885–97, 1899–1907
	(Hupa or Hoopa, Klamath, and other Indians):
183	1915–22
184	1923–29
185	1930–32
186	1933–35
187	1936–39
	Hopi:
188	1924–26
189	1927–29
	(Hopi and Navajo Indians):
190	1930
191	1931
192	1932 (with birth and death rolls, 1925–31)
193	1933
194	1934–36

Roll	*Jurisdiction and Dates*
195	Hopi, 1937–39
196	Hualapai (Walapai or Hualapai and Havasupai Indians), 1896–99
	Jicarilla:
	1900–15
197	1916–29
198	1930–39
199	Kaibab (Paiute and Goshute Indians), 1910–19, 1921–27; Kaw, 1905, 1909–11
	Keshena:
200	(Menominee and Stockbridge and Munsee Indians), 1909–14
201	(Menominee and Stockbridge Indians), 1915–19
	(Menominee and Oneida Indians):
202	1920–24
203	1925–29
204	1930–31
205	1932 (with birth and death rolls, 1924–32)
206	1933
207	1934–39
	Keshena (Menominee Indians):
208	1936–37
209	1938–42
210	Kickapoo (Kickapoo, Iowa, and Sauk and Fox of the Missouri Indians; Potawatomi Indians for 1920), 1903–20
	Kiowa:
211	(Kiowa, Comanche, Apache, Caddo, and Wichita and affiliated Indians), 1895–99
	(Kiowa, Comanche, Apache, Caddo, and Wichita Indians):
212	1900–4
213	1905–6, 1909–13
	(Kiowa, Comanche, Apache, Wichita, and Caddo Indians, and Apache prisoners of war):
214	1914–17
215	1918–21
	(Kiowa, Comanche, Apache, Wichita, and Caddo Indians, and Apache prisoners of war or Fort Sill Apache):
216	1922–25
217	1926–29
218	(Kiowa, Comanche, Apache, Fort Sill Apache, Wichita, and Caddo Indians), 1930
	(Kiowa, Comanche, Apache, Fort Sill Apache, Wichita, Caddo, and Delaware Indians):
219	1931
220	1932 (with birth and death rolls, 1924–32)
221	1933
222	1934–36
223	1937–39
	Klamath:
224	(Klamath, Modoc, Paiute or Snake, and Pit River Indians), 1885–1906
	(Klamath, Modoc, and Yahooskin Band of Paiute or Snake Indians):
225	1907–20
226	1921–29
	(Klamath, Modoc, Paiute, and other Indians):
227	1930–33
228	1934–39
	Lac du Flambeau:
229	(Chippewa Indians), 1910–27

Roll	*Jurisdiction and Dates*
	(Lac du Flambeau, Bad River, and Red Cliff Chippewa Indians, and Potawatomi Indians):
230	1928–30
231	1931, 1932 (with birth and death rolls, 1924–32)
232	(Lac du Flambeau, Bad River, Lac Courte Oreilles, and Red Cliff Chippewa Indians, and Potawatomi Indians), 1933–35
233	Laona (Potawatomi Indians), 1916–27
	La Pointe:
234	(Bad River, Bois Fort, Fond du Lac, Grand Portage, Lac Courte Oreilles, Lac du Flambeau, and Red Cliff Chippewa Indians), 1886–89
235	(Bad River, Bois Fort or Vermillion Lake, Fond du Lac, Grand Portage, Lac Courte Oreilles, Lac du Flambeau, and Red Cliff Chippewa Indians), 1890–92
	(Bad River, Fond du Lac, Grand Portage, Lac Courte Oreilles, Lac du Flambeau, Red Cliff, and Vermillion Lake Chippewa Indians):
236	1893–94
237	1895–97
	(Bad River, Fond du Lac, Grand Portage, Lac Courte Oreilles, Lac du Flambeau, Red Cliff, Rice Lake, and Vermillion Lake Chippewa Indians):
238	1898–1902
239	1903–7
240	(Bad River, Fond du Lac, Grand Portage, Lac Courte Oreilles, Lac du Flambeau, Red Cliff, and Rice Lake Chippewa Indians), 1908–15
241	(Bad River Chippewa Indians), 1916–22
242	(Bad River and Red Cliff Chippewa Indians), 1923–27
	Leech Lake (Chippewa Indians):
243	1899–1902
244	1903–5
245	1906–12
246	1913–17
247	1918–22
248	Lemhi (Shoshoni, Bannock, and Sheepeater Indians), 1885, 1887–1906
	Leupp (Navajo Indians):
249	1915–17, 1920–25, 1927, 1929
250	1930–32
251	1933–35
252	Lovelocks (Paiute Indians), 1910–12, Lower Brule, 1897–1924
253	Mackinac (Chippewa Indians), 1902–3, 1910, 1915–27
254	Malki, 1916–19
	Mescalero:
	1885–1914
255	1915–29
256	1930–39
257	Mexican Kickapoo (Mexican Kickapoo and Big Jim Band of Absentee Shawnee Indians), 1899–1901
	Mission Tule River:
	1886, 1888, 1890, 1893
258	1894–97
259	1898–1903
	Mission:

Roll	Jurisdiction and Dates
260	1922–25
261	1926–29
262	1930–31
263	1932 (with birth and death rolls, 1924–32)
264	1933
265	1934–35
266	1936
267	1937–39
268	Moapa River (Paiute Indians), 1910–19, 1921, 1923–26
	Moqui:
	1906, 1908–14
269	1915–16, 1918
270	1919–20
271	1921–23
	Navajo:
272	(Moqui Pueblo, or Hopi, and Navajo Indians), 1885 (with 1891 general schedule, and letter, 1898)
	Navajo:
273	1915 (with letters, 1919 and 1923)
274	1936 (supplements only)
275	Eastern Navajo Reservation, 1937
276	Leupp Reservation, 1937
277	Northern Navajo Reservation, 1937
	Southern Navajo Reservation:
278	1937 (Arizona (pt.))
279	1937 (Arizona (pt.))
280	1937 (New Mexico and supplements)
281	Western Navajo Reservation, 1937
282	Navajo, 1938–39
	Navajo Springs, 1909–14
	Neah Bay (Makah, Ozette, Quileute, and Hoh Indians):
283	1885–99
284	1900–13
285	1914–28
286	(Makah, Ozette, and Hoh Indians), 1930–33
287	Nett Lake (Bois Fort Band of Chippewa Indians), 1908–18
	Nevada (Paiute Indians):
288	1886–1905
289	1906–7, 1909–21
	New York:
290	1885–87
291	1888–89, 1891–93
292	1894–97
293	1898–1901
294	1903–6
295	1907–9
296	1910–12
297	1913–15
298	1916–18
299	1919–21
300	1922–24
301	Nez Perce, 1890–1901
302	Nisqually and Skokomish (Puyallup, Skokomish, Nisqualli, Squaxon, Sklallam, and Chehalis Indians), 1885–87
	Northern Idaho (Coeur d'Alene, Kalispel, Kutenai, and Nez Perce Indians), 1938, 1939 (supplemental rolls only)
	Northern Navajo:
303	1930
304	1931
305	1932

Roll	Jurisdiction and Dates
306	1933
307	1934–35
	Northern Pueblo:
308	1920–24
309	1925–28
310	1929–30
	Omaha (Omaha and Winnebago Indians):
311	1886–91
312	1892–98
313	1899–1909
314	Omaha, 1915–24
	Oneida:
315	1900–10
316	1911–20
	Osage:
317	(Osage, Kansa or Kaw, and Quapaw Indians), 1887–88, 1890–96
318	(Osage and Kansa or Kaw Indians), 1897–1905
	Osage:
319	1906–7, 1909–13
320	1914–18
321	1919–22
322	1923–26
323	1927–29
324	1930–31
325	1932
326	1933
327	1934–36
328	1937–39
329	Otoe (Oto and Missouri Indians), 1906–10, 1912, 1915–19
	Paiute (Paiute, Goshute, and Ute Indians):
330	1928–31
331	1932–33
332	1934–35
333	1936–37
334	1938–39
335	Pala (Mission Indians), 1905–7, 1916–20
336	Pawnee:
	1902–19
337	(Kansa or Kaw, Oto and Missouri, Pawnee, and Ponca Indians), 1920–27
	(Kansa or Kaw, Oto, Pawnee, Ponca, and Tonkawa Indians):
338	1928–30
339	1931
340	1932 (with birth and death rolls, 1924–32)
341	1933
342	1934–36
343	1937–39
	Phoenix:
	(Pima, Apache, and Mohave-Apache Indians of the Camp Verde, Fort McDowell, and Salt River Reservations):
344	1928–31
345	1932–33 (with birth and death rolls, 1924–32)
346	(Apache Indians of the Camp Verde Reservation), 1934–37
	Pima:
	(Pima, Papago, and Maricopa Indians):
347	1887, 1890–91, 1894
348	1895–96, 1899, 1901
349	1919–21 (with letters, 1912 and 1916)
350	1922–24

Roll	Jurisdiction and Dates
351	1925–26
352	1927–28
	(Pima, Papago, and Maricopa Indians of the Gila River, Ak Chin, and Gila Bend Reservations):
353	1929
354	1930
355	1931
356	1932 (with birth and death rolls, 1924–32)
357	1933
358	(Pima, Papago, Maricopa, and Mohave-Apache Indians of the Fort McDowell, Gila River, Maricopa or Ak Chin, and Salt River Reservations), 1934
	(Pima, Papago, Maricopa, and Mohave-Apache Indians of the Fort McDowell, Gila River, Maricopa, and Salt River Reservations):
359	1935–36
360	1937
361	1938, 1939 (supplemental rolls only)
	Pine Ridge:
	(Sioux and Cheyenne Indians):
362	1886 (two census rolls)
363	1887–88
364	1890, 1891 (summary only), 1892
365	1893 (two census rolls)
366	1894–95
367	1896–99
	Pine Ridge:
368	1900–3
369	1904–5, 1907, letters for 1909
	(Oglala Sioux Indians):
370	1913, 1915–17
371	1918–20
372	1921–23
373	1924–26
374	1927–28
375	1929
376	1930
377	1931
378	1932
379	1924–32 (birth and death rolls)
380	1933
381	1934
382	1934–36 (supplemental census rolls)
383	1937
384	1937–39, 1942–43 (supplemental census rolls)
385	Pipestone (Mdewakanton Sioux Indians), 1914, 1915 letter, 1918–19 and 1923 letters, 1924–39
	Ponca (Ponca, Oto and Missouri, Pawnee, and Tonkawa Indians):
386	1886–90
387	1891–96
388	1897–1903
389	(Ponca and Tonkawa Indians), 1904–12
390	(Ponca, Tonkawa, and Kansa or Kaw Indians), 1913–19
391	(Ponca, Tonkawa, and Oto and Missouri Indians), 1922–27
	Potawatomi:
392	(Prairie Band of Potawatomi, Iowa, Kickapoo, Sauk and Fox of the Missouri, and Chippewa and Christian or Munsee Indians), 1891–93, 1895–1902
393	(Prairie Band of Potawatomi Indians), 1903–19

Roll	Jurisdiction and Dates
	(Potawatomi, Iowa, Kickapoo, and Sauk and Fox Indians):
394	1921–26
395	1935–40, 1942 (supplement)
	Pueblo:
396	1885–86
397	1887–88
398	1889–90
399	1891–92, Pueblo Indians; 1892, Jicarilla Apache Indians
400	1898–99, Pueblo Indians; 1893–95, 1897–99, Jicarilla Apache Indians
	Pueblo Bonito (Navajo Indians):
401	1909–12, 1914
402	1915–19
403	1920–24, 1926
	Pueblo Day Schools (Pueblo and Navajo Indians):
404	1912–14
405	1915–16
406	1917–19
	Puyallup (Chehalis, Clallam or Sklallam, Nisqualli, Puyallup, Quinaielt, Skokomish, Squaxon, and other Indians):
407	1888–93
408	1894–1900
409	1901–9
410	Pyramid Lake (Paiute Indians), 1931–32
	Quapaw (Eastern Shawnee, Miami, Modoc, Ottawa, Peoria, Quapaw, Seneca, and Wyandot Indians):
411	1885–92
412	1893–1900
	(Eastern Shawnee, Ottawa, Quapaw, Seneca, and Wyandot Indians):
413	1922–29
414	1930–32
415	1933–35
416	(Eastern Shawnee, Miami, Ottawa, Peoria, Quapaw, Seneca, and Wyandot Indians), 1936–39
417	Quinaielt (Quinaielt and other Indians), 1885, 1887
	Red Cliff (Chippewa Indians), 1912, 1914–17, 1919–22
	Red Lake (Red Lake and Pembina Chippewa Indians):
418	1907–12
419	1913–17, 1919
420	(Red Lake and Pembina, Fond du Lac, Grand Portage, Bois Fort, Vermillion Lake, and Deer Creek Chippewa Indians), 1920–23
	(Chippewa Indians):
421	1924–29
422	1930–32
423	1933–35
424	1936–39
425	Red Moon (Cheyenne Indians), 1909–12, 1914–16
	Reno (Paiute Indians), 1922–24 (with letters 1915, 1917–20)
426	Rocky Boy, 1919–39
	Rosebud:
427	(Brule and other bands of Sioux Indians), 1886 (totals only), 1887, 1891
	(Brule Sioux Indians):
428	1892, 1895–96
429	1897–1900

Roll	Jurisdiction and Dates
430	1901–5
	(Sioux Indians):
431	1906–7, 1909–10
432	1911–12, 1915
433	1916–17
434	1918–20
435	1921–23
436	1924–25
437	1926
438	1927–28
439	1929
440	1930
441	1931 (with birth and death rolls, 1924–31)
442	1932
443	1933
	(Rosebud and Yankton Sioux Indians):
444	1934–35
445	1936–39, 1942–43
446	Roseburg (Shasta, Klamath, Pit River, Wintu, and other Indians)
	Round Valley:
447	(Concow, Little Lake, Redwood, Pit River, Potter Valley, Yuki, Wailaki, and Nomelaki Indians), 1885–1905, 1909
	(Concow, Little Lake, Redwood, Pit River, Nomelaki, Yuki, Wailaki, and other Indians):
448	1915–19
449	1920–23
	Sac and Fox, Iowa:
450	1888–1910
451	1911–20, 1922–29
452	1930–39
	Sac and Fox, Oklahoma:
453	(Sauk and Fox, Iowa, Citizen Potawatomi, Absentee Shawnee, and Mexican Kickapoo Indians), 1885 (letter only), 1889–98
454	(Sauk and Fox, Iowa, Citizen Potawatomi, and Absentee Shawnee Indians), 1899–1904
455	(Sauk and Fox and Iowa Indians), 1905–19
	Sacramento:
456	(Indians of Fort Bidwell, Round Valley, and Tule River Reservations, and public domain Indians), 1924 (letter only), 1926, 1930, 1932–33
457	(Indians of Fort Bidwell, Round Valley, and Tule River Reservations and of Modoc County), 1934–39
	Salem (Indians of Grande Ronde and Siletz Reservations and non-reservation Indians):
458	1926–32
459	1933–39
460	Salt Lake Special (Paiute Indians), 1913, and letter for 1915
	Salt River (Camp McDowell, Lehi, and Salt River Indians), 1913–27
	San Carlos (Apache, Mohave, and Yuma Indians):
461	1887–90, 1892
462	1893–96
463	1897–1902
464	1904–12
	(Apache and Mohave Indians):
465	1914–15
466	1916–19
467	1920–24

Roll	Jurisdiction and Dates
468	1925–29
469	1930–33
470	(Apache Indians), 1934–39
471	San Jacinto (Mission and other Indians), 1904–6
	San Juan (Navajo Indians), 1916 and letters for 1905, 1909, 1918–20, 1922–24
	Santa Fe (Pueblo Indians):
472	1904, 1906, 1910–14
473	1931–32
474	1933–35
	Santee:
475	(Santee and Flandreau Sioux and Ponca Indians), 1885–98
	(Santee Sioux and Ponca Indians):
476	1899–1907, 1909–10
477	1911–17
478	San Xavier (Papago Indians), 1904, 1910–17
479	Seger (Cheyenne and Arapahoe Indians), 1903–12, 1914–27
	Sells (Papago Indians):
480	1918–21
481	1922–24
482	1925–28 (letters only for 1927)
483	1929–30
484	1931–32
485	1933–34, 1937–39
	Seminole (Florida):
486	1913–29
487	1930–40
	Seneca (Eastern Shawnee, Miami, Modoc, Ottawa, Peoria, Quapaw, Seneca, and Wyandot Indians):
488	1901–7
489	1910–21
	Shawnee:
490	(Absentee Shawnee, Mexican Kickapoo, and Citizen Potawatomi Indians), 1904–6, 1915–19
	(Absentee Shawnee, Mexican Kickapoo, Citizen Potawatomi, Iowa, and Sauk and Fox Indians):
491	1920–23
492	1924–29
493	1930–31
494	1932–33
495	1934–36
496	1937–39
497	Shivwits, 1910–17, 1919, 1921–22
	Shoshoni (Shoshoni and Arapahoe Indians):
498	1885, 1890–93, 1895–99
499	1900–11
500	1912–18
501	1919–25
502	1926–29
503	1930–32
504	1933–37
	Siletz:
505	1885–1908
506	1909–25
	Sisseton (Sisseton and Wahpeton Sioux Indians):
507	1886–91, 1893, 1895, 1897–98
508	1899–1907
509	1909–14
510	1915–18
511	1919–24

Roll	Jurisdiction and Dates
512	1925–27, 1929
	(Sioux Indians):
513	1930–31
514	1932–33
515	1934–36
516	1937–39
517	1916–20
	Southern Navajo:
518	1929 (transmittal letter and recapitulation)
	1930 (A–G)
519	1930 (H–Z)
520	1931 (A–G)
521	1931 (H–Z and supplemental rolls)
522	1932 (A–B)
523	1932 (C–M)
524	1932 (N–Z and supplemental rolls)
525	1933 (Arizona, A–G)
526	1933 (Arizona, H–Z)
527	1933 (New Mexico and supplemental rolls)
528	1934 (Arizona, A–G)
529	1934 (Arizona, H–Z)
530	1934 (New Mexico)
531	1934–35 (supplemental rolls)
	Southern Pueblo:
532	1920–21
533	1922–23
534	1924–25
535	1926–27
536	1928
537	1929
538	1930
539	1931 (with birth and death rolls, 1924–31)
540	1932 (with birth and death rolls, 1926–32)
541	1933
542	1934–35
543	Southern Utah (Shivwits or Shebits and Kaibab Indians), 1897–1905
	Southern Ute (Ute and Jicarilla Apache Indians), 1885–92
	Southern Ute:
544	1893–95, 1897–1908
545	1909–23
546	Spokane, 1913–24
	Standing Rock (Sioux Indians):
547	1885–88
548	1889–93
549	1894–99
550	1900–4
551	1905–8
552	1909–11
553	1912–13, 1915–16
554	1917–20
555	1921–24
556	1925–29
557	1930–31
558	1932 (with birth and death rolls, 1924–32)
559	1933
560	1934–35
561	1936
562	1937–38
563	1939
	Taholah:
564	(Quinaielt, Chehalis, Nisqualli, Skokomish, and Squaxin Island Indians), 1915–25

Roll	Jurisdiction and Dates
	(Chehalis, Nisqualli, Quileute, Quinaielt, Skokomish, and Squaxin Island Indians):
565	1926–29
566	1930–32
567	(Chehalis, Nisqually, Quinaielt, Skokomish, and Squaxin Island Reservations), 1933
	(Chehalis, Makah, Nisqually, Ozette, Quinaielt, Skokomish, and Squaxin Island Reservations):
568	1934–36
569	1937–39
	Tomah (Winnebago Indians):
570	1911–15, letter for 1916, 1927–29
571	1930–33
572	(Winnebago and Oneida Indians), 1934–36
573	(Winnebago and Oneida Indians and Stockbridge-Munsee Community for 1938), 1937–39
	Tongue River (Northern Cheyenne Indians):
574	1886, 1888–1900
575	1901–8
576	1909–20
577	1922–29
578	1930–33
579	1934–39
	Truxton Canon:
580	(Walapai and Havasupai Indians), 1901–7, 1910–26, 1928–29
581	(Walapai, Havasupai, Yavapai, and Camp Verde Apache Indians), 1930–39
	Tulalip (Lummi, Muckleshoot, Port Madison, Swinomish, and Tulalip Reservations):
582	1885–97
583	1898–1910
584	(Lummi, Muckleshoot, Port Madison, Swinomish, and Tulalip Reservations, and Clallam Indians for 1912), 1911–15
585	(Lummi, Port Madison, Swinomish, and Tulalip Reservations), 1916–20
	(Clallam, Lummi, Muckleshoot, Nooksak, Port Madison or Suquamish, Skagit-Suiattle, Swinomish, and Tulalip or Snohomish Indians):
586	1921–23
587	1924–26
	(Clallam, Lummi, Muckleshoot, Nooksak, Port Madison or Suquamish, Puyallup, Skagit-Suiattle, Swinomish, and Tulalip or Snohomish Indians):
588	1927–29
589	1930
590	1931 (with birth and death rolls, 1924–31)
591	1932–33
592	1934–36
593	1937–39
594	Tule River, 1885–87, 1915–23
	Turtle Mountain (Chippewa Indians):
595	1910–12
596	1913–15
597	1916–18
598	1919–21
599	1922–24
600	1925–27
601	1928–29
602	1930
603	1931

Roll	Jurisdiction and Dates

604 1932 (with birth and death rolls, 1924–32)
605 1933
606 1934–36
607 1937–39

Uintah and Ouray:
(Uintah, Uncompahgre, and White River Ute Indians):
608 1885–89, 1891–92, 1894–95
609 1896–1902
610 1903–11
611 1912–20
612 1921–29
(Ute Indians):
613 1930–33
614 1934–39
615 (Paiute and Ute Indians), 1940, 1942–44

Umatilla:
(Cayuse, Umatilla, and Wallawalla Indians):
616 1886–94, 1896, 1898–1900
617 1901–5, 1910–12
618 1913–17
619 1918–23
620 1924–29
(Cayuse, Umatilla, Wallawalla, and other Indians):
621 1930–32
622 1933–39
623 Union (Choctaw Indians only) 1885

United Pueblos:
624 1936 (supplemental rolls only)
625 1937
626 (Laguna Pueblo), 1938 (with supplemental rolls for other Pueblos)
627 United Pueblos 1939
628 Ute Mountain (Ute Indians) 1915–22

Vermillion Lake (Bois Fort Band of Chippewa Indians) 1907

Walker River:
(Paiute Indians):
629 1897–1912
630 1914–24
631 (Paiute, Monache, Shoshoni, and Washo Indians), 1925–29
(Paiute and other Indians):
632 1930–31
633 1932–33
634 1934–35

Warm Springs:
635 (Warm Springs, John Day, Paiute, Tenino, and Wasco Indians), 1886–91, 1895, 1897–1908
(Warm Springs and other Indians):
636 1909–11, 1913–21
637 1922–29
(Warm Springs, Paiute, and other Indians):
638 1930–33
639 1934–39

Western Navajo:
640 (Hopi Indians, and Navajo and Paiute Indians for 1929),

1905 (letter), undated Hopi roll, 1915–20, 1922, 1923 (letter), 1924–27, 1929 (Navajo, Hopi, and Paiute Indians):
641 1930
642 1931
643 1932
644 1933 (with birth and death rolls, 1925–33)
645 1934–35
Western Shoshone (Shoshoni and Paiute Indians):
646 1885, 1887–90, 1892–1909
647 1910–29
648 1930–39
White Earth (Chippewa Indians):
649 1885–88
650 1890–92
651 1894–95
652 1896–97
653 1898–1900
654 1901–4
655 1905–9
656 1910–11
657 1912–13
658 1914–15
659 1916–17
660 1918–19
661 1920–21
662 1922
663 Wind River (Shoshoni and Arapahoe Indians) 1938–39 (supplemental rolls)
Winnebago: 1904–7, 1909
664 (Omaha and Winnebago Indians), 1910–14
Winnebago:
665 1915–24
(Omaha and Winnebago Indians):
666 1925–29
667 1930–31
668 1932–33
(Omaha, Ponca, Santee, and Winnebago Indians):
669 1934–36
670 1937–39
671 Wittenberg (Winnebago Indians of Wisconsin), 1905, 1910
Yakima (Yakima and other Indians), 1885, 1887–91, 1893–97
Yakima:
672 1898–1907
673 1910–16
674 1917–21
675 1922–25
676 1926–29
677 1930–31
678 1932–33
679 1934–39
Yankton:
680 1885–87, 1890, 1892–94
681 1895–1905
682 1906–7, 1909–11
683 1913–17
(Ponca and Santee and Yankton Sioux Indians):
684 1918–20

Roll	Jurisdiction and Dates
685	1921–24
686	1925–27
687	1928–29
688	1930–31
	Zuni:
689	1904–5, 1907, 1915 (letter), 1916–20
690	1921–24, 1926–29
691	1930–32
692	1933–35

Enrollment Cards of the Five Civilized Tribes, 1898–1914. M1186. 93 rolls. DP.

This microfilm publication reproduces the enrollment cards prepared by the staff of the Commission to the Five Civilized Tribes (Cherokee, Chickasaw, Choctaw, Creek, and Seminole) between 1898 and 1914. These records are part of the Records of the Office of Indian Affairs, Record Group 75, and are housed in the Archives Branch of the Federal Archives and Records Center, Fort Worth, Texas.

The Commission enrolled individuals as "citizens" of a tribe under the following categories: Citizens by Blood, Citizens by Marriage, New Born Citizens by Blood (enrolled under an act of Congress approved March 3, 1905, 33 Stat. 1071), Minor Citizens by Blood (enrolled under an act of Congress approved April 26, 1906, 34 Stat. 137), Freedmen (former black slaves of Indians, later freed and admitted to tribal citizenship), New Born Freedmen, and Minor Freedmen. Delaware Indians adopted by the Cherokee tribe were enrolled as a separate group within the Cherokee. Within each enrollment category, the Commission generally maintained three types of cards: "Straight" cards for persons whose applications were approved, "D" cards for persons whose applications were considered doubtful and subject to question, and "R" cards for persons whose applications were rejected. Persons listed on "D" cards were subsequently transferred to either "Straight" or "R" cards depending on the Commission's decisions. All decisions of the Commission were sent to the Secretary of the Interior for final approval.

An enrollment card, sometimes referred to by the Commission as a "census card," records the information provided by individual applications submitted by members of the same family group or household and includes notation of the actions taken. The information given for each applicant includes name, roll number (individual's number if enrolled), age, sex, degree of Indian blood, relationship to the head of the family group, parents' names, and references to enrollment on earlier rolls used by the Commission for verification of eligibility. The card often includes references to kin-related enrollment cards and notations about births, deaths, changes in marital status, and actions taken by the Commission and the Secretary of the Interior. Within each enrollment category, the cards are arranged numerically by a "field" or "census card" number which is separate from the roll number. The index to the final rolls, which is reproduced on roll 1 of this publication, provides the roll number for each person, while the final rolls themselves provide the census card numbers for each enrollee. No indexes have been located for the majority of the "D" and "R" cards. There are a few Mississippi Choctaw "Identified" and "Field Cards" as well as some Chickasaw "Cancelled" that refer to persons never finally enrolled.

Roll	Category	Census Card Number
1	Index to the Final Rolls and Final Rolls	
2	Cherokee by Blood	1–805
3	Cherokee by Blood	806–1645
4	Cherokee by Blood	1646–2461
5	Cherokee by Blood	2462–3293
6	Cherokee by Blood	3294–4027
7	Cherokee by Blood	4028–4847
8	Cherokee by Blood	4848–5661
9	Cherokee by Blood	5662–6303
10	Cherokee by Blood	6304–7140
11	Cherokee by Blood	7141–7961
12	Cherokee by Blood	7962–8794
13	Cherokee by Blood	8795–9634
14	Cherokee by Blood	9635–10461
15	Cherokee by Blood	10462–11132
16	Cherokee Minors by Blood	1–824
17	Cherokee Minors by Blood	825–1582
18	Cherokee Minors by Blood	1583–2331
19	Cherokee Minors	2332–3034
20	Cherokee Minors	3035–3684
21	Cherokee Minors	3685–4005
22	Delaware	1–382
	Delaware	D1–D50
	Delaware	R1–R5
	Cherokee by Marriage	1–188
23	Cherokee by Marriage	189–288
	Cherokee Freedmen	1–382
24	Cherokee Freedmen	383–814
25	Cherokee Freedmen	815–1231
26	Cherokee Freedmen	1232–1595
	Cherokee Freedmen Minors	1–93
27	Cherokee Freedmen Minors	94–542
	Cherokee	D1–D267
28	Cherokee	D268–D1062
29	Cherokee	D1063–D1879
30	Cherokee	D1880–D2711
31	Cherokee	D2712–D3207
	Cherokee	R1–R336
32	Cherokee	R337–R1168
33	Cherokee Freedmen	D1–D388
34	Cherokee Freedmen	D389–D811
35	Cherokee Freedmen	D812–D1225
36	Cherokee Freedmen	D1226–D1342
	Cherokee Freedmen	R1–R304
37	Cherokee Freedmen	R305–R730
38	Cherokee Freedmen	R731–R1276
39	Choctaw by Blood	1–858
40	Choctaw by Blood	859–1718
41	Choctaw by Blood	1719–2575
42	Choctaw by Blood	2576–3426
43	Choctaw by Blood	3427–4287
44	Choctaw by Blood	4288–5140
45	Choctaw by Blood	5141–5994
46	Choctaw by Blood	5995–6109
	Choctaw New Born by Blood	1–746
47	Choctaw New Born by Blood	747–1538
	Choctaw Minor by Blood	1–73

Roll	Category	Census Card Number
48	Choctaw Minor by Blood	74–914
49	Choctaw Minor by Blood	915–1325
	Choctaw Freedmen	1–225
50	Choctaw Freedmen	226–659
51	Choctaw Freedmen	660–1098
52	Choctaw Freedmen	1099–1540
53	Choctaw Freedmen	1541–1602
	Choctaw Minor Freedmen	1–521
	Choctaw	D1–D238
54	Choctaw	D239–D1009
	Choctaw	R1–R105
55	Choctaw	R106–R756
	Choctaw Freedmen	D1–D111
56	Choctaw Freedmen	D112–D234
	Choctaw Freedmen	R1–R45
	Mississippi Choctaw by Blood	1–540
57	Mississippi Choctaw by Blood	541–918
	Mississippi Choctaw New Born and Minor by Blood	1–372
	Mississippi Choctaw Identified	1–11
	Mississippi Choctaw Field Cards	1–110
58	Mississippi Choctaw Field Cards	111–564
	Mississippi Choctaw	D1–D74
	Mississippi Choctaw	R1–R351
59	Mississippi Choctaw	R352–R1215
60	Mississippi Choctaw	R1216–R2107
61	Mississippi Choctaw	R2108–R3016
62	Mississippi Choctaw	R3017–R3911
63	Mississippi Choctaw	R3912–R4811
64	Mississippi Choctaw	R4812–R5713
65	Mississippi Choctaw	R5714–R6622
66	Mississippi Choctaw	R6623–R7446
67	Chickasaw by Blood	1–662
68	Chickasaw by Blood	663–1424
69	Chickasaw by Blood	1425–1850
	Chickasaw New Born by Blood	1–331
70	Chickasaw New Born by Blood	332–553
	Chickasaw Minor by Blood	1–469
	Chickasaw Freedmen	1–35
71	Chickasaw Freedmen	36–415
72	Chickasaw Freedmen	416–799
73	Chickasaw Freedmen	800–1178
74	Chickasaw Freedmen	1179–1522
	Chickasaw Freedmen Minor	1–84
75	Chickasaw Freedmen Minor	85–517
	Chickasaw Freedmen	D1–D130
	Chickasaw Freedmen	R1–R9
	Chickasaw	R1–R57
76	Chickasaw	R58–R111
	Chickasaw Cancelled	1–219
	Chickasaw	D1–D455
77	Creek by Blood	1–662
78	Creek by Blood	663–1398
79	Creek by Blood	1399–2125

Roll	Category	Census Card Number
80	Creek by Blood	2126–2867
81	Creek by Blood	2868–3611
82	Creek by Blood	3612–4059
	Creek New Born by Blood	1–289
83	Creek New Born by Blood	290–1171
84	Creek Minor by Blood	1–688
85	Creek Freedmen	1–358
86	Creek Freedmen	359–740
87	Creek Freedmen	741–1081
88	Creek Freedmen	1082–1456
89	Creek Freedmen	1457–1833
90	Creek Freedmen	1834–1917
	Creek Freedmen New Born by Blood	1–468
91	Creek Freedmen New Born by Blood	469–748
	Creek Freedmen Minor by Blood	1–435
92	Seminole by Blood	1–607
	Seminole Freedmen	608–670
93	Seminole Freedmen	671–855
	Seminole New Born by Blood	1–181
	Seminole Freedmen	1–R5
	Seminole New Born Freedmen	1–91

Indian Division of the Office of the Secretary of the Interior (Record Group 48)

Final Rolls of Citizens and Freedmen of the Five Civilized Tribes in Indian Territory, 1907, 1914. T529. 3 rolls.

The rolls were prepared by the Commission and the Commissioner to the Five Civilized Tribes and submitted to the Secretary of the Interior for approval as provided by several acts of Congress. Both approved and disapproved names are included. Most rolls give name, age, sex, degree of Indian blood, and roll and census card number of each individual. This series is arranged by name of tribe and thereunder divided into rolls for citizens by blood, citizens by marriage, and freedmen. There are also rolls for the Mississippi Choctaw and the Delaware Cherokee. In many of the groups there are separate rolls for minor children and newborn babies. The names on the rolls are arranged numerically by roll numbers.

Roll	Contents
1	Choctaw and Chickasaw rolls
2	Cherokee rolls
3	Creek and Seminole rolls

U.S. Court of Claims (Record Group 123)

The U.S. Court of Claims was established by an act of February 24, 1855, (10 Stat. 612) to hear claims against the United States including those referred to the court by Congress. An act approved July 1, 1902 (32 Stat. 726), gave the Court of Claims jurisdiction over any claim arising under treaty stipulations that the Cherokee Tribe, or any band thereof, might have against the United States. Within 2 years after the act was approved, three suits were brought before the court concerning grievances arising out of the treaties: (1) *The Cherokee Nation* v. *The United States*, General Jurisdiction Case No. 23199; (2) *The Eastern and Emigrant Cherokees* v. *The United States*, General Jurisdiction Case No. 23212; and (3) *The Eastern Cherokees* v. *The United States*, General Jurisdiction Case No. 23214.

On May 18, 1905, the court decided in favor of the Eastern Cherokee and instructed the Secretary of the Interior to identify the persons entitled to participate in the distribution of funds for payment of the claims. On June 30, 1906, Congress appropriated more than $1 million for this purpose. Guion Miller, special agent of the Interior Department, began compiling a roll of all Eastern and Western Cherokee Indians who were alive on May 28, 1906, and could establish that at the time of the treaties they were members or descendants of members of the Eastern Cherokee. They also had to prove that they had not been affiliated with any tribe of Indians other than the Eastern Cherokee or the Cherokee Nation. In his report of May 28, 1909, Miller stated that 45,847 separate applications had been filed, representing a total of about 90,000 individual claimants, 30,254 of whom were entitled to share in the fund.

Eastern Cherokee Applications of the U.S. Court of Claims, 1906–1909. M1104. 348 rolls. DP.

The applications required each claimant to state full English and Indian names, residence, age, place of birth, name of husband or wife, name of tribe, and names of children. It also required information on the claimant's parents, grandparents, brothers, sisters, uncles, and aunts. The index to the applications is arranged alphabetically by name (either English or Indian) of claimant.

Roll	Contents
1	Roll of Eastern Cherokee
	General index to Eastern Cherokee
	Applications, vols. 1 and 2
	Application numbers 1–145
2	146–136
3	137–224
4	225–331
5	332–420
6	421–514
7	515–596
8	597–681
9	682–778
10	779–859
11	860–964
12	965–1082
13	1083–1175
14	1176–1267
15	1268–1362
16	1363–1455

Roll	Contents
17	1456–1545
18	1546–1642
19	1643–1735
20	1736–1820
21	1821–1910
22	1911–2001
23	2002–2113
24	2114–2229
25	2230–2339
26	2340–2432
27	2433–2534
28	2535–2637
29	2638–2743
30	2744–2841
31	2842–2947
32	2948–3049
33	3050–3147
34	3148–3250
35	3251–3342
36	3343–3442
37	3443–3540
38	3541–3647
39	3648–3747
40	3748–3847
41	3848–3949
42	3950–4057
43	4058–4157
44	4158–4228
45	4229–4327
46	4328–4426
47	4427–4555
48	4556–4661
49	4662–4771
50	4772–4879
51	4880–4984
52	4985–5089
53	5090–5189
54	5190–5289
55	5290–5394
56	5395–5492
57	5493–5591
58	5592–5690
59	5691–5789
60	5790–5889
61	5890–5989
62	5990–6089
63	6090–6189
64	6190–6289
65	6290–6391
66	6392–6481
67	6482–6580
68	6581–6683
69	6684–6787
70	6788–6888
71	6889–6991
72	6992–7091
73	7092–7202
74	7203–7302
75	7303–7403
76	7404–7504
77	7505–7604
78	7605–7704
79	7705–7804
80	7805–7904

Roll	Contents
81	7905–8006
82	8007–8115
83	8116–8216
84	8217–8316
85	8317–8416
86	8417–8516
87	8517–8617
88	8618–8720
89	8721–8818
90	8819–8918
91	8919–9019
92	9020–9119
93	9120–9219
94	9220–9317
95	9318–9416
96	9417–9515
97	9516–9615
98	9616–9715
99	9716–9815
100	9816–9900
101	9901–10000
102	10001–10100
103	10101–10200
104	10201–10300
105	10301–10400
106	10401–10500
107	10501–10600
108	10601–10700
109	10701–10800
110	10801–10900
111	10901–11000
112	11001–11100
113	11101–11200
114	11201–11300
115	11301–11400
116	11401–11500
117	11501–11600
118	11601–11700
119	11701–11806
120	11807–11900
121	11901–12000
122	12001–12100
123	12101–12200
124	12201–12350
125	12351–12500
126	12501–12650
127	12651–12800
128	12801–12950
129	12951–13100
130	13101–13250
131	13251–13400
132	13401–13550
133	13551–13700
134	13701–13850
135	13851–14000
136	14001–14150
137	14151–14300
138	14301–14450
139	14451–14600
140	14601–14750
141	14751–14900
142	14901–15050
143	15051–15200
144	15201–15350

Roll	Contents
145	15351–15500
146	15501–15650
147	15651–15800
148	15801–15950
149	15951–16100
150	16101–16250
151	16251–16400
152	16401–16550
153	16551–16700
154	16701–16850
155	16851–17000
156	17001–17150
157	17151–17300
158	17301–17450
159	17451–17600
160	17601–17750
161	17751–17900
162	17901–18050
163	18051–18200
164	18201–18350
165	18351–18500
166	18501–18650
167	18651–18800
168	18801–18950
169	18951–19100
170	19101–19250
171	19251–19400
172	19401–19550
173	19551–19700
174	19701–19850
175	19851–20000
176	20001–20150$\frac{1}{2}$
177	20151–20300
178	20301–20450
179	20451–20600
180	20601–20750
181	20751–20900
182	20901–21050
183	21051–21200
184	21201–21350
185	21351–21500
186	21501–21650
187	21651–21800
188	21801–21950
189	21951–22100
190	22101–22250
191	22251–22400
192	22401–22550
193	22551–22700
194	22701–22850
195	22851–23000
196	23001–23150
197	23151–23300
198	23301–23450
199	23451–23600
200	23601–23750
201	23751–23900
202	23901–24050
203	24051–24200
204	24201–24350
205	24351–24500
206	24501–24650
207	24651–24800
208	24801–24950

Roll	Contents
209	24951–25100
210	25101–25250
211	25251–25400
212	25401–25550
213	25551–25700
214	25701–25850
215	25851–26000
216	26001–26150
217	26151–26300
218	26301–26450
219	26451–26600
220	26601–26750
221	26751–26900
222	26901–27050
223	27051–27200
224	27201–27350
225	27351–27500
226	27501–27650
227	27651–27800
228	27801–27950
229	27951–28100
230	28101–28250
231	28251–28400
232	28401–28550
233	28551–28700
234	28701–28850
235	28851–29000
236	29001–29150
237	29151–29300
238	29301–29450
239	29451–29600
240	29601–29750
241	29751–29900
242	29901–30050
243	30051–30200
244	30201–30350
245	30351–30500
246	30501–30650
247	30651–30800
248	30801–30950
249	30951–31100
250	31101–31250
251	31251–31400
252	31401–31550
253	31551–31700
254	31701–31850
255	31851–32000
256	32001–32150
257	32151–32300
258	32301–32450
259	32451–32600
260	32601–32750
261	32751–32900
262	32901–33050
263	33051–33200
264	33201–33350
265	33351–33500
266	33501–33650
267	33651–33800
268	33801–33950
269	33951–34100
270	34101–34250
271	34251–34400
272	34401–34550
273	34551–34700
274	34701–34850
275	34851–35000
276	35001–35150
277	35151–35300
278	35301–35450
279	35451–35600
280	35601–35750
281	35751–35900
282	35901–36050
283	36051–36200
284	36201–36350
285	36351–36500
286	36501–36650
287	36651–36800
288	36801–36950
289	36951–37100
290	37101–37250
291	37251–37400
292	37401–37550
293	37551–37700
294	37701–37850
295	37851–38000
296	38001–38150
297	38151–38300
298	38301–38450
299	38451–38600
300	38601–38750
301	38751–38900
302	38901–39050
303	39051–39200
304	39201–39350
305	39351–39500
306	39501–39650
307	39651–39800
308	39801–39950
309	39951–40100
310	40101–40250
311	40251–40400
312	40401–40550
313	40551–40700
314	40701–40850
315	40851–41000
316	41001–41150
317	41151–41300
318	41301–41450
319	41451–41600
320	41601–41750
321	41751–41900
322	41901–42050
323	42051–42200
324	42201–42350
325	42351–42500
326	42501–42650
327	42651–42800
328	42801–42950
329	42951–43100
330	43101–43250
331	43251–43400
332	43401–43550
333	43551–43700
334	43701–43850
335	43851–44000
336	44001–44150

Roll	Contents
337	44151–44300
338	44301–44450
339	44451–44600
340	44601–44750
341	44751–44900
342	44901–45050
343	45051–45200
344	45201–45350
345	45351–45500
346	45501–45650
347	45651–45750
348	45751–45857

Records Relating to Indian Treaties

Ratified Indian Treaties, 1722–1869. M668. 16 rolls. DP.

This microfilm publication reproduces ratified Indian treaties, 1722–1869, with related papers; eight unperfected treaties, 1854–55; a chronological list of the treaties; and indexes by place and by tribe. The list and indexes include a few entries dated as late as 1883. These documents are contained in General Records of the U.S. Government, Record Group 11.

This series of Indian treaties and related papers is arranged chronologically by the date of the signing of the treaty, and the treaties are numbered in that order. On the envelope containing each treaty is a label giving the name of tribe, the date, the date of ratification, the place of treaty, and, occasionally, added information. Each envelope is shown on the film before the treaty and other records it contains. The first seven treaties are copies. The first original treaty is that of September 17, 1778, with the Delaware Indians. Usually the accompanying papers consist of the Presidential proclamation of the treaty (with which the treaty is often fastened in order to incorporate it as part of the proclamation), the resolution of consent to ratification by the Senate, and printed copies of the treaty (duplicates have not been filmed). Sometimes there are copies of messages from the President to the Senate, copies of messages or letters of instruction to the treaty commissioners, and journals and correspondence concerning the treaty. In a few cases, the original treaty is missing. Envelope 247-A, on roll 10, contains eight unperfected treaties dated 1854–55.

Roll	Contents	Dates
1	Chronological list, index by place, and index by tribe, 1722–1883	

Numbered treaties and inclusive dates:

Roll	Contents	Dates
2	1–30	Aug. 14, 1772–Oct. 24, 1801
3	31–60	Dec. 27, 1801–July 22, 1814
4	61–95	Aug. 9, 1814–June 22, 1818
5	96–143	Aug. 24, 1818–Nov. 7, 1825
6	144–170	Jan. 24, 1826–Sept. 21, 1832
7	171–196	Oct. 11, 1832–Dec. 17, 1834
8	197–229	July 1, 1835–Nov. 23, 1837
9	230–252	Jan. 15, 1838–Aug. 6, 1848
10	253–276	Oct. 14, 1848–Nov. 4, 1854
11	277–300	Nov. 15, 1854–Dec. 21, 1855
12	301–320	Feb. 5, 1856–June 24, 1862
13	321–338	June 28, 1862–Sept. 29, 1865
14	339–354	Oct. 10, 1865–Apr. 7, 1866
15	355–363	Apr. 28, 1866–Mar. 19, 1867
16	364–374	Oct. 21, 1867–Aug. 13, 1868

Documents Relating to the Negotiation of Ratified and Unratified Treaties with Various Indian Tribes, 1801–1869. T494. 10 rolls.

These documents are part of Records of the Office of Indian Affairs, Record Group 75. They consist of journals of treaty commissioners, proceedings of councils, reports, and other records relating to the negotiation of Indian treaties that were ratified by the Senate plus similar records pertaining to Indian treaties that were never ratified by the Senate. Some of these treaties were made between Indian tribes without the United States as signatory. Most of the records in these files were taken from the incoming correspondence of the Office of Indian Affairs and that of the Secretary of War relating to Indian affairs. The ratified treaty files are arranged by treaty number assigned by the State Department (the custodian of the original treaties), thereby making the files the equivalent of a chronological arrangement by date of signing of the treaties. The unratified treaty files are arranged chronologically. The original ratified treaties are reproduced as M668.

Roll	Contents	Date
1	Introduction and ratified treaties	1801–26
2	Ratified treaties	1827–32
3	"	1833–37
4	"	1838–53
5	"	1854–55
6	"	1856–63
7	"	1864–68
8	Unratified treaties	1821–65
9	"	1866–67
10	"	1868–69

Records Relating to Territories

Territorial Papers of the United States

The *Territorial Papers of the United States* is a multi-volume documentary historical publication containing archival materials selected from many record groups of the National Archives. The objective of the series is to document the administrative history of the U.S. Territories with texts that are annotated, exact, representative, and particularly significant. In addition to governmental operations, the records relate to genealogy, economic development, Indian affairs, geographical features, and partisan politics.

Listed below are the principal rolls in each publication that contain material relating to American Indians. Other unlisted rolls may also contain small amounts of relevant material.

Wisconsin, 1836–1848. M236. 122 rolls. DP.

Roll	Contents
38	Records of the Bureau of Indian Affairs Letters received by the Office of Indian Affairs, 1836–48 Miscellaneous file: 1836–40
39	1841–48, miscellaneous emigration file, miscellaneous reserves
40	Schools file
41	"Special Files of the Office of Indian Affairs," 1836–46: special files no. 7, 16, 20, 29, 47, 49, 65, 81, 82, 98, 145, 161, 162
42	186, 190, 197, 200, 206
43	Letters sent: 1836–40
44	1841–48
45	Report books, 1838–48; miscellaneous record books, 1836–48
46	Segregated records relating to ratified Indian treaties, 1836–47, treaties no. 209, 216, 218, 223, 224, 225, 228, 233, 238, 242, 249, 250

Iowa, 1838–1846. M325. 102 rolls. DP.

Roll	Contents
56	Records of the Bureau of Indian Affairs Letters received by the Office of Indian Affairs, subject files "Schools," 1838–47 (0–619) "Stocks," 1840–47 (626–739) "Miscellaneous," 1838–46 (740–1266) "St. Louis Emigration," 1838–39 (1267–1279) "Miscellaneous Emigration," 1839 (1280–1290)
57	Letters sent by the Office of Indian Affairs, 1838–43
58	Letters sent by the Office of Indian Affairs, 1843–47
59	Report books, 1838–46 (0–335) Miscellaneous records, 1838–46 (336–642) Letters sent by the Winnebago Agency, 1846 (642A–642C) Register of applications and recommendations for appointment, 1838–46 (643–697)
74	Second Comptroller of the Treasury Letters received by the Second Comptroller of the Treasury, 1839–47 (0–74) Letters sent by the Second Comptroller of the Treasury, 1840–48 (75–138) Army contracts, 1838–47 (139–473) Second Auditor of the Treasury Second Auditor's letterbooks, 1839–47 (474–801) Second Auditor's Indian letters, 1846–51 (802–862) Accounts of the Second Auditor of the Treasury Office of Indian Affairs related accounts Superintendent of Indian Affairs for the Iowa Superintendency Settlement nos. 5,373/41–2, 636/45 Settlement nos. 2,747/45–9, 083/49
75	Military disbursing agent at St. Louis and Superintendent of Indian Affairs at St. Louis Settlement nos. 5,070/40–6, 317/41 (part)
76	Settlement nos. 6,317/41 (part)–1,150/44
77	Settlement nos. 1,799/45–3,261/44
78	Settlement nos. 3,658/46–9,258/49 (1–323) Council Bluffs Subagency Settlement nos. 4,741/40–3,509/56 (324–1269)

Roll	Contents
79	Sac and Fox Agency Settlement nos. 2,349/38–197/43
80	Settlement nos. 219/43–10,911/50
81	St. Peters Agency Settlement nos. 2,347/38–10,921/50
82	Turkey River Subagency Settlement nos. 4,908/40–1,200/44
83	Settlement nos. 1,393/44–3,885/46
84	Settlement nos. 3,900/46–13,496/52 (1–522) Upper Missouri Agency Settlement nos. 2,389/45–7,189/48 (523–771) U.S. Army Paymaster accounts Settlement nos. 2,524/39–5,729/41 (772–1298)

Oregon, 1849–1859. M1049. 12 rolls.

Roll	Contents
7	Interior Department Appointment Papers: Indian Division (Mar. 10, 1849–Feb. 11, 1859)
8	Records of the Bureau of Indian Affairs

Minnesota, 1849–1858. M1050. 19 rolls.

Roll	Contents
10	Records of the Office of the Secretary of the Interior Appointments Division: Press copies of letters sent, vol. 1, Oct. 31, 1856–Nov. 14, 1860; executive nominations, 2 vols., Mar. 12, 1849–Mar. 2, 1853, and Mar. 9, 1857–June 11, 1860; executive nominations, judiciary, 1 vol., Apr. 2–Oct. 13, 1849; executive commissions confirmed, vols. 1 and 2, Mar. 16, 1849–Mar. 25, 1861; executive commissions, temporary, 2 vols., Mar 25, 1849–June 26, 1861; and Minnesota Territory appointment papers, Milton H. Abbott–E. O. Jackson, Jan. 17, 1849–Sept. 1, 1858 Minnesota Territory appointment papers Isaac Jewett–Jeremiah Zander, Mar. 20, 1848–June 5, 1858, and charges file Willis A. Gorman and Henry C. Lowell, Jan. 17, 1854, and Apr. 6, 1857
11	Presidential proclamations Ratified Indian treaties Unratified Indian treaies Documents relating to negotiations of Indian treaties
14	Records of the Bureau of Indian Affairs: Letters sent, June 1, 1848–Mar. 19, 1856
15	Letters sent, Mar. 20, 1856–Oct. 23, 1858
16	Records of the Northern Superintendency, 1848–58
17	Accounts and records of the Northern Superintendency, 1857–58

State Department Territorial Papers

The Department of State supervised affairs in the Territories of the United States from 1789 to 1873. The Department attended to such matters as correspondence between the President and Territorial officials, the printing of Territorial laws, and the provision of seals for the official use of the Territories. In 1873, Congress transferred the supervision of the Territories to the Office of the Secretary of the Interior. Records of the period of Territorial administration by the Department of State are among the General Records of the Department of State, Record Group 59.

These records include correspondence, reports, copies of journals of proceedings of legislative assemblies, and other records relating to Territorial administration.

Arizona, 1864–1872. M342. 1 roll. DP.

Colorado series. M3. 1 roll. DP.

Dakota, 1861–1873. M309. 1 roll. DP.

Florida, 1777–1824. M116. 11 rolls.

Roll	Dates
1	Oct. 13, 1777–Dec. 1811
2	Jan.–Dec. 1812
3	Feb. 1813–Dec. 1817
4	Jan. 1818–Oct. 1820
5	Mar. 15–July 29, 1821
6	July 30, 1821
7	Aug. 4–Sept. 30, 1821
8	Oct. 1821
9	Nov.–Dec. 1821
10	Jan. 5, 1821–Nov. 5, 1822
11	Jan. 17, 1823–Sept. 9, 1824

Idaho, 1863–1872. M445. 1 roll. DP.

Kansas, 1854–1861. M218. 2 rolls. DP.

Roll	Contents
1	Official correspondence, May 30, 1854–Apr. 30, 1861
2	Executive minutes, June 29, 1854–Jan. 13, 1859

Missouri, 1812–1820. M1134. 1 roll.

Montana, 1864–1872. M356. 2 rolls.

Roll	Contents
1	Official correspondence, Oct. 14, 1864–July 16, 1872 (1 vol.), chiefly letters received by the Department of State, often transmitting records of proceedings of the Executive Office and the Legislative Assembly as well as messages from the Governors to the Assembly. There are also letters from officials in the Departments of the Interior, Justice, and War.
2	Second Legislative Assembly, Mar. 5–Apr. 13, 1866 (3 vols.). Copies of acts and resolutions of the Assembly and of the daily proceedings of the Territorial Council and the House of Representatives.

Nebraska, 1854–1867. M228. 1 roll. DP.

Nevada, 1861–1864. M13. 1 roll.

New Mexico, 1851–1872. T17. 4 rolls.

Roll	Dates
1	Mar. 3, 1851–Dec. 8, 1860
2	Jan. 2, 1861–Dec. 23, 1864
3	Jan. 6, 1865–Mar. 15, 1871
4	Apr. 28, 1871–Nov. 16, 1872

Oregon, 1848–1858. M419. 1 roll.

Orleans , 1764–1823. T260. 13 rolls.

Roll	Dates
1	Apr. 24, 1764–Dec. 12, 1833
2	Aug. 19–Dec. 27, 1803
3	Jan. 2–Mar. 30, 1804
4	Apr. 7–Aug. 29, 1804
5	Sept. 1–Dec. 31, 1804
6	Jan. 1–June 21, 1805
7	July 5–Dec. 15, 1805
8	Jan. 2–Dec. 31, 1806
9	Jan. 15, 1807–Dec. 27, 1808
10	Jan. 1–Dec. 31, 1809
11	Feb. 12–Dec. 28, 1810
12	Jan. 3–Dec. 20, 1811
13	Jan. 2, 1812–Dec. 6, 1813

Territory Northwest of the River Ohio, 1787–1801. M470. 1 roll.

Territory Southwest of the River Ohio, 1790–1795. M471. 1 roll.

Utah, 1853–1873. M12. 2 rolls. DP.

Roll	Dates
1	Apr. 30, 1853–Dec. 24, 1859
2	Jan. 5, 1860–Jan. 3, 1873

Washington Territory, 1854–1872. M26. 2 rolls.

Roll	Dates
1	July 1, 1854–Jan. 8, 1859
2	Feb. 18, 1859–Dec. 4, 1872

Wyoming, 1868–1873. M85. 1 roll.

Interior Department Territorial Papers

Congress delegated supervision of the Territories to the Secretary of State until 1873 when they were assigned to the Department of the Interior. The papers described below are chiefly original letters from the Territorial Governors and secretaries to the President or to the Secretaries of State or the Interior; journals of executive proceedings in Territories; acts of Territorial legislatures; and letters and documents predating the establishment of a Territory. These papers are from the Records of the Office of the Secretary of the Interior, Record Group 48.

Alaska, 1869–1913. M430. 17 rolls. DP.

Roll　　　　*Dates*

Letters received relating to the District of Alaska, Feb. 3, 1869–July 2, 1907:

Roll	Dates
1	Feb. 3 and Dec. 3, 1869, and Apr. 20, 1880–Dec. 21, 1889
2	Jan. 21, 1890–Dec. 21, 1892
3	Dec. 30, 1892–Dec. 30, 1896
4	Feb. 1–Dec. 27, 1897
5	Dec. 13, 1897–Dec. 20, 1898
6	Jan. 5–Dec. 24, 1899
7	Jan. 3–Dec. 29, 1900
8	Jan. 4–Dec. 21, 1901
9	Jan. 7, 1902–Dec. 15, 1903
10	Jan. 14–Dec. 23, 1904
11	Dec. 28, 1904–May 3, 1905
12	Mar. 13–July 11, 1905
13	July 1–Dec. 16, 1905
14	Nov. 22, 1905–May 5, 1906
15	May 7, 1906–July 2, 1907

Letters received, Oct. 26, 1899–Jan. 21, 1911, relating to:

Roll	
16	(1) Alaska-Canada boundary disputes, Oct. 26, 1899–June 15, 1906; (2) the Alaskan insane, June 27, 1900–Dec. 15, 1904;
17	Jan. 17, 1905–Jan. 21, 1911

Arizona, 1868–1913. M429. 8 rolls. DP.

Roll	Contents
1	Executive proceedings and official correspondence, July 1, 1877–Dec. 31, 1903
2	Messages of the Governor and reports of Territorial officials, 1905–7
3	Letters received, Feb. 14, 1868–Jan. 24, 1888, relating to: (1) disturbances along the Mexican border, Dec. 13, 1878–Jan. 25, 1884, and (2) miscellaneous subjects, Feb. 14, 1868–Jan. 24, 1888

Letters received relating to miscellaneous subjects:

4	Apr. 2, 1889–Oct. 27, 1898
5	Mar. 11, 1899–June 25, 1907

Subject-classified files of the Office of the Secretary of the Interior, 1907–13 and 1919:

6	9–2–1	Annual reports of Governors and Territorial officials, parts 1–2, and supplements A–1–4, 1907–12 and 1919
7	9–2–2	Claims against Territory, 1907
	9–2–3	Smuggling of arms to Yaqui Indians, 1907–9
	9–2–4	Comptroller's decisions, 1907
	9–2–5	Toll road through Grand Canyon Forest Reserve, 1907
	9–2–6	Extradition with Mexico for escaped convicts, 1907–11
	9–2–7	Arizona Corporation Charter Guarantee Co., 1907
	9–2–8	Acts of legislature, 1907–12
	9–2–9	Miscellaneous, parts 1–3, 1907–12
	9–2–10	Federal appointments, 1907–8
	9–2–11	Leave granted Governor, 1907–12
	9–2–12	Observatory land tract, 1908
	9–2–13	Protection of Mexican citizens, improper treatment of Mexicans, parts 1–2, 1908–11

Roll	Contents
	9–2–15	Bond issue, general, 1908-10; legislation, 1909–11
8	9–2–16	Statehood, general, parts 1–6, 1908–13; legislation, 1911–12
	9–2–17	Judicial affairs, 1909–11
	9–2–18	Professional practice in Territory, 1909–11
	9–2–19	National forests, 1909
	9–2–21	General legislation, 1909–11

Colorado, 1861–1888. M431. 1 roll. DP.

Dakota, 1863–1889. M310. 3 rolls. DP.

Roll	Dates
1	July 1, 1877–June 30, 1886
2	Jan. 1, 1887–Dec. 31, 1888
3	Letters received, June 25, 1863–Dec. 26, 1889, relating to: (1) the U. S. penitentiary in Dakota Territory, Feb. 25, 1881–Feb. 27, 1886, and (2) miscellaneous subjects, June 25, 1863–Dec. 26, 1889

Idaho, 1864–1890. M191. 3 rolls. DP.

Roll	Contents
1	Executive proceedings and official correspondence, July 6, 1880–Dec. 14, 1885
2	Executive proceedings and official correspondence, Jan. 12, 1886–Dec. 23, 1889
3	Letters received, June 21, 1864–Nov. 24, 1890, relating to: (1) miscellaneous subjects, June 21, 1864–Oct. 28, 1890, and (2) the penitentiary at Boise City, Jan. 14, 1869–June 8, 1872, and Jan. 18, 1889–Nov. 24, 1890

Montana, 1867–1889. M192. 2 rolls. DP.

Roll	Contents
1	Executive proceedings and official correspondence, June 1, 1877–June 24, 1887
2	Letters received, Feb. 5, 1867–Nov. 25, 1889, relating to: (1) the U.S. penitentiary in Montana Territory, Feb. 5, 1867–May 21, 1886, (2) the Deer Lodge Telegraph Co. of Montana, Nov. 9, 1877–Apr. 9, 1878, and (3) miscellaneous subjects, May 21. 1867–Nov. 25, 1889

New Mexico, 1851–1914. M364. 15 rolls. DP.

Roll　　　　*Contents*

Executive proceedings:

1	Oct. 8, 1874–Dec. 31, 1888
2	July 1, 1889–Dec. 31, 1899
3	Jan. 1, 1900–Dec. 31, 1906
4	Letters received relating to: (1) public buildings and grounds, Sept. 18, 1858–Feb. 16, 1899, and (2) Adobe Palace, Sept. 1867–Dec. 14, 1900

Letters received relating to inspection of coal mines:

5	Nov. 12, 1892–Dec. 14, 1896
6	Jan. 14, 1897–Dec. 9, 1901
7	Jan. 10, 1902–May 9, 1907

Letters received relating to miscellaneous subjects:

8	Apr. 1851–Nov. 20, 1900
9	Mar. 30, 1901–May 29, 1907

Roll		Contents

Subject-classified files of the Office of the Secretary of the Interior, 1906–14 and 1923:

10	9–5–2	Extradition with Mexico, 1908–9
	9–5–3	Progress and development, annual reports, Executive proceedings, etc., 1907–13, parts 1–3 and supplements
	9–5–4	Depository for Territorial funds, 1907
11	9–5–5	Investigation of land transactions, American Lumber Co., parts 1–3, 1907–13; general, parts 1–12, 1906–7
12		General, parts 13–17, supplements A2–A5, and special memorandums, 1906–9; Pennsylvania Development Co., New Mexico Fuel and Iron Co., and W. S. Hopewell, 1906–9; Rio Mimbres Irrigation Co., parts 1–2, 1908
13	9–5–6	Miscellaneous matters, parts 1–2, 1907–12, 1923
	9–5–7	Legislation, acts of legislature, journal of legislative proceedings, general, 1906–12 Legislative Assembly of New Mexico—legislation, 60th and 61st Congresses, parts 1–2, 1908–10
	9–5–8	Statehood, general, parts 1–5, 1907–11;
14		General, parts 6–8, 1911–14 Legislation, 1909–14
	9–5–9	Investment of Territorial funds, 1907–11
	9–5–10	Proclamations of Governor, 1907–10
15	9–5–11	Normal University, 1907
	9–5–12	Attorney General, 1907
	9–5–13	Leave granted Territorial officials, 1907–11
	9–5–14	Cruelty to animals, 1908
	9–5–15	Protection of Mexican citizens: improper treatment of Mexicans, etc., 1908–11
	9–5–16	Liquor traffic, regulation, prohibition, etc., 1908
	9–5–17	New Mexico College of Agriculture and Mechanic Arts, 1908
	9–5–18	Territorial and school lands, general, 1907–12; leases; forms, 1907; Gaar, James M. et al., 1908–10; general, parts 1–3, 1907–11; legislation, 1910
	9–5–19	Judicial affairs, 1908–10
	9–5–20	Messages of Governor to Legislative Assembly, 1909
	9–5–21	Bond issues, general, 1909; legislation, 60th and 61st Congresses, parts 1–2, 1908–10

Roll		Contents
	9–5–22	Sale of timber on Territorial lands, 1908
	9–5–23	Professional practice in Territory, 1908–10
	9–5–24	National forests, proceeds from, etc., 1909
	9–5–25	New Mexico Institute for the Blind, 1909
	9–5–26	General legislation, 1908–12
	9–5–27	Construction of public wells, legislation, 1910
	9–5–28	Official seal, 1911
	9–5–29	Court of Private Land Claims, 1911

Oklahoma, 1889–1912. M828. 5 rolls. DP.

1	Letters received by the Patents and Miscellaneous Division, May 5, 1889–July 20, 1907, relating to: Cheyenne and Arapahoe Strip Land Opening, Mar. 30, 1892–Nov. 15, 1894 Cherokee Outlet Land Opening, May 5, 1889–June 19, 1894 Miscellaneous subjects: May 16, 1890–Nov. 10, 1900
2	Jan. 18, 1901–Apr. 22, 1904
3	May 10, 1904–Dec. 12, 1905
4	Jan. 2–Dec. 11, 1906
5	Jan. 2–July 20, 1907

Subject-classified files of the Office of the Secretary of the Interior, 1905, 1907–12, 1918:

	9–6–1	Proposed constitution, parts 1 and 2, 1905, 1907–8
	9–6–2	Oil inspection laws, 1907
	9–6–3	Town lot fund, parts 1–3, 1907–12
	9–6–4	Reports of treasurer and secretary of board for leasing school lands, parts 1–4, 1907
	9–6–5	Census, 1907
	9–6–6	Progress and development, 1907–8
	9–6–7	Miscellaneous, 1907–9
	9–6–8	Complaint, *Sarah Frey* v. *Dave McClure*, 1907
	9–6–9	Election expenses, constitutional convention, 1907–9
	9–6–10	Acts of legislature, 1907–8
	9–6–11	"Enabling Act," 1907
	9–6–12	Appointment of townsite trustees, 1907
	9–6–13	Appointment of notaries public, 1907
	9–6–14	Statehood, 1907–9, 1918
	9–6–15	Bank holiday, 1907
	9–6–16	Newspaper clippings, 1907

Utah, 1850–1902. M428. 6 rolls. DP.

Roll	Contents

Executive proceedings:

1	Mar. 12, 1877–Dec. 31, 1888
2	Jan. 1, 1889–Dec. 31, 1893

Letters received relating to:

3	The U.S. penitentiary in Utah, Sept. 30, 1885–July 8, 1896
4	Polygamy, Jan. 27, 1879–Dec. 17, 1897

Roll	Contents
5	Inspection of coal mines, Nov. 12, 1892–Feb. 7, 1896
6	Miscellaneous subjects, Jan. 1, 1850–Apr. 3, 1886, and June 20, 1902

Washington, 1854–1902. M189. 4 rolls. DP.

Roll	Contents
1	Executive proceedings, Mar. 28, 1877–Dec. 27, 1884, and official correspondence, Mar. 4–June 19, 1878
2	Executive proceedings, Jan. 2, 1885–June 29, 1889
3	Letters received, Aug. 15, 1854–Oct. 4, 1890, relating to: (1) anti-Chinese disturbances, Oct. 12, 1885–Feb. 12, 1887, (2) an alleged lynching of an Indian in British Columbia by residents of Washington Territory, May 8–July 17, 1884, and (3) miscellaneous subjects, Aug. 15, 1854–Oct. 4, 1890
4	Letters received, Jan. 28, 1867–Aug. 9, 1902, relating to: (1) the Territorial penitentiary at McNeil Island, Jan. 28, 1867–Oct. 23, 1888, and (2) the penitentiary at Walla Walla, July 21, 1892–Aug. 9, 1902

Wyoming, 1870–1890. M204. 6 rolls. DP.

Roll	Contents
1	Executive proceedings, Jan. 1, 1878–Dec. 30, 1884, and official correspondence, June 21, 1878–Dec. 22, 1884
2	Executive proceedings, Jan. 2, 1885–Dec. 22, 1886, and official correspondence, Jan. 2, 1885–Dec. 27, 1886
3	Executive proceedings, Jan. 3, 1887–Dec. 26, 1888, and official correspondence, Jan. 3, 1887–Dec. 31, 1888
4	Executive proceedings, Jan. 2–Dec. 31, 1889, and official correspondence, Jan. 2–Dec. 31, 1889
5	Executive proceedings, Jan. 4–Aug. 7, 1890, and official correspondence, Jan. 1–Oct. 13, 1890
6	Letters received, June 4, 1870–Sept. 25, 1890, relating to: (1) Territorial matters prior to 1873, Dec. 20, 1870–May 14, 1873, (2) the penitentiary at Laramie, June 4, 1870–Jan. 1, 1878, and Apr. 22, 1886–May 2, 1890, and (3) miscellaneous subjects, Jan. 17, 1876–Sept. 25, 1890

Records Relating to Appointments

State Department Letters of Application and Recommendation

Letters of application and recommendation were submitted by applicants, supporters, and occasionally opponents, for positions within the State Department. They are arranged by Presidential administration in 4- and 8-year blocks and thereunder alphabetically by surname of the applicant or person recommended. The applications are mainly for posi-tions with the State Department or its Foreign Service. However, since the Department was once responsible for most aspects of domestic administration not related to war or finance, the positions applied for include most of those within the Federal service, including positions relating to Indian affairs.

These records are from the General Records of the Department of State, Record Group 59. For a complete roll listing of these microfilm publications see *Genealogical and Biographical Research: A Select Catalog of National Archives Microfilm Publications* or the individual descriptive pamphlets. The letters of application and recommendation for the Washington administration are held by the Manuscript Division of the Library of Congress.

During the Administration of:

John Adams, 1797–1801. M406. 3 rolls. DP.

Thomas Jefferson, 1801–1809. M418. 12 rolls.

James Madison, 1809–1817. M438. 8 rolls. DP.

James Monroe, 1817–1825. M439. 19 rolls. DP.

John Quincy Adams, 1825–1829. M531. 8 rolls. DP.

Andrew Jackson, 1829–1837. M639. 27 rolls. DP.

Martin Van Buren, William Henry Harrison, and John Tyler, 1837–1845. M687. 35 rolls. DP.

James Polk, Zachary Taylor, and Millard Fillmore, 1845–1853. M873. 98 rolls. DP.

Franklin Pierce and James Buchanan, 1853–1861. M967. 50 rolls. DP.

Abraham Lincoln and Andrew Johnson, 1861–1869. M650. 53 rolls. DP.

Ulysses S. Grant, 1869–1877. M968. 69 rolls. DP.

Interior Department Appointment Papers

The records cited pertain only to superintendents of Indian affairs and Indian agents, positions normally filled by Presidential appointment. Among the records are letters of application and recommendation, petitions, reports, oaths of office, bonds, notices of dates of succession, and applications for leaves of absence. Also, the records document such matters as resignations, removals, and the investigation of charges against officials. Several documents pertain to the establishment or discontinuance of offices rather than to filling positions, and some concern the assignment of Army officers as acting Indian agents. The records are arranged by title of office or position and thereunder alphabetically by name of applicant or incumbent. These records are from the Records of the Office of the Secretary of the Interior, Record Group 48.

Arizona, 1857–1907. M576. 22 rolls. DP.

Roll	Contents
16	Arizona Superintendency of Indian Affairs. 1861–73; Camp Apache Indian Agency, 1872–76; Camp Grant Indian Agency. 1872–73; Camp Verde Indian Agency. 1872–75; Chiricahua Indian Agency 1873–74. Colorado River Indian Agency, A–B, 1870–97
17	Colorado River Indian Agency, C–W, 1865–1903
18	Fort Apache Indian Agency. 1896–1905; Moqui Pueblo Indian Agency. 1869–83; Papago Indian Agency, 1871–78
19	Pima Indian Agency, A–H, 1865–1907
20	Pima Indian Agency, J–Y, 1866–1905
21	San Carlos Indian Agency, A–K, 1873–1906
22	San Carlos Indian Agency, L–W, 1876–1903: Supervisor of the Census, 1889–90

California, 1849–1907. M732. 29 rolls. DP.

Roll	Contents
20	California Superintendency of Indian Affairs, 1852–67; Superintending Agent: Northern District, 1858–63, Southern District, 1858–66
21	Fresno Indian Subagency, 1850–57; Hoopa Valley Indian Agency, 1864–98; Klamath Indian Agency, 1856–61; Mendocino Indian Subagency, 1860–61 Mission Indian Agency
22	A–L, 1871–97
23	M–Y, 1874–1903
24	Nome Lake Indian Agency, 1857–61; Round Valley Indian Agency, 1864–94
25	Smith River Indian Agency, 1866; Tejon (Sebastian) Indian Agency, 1855–59; Tule River Indian Agency, 1866–89
26	Early Indian Agents, 1849–52; unspecified Indian agency, 1853–97

Colorado, 1857–1907. M808. 13 rolls.

Roll	Contents
13	Los Pinos, Middle Park-White River, Southern Ute, and Upper Arkansas Indian Agencies, 1857–1903; unspecified Indian agency, 1861–69; Supervisor of the Census, 1889–90, and Pension Agent, 1866–77

Florida, 1849–1907. M1119. 6 rolls.

Roll	Contents
6	General Land Office registers and receivers, Tallahassee (H–W), 1849–82; Tampa, 1854–59; Supervisors of the Census, 1879–80 and 1889–90; Indian Agent, 1849–96; miscellaneous Indian Agents, 1849–94; appraisers of abandoned military reservations, 1886–96; timber agent, 1852–79; unspecified offices, 1857–93

Idaho, 1862–1907. M693. 17 rolls. DP.

Roll	Contents
13	Idaho Superintendency of Indian Affairs; unspecified Indian agency; Fort Hall Indian Agency: A–H
14	I–W
15	Lemhi Indian Agency Nez Perce Indian Agency:
16	A–M
17	N–W Supervisor of the Census

Missouri, 1849–1907. M1058. 9 rolls. DP.

Roll	Contents
1	Supervisor of the Census Superintendent of Indian Affairs

Nevada, 1860–1907. M1033. 3 rolls. DP.

Roll	Contents
Indian Agencies:	
3	Nevada; Pyramid Lake; Southeast Pi-Ute; Walker River; Western Shoshoni

New Mexico, 1850–1907. M750. 18 rolls. DP.

Roll	Contents
Indian Agencies:	
12	New Mexico Superintendency of Indian Affairs, 1861–69; Abiquiu Indian Agency, 1870–78; Cimarron Indian Agency, 1869–77; Mescalero Indian Agency, 1869–99, A–B
13	C–Y
Navajo Indian Agency:	
14	A–J, 1872–1902
15	K–Z, 1872–1903
Pueblo Indian Agency:	
16	A–S, 1863–1902
17	T–Y, 1857–1902; Southern Apache Indian Agency, 1872–76; unspecified Indian agencies, 1857–67

New York, 1849–1906. M1022. 5 rolls. DP.

Roll	Contents
1	Supervisor of the Census, 1879–95; Indian Agent, 1849–1902, A–G
2	Indian Agent, 1849–1902, H–S
3	Indian Agent, 1849–1902, T–W; Pension Agent, 1849–1906, Albany-Buffalo

North Carolina, 1849–1892. M950. 1 roll. DP.

Oregon, 1849–1907. M814. 10 rolls. DP.

Roll	Contents
8	Superintendent of Indian Affairs, 1849–76; Alsea Indian Subagency, 1872–76; Grand Ronde Indian Agency, 1872–97; Klamath Indian Agency, 1871–98
9	Malheur Indian Agency, 1873–80; Siletz Indian Agency, 1874–97; Umatilla Indian Agency, 1865–1902
10	Warm Springs Indian Agency, 1860–98; unspecified Indian agency, 1849–71; Pension Agent, 1852–74; Supervisor of the Census, 1889–90

Wisconsin, 1849–1907. M831. 9 rolls. DP.

Roll	Contents
7	Green Bay Indian Agency, 1849–1904
8	La Pointe Indian Agency, 1849–1906; unspecified, 1861

Wyoming, 1869–1907. M830. 6 rolls. DP.

Roll	Contents
6	Shoshone Indian Agency, 1870–1907; Supervisor of the Census, 1889–90

Records of Miscellaneous Civilian Agencies

Consular Despatches

Consular despatches are the official communications sent by United States consuls to the Department of State. It is difficult to ascertain the number of consular records that contain material relating to American Indians, but generally despatches from consular posts in Canada and Mexico located on or near the border contain at least scattered references to difficulties of American citizens with Indian bands ranging across the border. After 1876, the principle of "hot pursuit" was in effect in the United States' dealings with Mexico. Despatches from Winnipeg contain many references to Sitting Bull and efforts to return him to the United States (1876–82). Consular despatches should supplement Army records relating to the pursuit of Indians.

The following microfilmed consular despatches may contain materials relating to American Indians. For each post, the rolls are arranged chronologically. For a complete listing of microfilmed consular despatches see *Diplomatic Records: A Select Catalog of National Archives Publications* or the individual descriptive pamphlets. Consular despatches are found in the General Records of the Department of State, Record Group 59.

Mexico

Guaymas, 1832–1896. M284. 5 rolls. DP.

Roll	Dates
1	Nov. 27, 1832–June 30, 1872
2	July 7, 1872–Mar. 31, 1880
3	Apr. 11, 1880–Oct. 30, 1886
4	Nov. 1, 1888–July 20, 1889
5	Aug. 2, 1889–Feb. 27, 1896

Guerrero, 1871–1888. M292. 1 roll. DP.

Matamoras, 1826–1906. M281. 12 rolls. DP.

Roll	Dates
1	July 24, 1826–Dec. 24, 1839
2	Jan. 1, 1840–Dec. 12, 1857
3	Jan. 1, 1858–Dec. 28, 1869

Roll	Dates
4	Jan. 1, 1870–Mar. 10, 1874
5	Mar. 19, 1874–Apr. 28, 1879
6	May 7, 1879–July 15, 1881
7	Aug. 3, 1881–June 30, 1883
8	July 2, 1883–Dec. 31, 1884
9	Jan. 1, 1885–Mar. 31, 1887
10	Apr. 1, 1888–June 30, 1888
11	July 6, 1888–Dec. 31, 1892
12	Jan. 3, 1893–Aug. 3, 1906

Mexico City, 1822–1906. M296. 15 rolls. DP.

Roll	Dates
1	July 30, 1822–Dec. 28, 1836
2	Jan. 4, 1837–June 24, 1838
3	July 3, 1838–May 16, 1839
4	May 16, 1839–Dec. 30, 1845
5	Jan. 11, 1846–Apr. 19, 1859
6	Jan. 15, 1861–Dec. 10, 1869
7	Jan. 26, 1870–Jan. 25, 1875
8	Feb. 15, 1875–Dec. 31, 1879
9	Jan. 2, 1880–Oct. 13, 1886
10	Nov. 12, 1886–Apr. 29, 1893
11	May 10, 1893–June 28, 1897
12	July 5, 1897–Dec. 23, 1899
13	Jan. 2, 1900–Dec. 18, 1901
14	Jan. 6, 1902–Mar. 30, 1905
15	Apr. 4, 1905–Aug. 16, 1906

Mier, 1870–1878. M297. 1 roll. DP.

Monterey, Upper California, 1834–1848. M138. 1 roll.

Monterrey, 1849–1906. M165. 7 rolls. DP.

Roll	Dates
1	Nov. 15, 1849–Dec. 9, 1869
2	Jan. 1, 1870–Sept. 18, 1873
3	Oct. 1873–Dec. 31, 1880
4	Feb. 13, 1881–June 30, 1889
5	Jan. 31, 1898–Aug. 31, 1901
6	Sept. 2, 1901–Dec. 31, 1903
7	Jan. 1, 1904–Aug. 7, 1906

Nogales, 1889–1906. M283. 4 rolls. DP.

Roll	Dates
1	July 5, 1889–Feb. 28, 1893
2	Mar. 15, 1893–Apr. 27, 1897
3	May 11, 1897–Dec. 29, 1902
4	Jan. 2, 1903–July 26, 1906

Nuevo Laredo, 1871–1906. M280. 4 rolls. DP.

Roll	Dates
1	Nov. 30, 1871–May 31, 1889
2	June 1, 1889–May 31, 1891
3	June 4, 1891–June 30, 1893
4	July 3, 1893–July 30, 1906

Piedras Negras, 1868–1906. M299. 5 rolls.

Roll	Dates
1	Jan. 8, 1868–July 14, 1881
2	Sept. 7, 1881–Nov. 25, 1889
3	Dec. 6, 1889–Dec. 31, 1893
4	Jan. 4, 1894–June 16, 1897

Roll	Dates
5	July 10, 1897–July 30, 1906

Santa Fe, 1830–1846. M199. 1 roll. DP.

Texas
Galveston, 1832–1846. T151. 2 rolls.

Roll	Dates
1	Sept. 15, 1832–Dec. 22, 1841
2	Jan. 1, 1842–Nov. 20, 1846

Canada
Fort Erie, 1865–1906. T465. 3 rolls.

Roll	Dates
1	Mar. 9, 1865–Dec. 31, 1869
2	Jan. 11, 1870–Dec. 22, 1882
3	Jan. 4, 1883–Aug. 14, 1906

Moncton, 1885-1905. T636. 2 rolls.

Roll	Dates
1	Oct. 31, 1885–Dec. 28, 1900
2	Feb. 13, 1901–Dec. 5, 1905

Sherbrooke, 1879–1906. T680. 3 rolls.

Roll	Dates
1	Mar. 31, 1879–Dec. 20, 1887
2	Jan. 4, 1888–July 11, 1900
3	Jan. 11, 1901–July 26, 1906

Sorel, 1882–1898. T684. 1 roll.

Toronto, 1864–1906. T491. 9 rolls.

Roll	Dates
1	Jan. 15, 1864–Dec. 29, 1866
2	Jan. 3, 1867–Jan. 2, 1868
3	Jan. 1–Dec. 22, 1868
4	Dec. 23, 1868–Dec. 28, 1869
5	Oct. 4, 1865–June 20, 1873
6	July 18, 1873–Dec. 31, 1884
7	Jan. 2, 1885–Dec. 21, 1892
8	Jan. 3, 1893–Dec. 31, 1902
9	Feb. 20, 1903–July 20, 1905

Victoria, 1862–1906. T130. 16 rolls.

Roll	Dates
1	Apr. 14, 1862–Dec. 31, 1869
2	Jan. 6, 1870–Oct. 3, 1872
3	Oct. 10, 1872–Dec. 23, 1874
4	Jan. 2, 1875–Jan. 25, 1877
5	Feb. 10, 1877–Sept. 25, 1884
6	Oct. 5, 1884–Mar. 31, 1886
7	Apr. 4, 1886–June 28, 1887
8	July 1, 1887–Dec. 31, 1888
9	Jan. 7, 1889–Dec. 31, 1890
10	Jan. 2, 1891–July 26, 1892
11	Aug. 2, 1892–June 23, 1894
12	July 2, 1894–June 29, 1898
13	Report, Sept. 24, 1897
14	July 5, 1898–May 31, 1901
15	June 11, 1901–Feb. 25, 1905
16	Mar. 14, 1904–Aug. 9, 1906

Windsor, 1864–1906. T492. 4 rolls.

Roll	Dates
1	Nov. 8, 1864–Dec. 10, 1869
2	Jan. 4, 1870–Dec. 26, 1882
3	Jan. 1, 1883–Dec. 31, 1894
4	Feb. 8, 1895–Aug. 8, 1906

Winnipeg, 1869–1906. T24. 10 rolls.

Roll	Dates
1	June 11, 1869–Dec. 19, 1871
2	Dec. 21, 1871–May 3, 1873
3	May 21, 1873–Mar. 23, 1874
4	Mar. 25, 1874–Feb. 3, 1875
5	Apr. 6, 1875–Dec. 31, 1881
6	Jan. 2, 1882–Aug. 28, 1885
7	Sept. 1, 1885–Aug. 16, 1889
8	Sept. 2, 1889–Sept. 30, 1895
9	Oct. 10, 1895–Nov. 24, 1902
10	Feb. 13, 1903–Aug. 11, 1906

Other Records of the Department of State

Journal of Charles Mason Kept During the Survey of the Mason and Dixon Line, 1763–1768. M86. 1 roll.

The journal kept by Charles Mason during the Mason and Dixon survey of the boundary between Pennsylvania and Maryland includes comments on Indians.

"War of 1812 Papers" of the Department of State, 1789–1815. M588. 7 rolls. DP.

The War of 1812 papers include some intercepted correspondence of British military officers relating to Indian affairs on the U.S.-Canadian frontier.

Domestic Letters of the Department of State, 1784–1906. M40. 171 rolls.

This series consists of letters sent to persons other than U.S. and foreign diplomats and contains some documents relating to Indian treaties.

Miscellaneous Letters of the Department of State, 1789–1906. M179. 1,310 rolls. DP.

This series consists of letters received from persons other than U.S. and foreign diplomats and contains some documents relating to Indian treaties.

Records of the Continental Congress and the Constitutional Convention (Record Group 360)

Papers of the Continental Congress, 1774–1789. M247. 204 rolls. DP.

The records of the Continental and Confederation Congresses, known informally as the Papers of the Continental Congress, are the basic governmental records of the United States before the establishment of the Federal

Government in 1789. A number of these documents relate to Indians.

Material pertaining to Indians is contained in the Journals of Congress; reports of Congressional committees; memorials and petitions submitted to Congress; and letters and reports from State governments, military and naval personnel, government officials, and private citizens. The records include information on the establishment of administrative machinery for supervising relations with the Indians, the negotiation of Indian treaties, the appointment and instruction of commissioners for Indian affairs, trade with the Indians, hostilities between Indians and white settlers, the protection of the frontier, and the enlistment of Indians in the Continental Army.

The Papers of the Continental Congress are indexed in the 5-volume *Index: Papers of the Continental Congress, 1774–1789*, compiled by John P. Butler (1978). The *Index* has major headings for Indians and Indian Affairs, Commissioner of. See also individual names, tribes, and States.

Records of the Supreme Court of the United States (Record Group 267)

The Supreme Court of the United States, provided for in article III, section 1, of the Constitution, was established by the Judiciary Act of September 24, 1789. The Court's jurisdiction extends to all cases in law or equity arising under the Constitution and laws of the United States, and treaties made under their authority.

The Court decided cases concerning almost every aspect of Indian life, including determination of a tribe's legal existence and an individual's membership in a tribe, tribal property rights, jurisdiction over criminal acts on reservations, treaties, the scope of Federal power over Indian affairs, claims, and other matters. Case files may include petitions for writs of error or certiorari; transcripts of records from lower courts; and exhibits, agreements of counsel, briefs, depositions, motions, orders, judgments, mandates to lower courts, correspondence, and other papers.

Index to the Appellate Case Files of the Supreme Court of the United States, 1792–1909. M408. 20 rolls. DP. 16 mm.

This publication reproduces an alphabetical card index of about 59,000 cards. The early appellate case files, 1792–1831, have been microfilmed separately.

Each card in the index gives the name of the party in the case, the file number, the title of the case, the date the case was docketed, and the date of the decision. Cards for other parties in a case are not always included in the index. For the parties involved in more than one case, such as the United States, individual States, cities, and many other subjects, the cards under each heading are arranged in numeric order by case file number.

Roll	Contents
1	A–Bars
2	Bart–Bri
3	Bro–Cha
4	Che–Cra
5	Cre–Eap
6	Ear–Fos
7	Fou–Gun
8	Gur–Hov
9	How–Ken
10	Keo–Lov
11	Low–Mem
12	Men–Nel
13	Nem–Pea
14	Pec–Rib
15	Ric–Sed
16	See–Ste
17	Sti–Ull
18	Ulm–U.S. (case 16011)
19	U.S. (case 16015)–Wei
20	Wel–Z

Appellate Case Files of the Supreme Court of the United States, 1792–1831. M214. 96 rolls. DP.

This microfilm publication reproduces the appellate case files of the Supreme Court of the United States, 1792–1831. These records consist chiefly of transcripts of record of the cases of lower courts, comprising copies of the papers filed and of minute entries of the lower courts' actions in the cases. The case files also include documents associated with the transcripts of record, and there are documents resulting from the proceedings. Case numbers, dates of docketing, and the terms in which the cases were settled are also provided.

Roll	Inclusive Case Nos. and Dates of Docketing	Terms
1	1–14; June 30, 1792–Jan. 28, 1796	Feb. 1793–Aug. 1796
2	15–23; Jan. 28, 1796	Feb. and Aug. 1796
3	24–48; Jan. 28, 1796–July 17, 1797	Feb. 1796–Feb. 1799
4	49–87; July 17, 1797–Aug. 4, 1800	Aug. 1797–Feb. 1807
5	88–131; Aug. 14, 1800–Feb. 8, 1803	Aug. 1801–Feb. 1805
6	132–174; Feb. 1, 1803–Feb. 1804	Feb. 1803–Feb. 1808
7	175–200; Feb. 7, 1804–Jan. 29, 1805	Feb. 1804–Feb. 1808
8	201–230; Jan. 29, 1805–Jan. 23, 1806	Feb. 1805–Feb. 1809
9	231–257; Jan. 28–June 10, 1806	Feb. 1806–Feb. 1809
10	258–282; July 21, 1806–Feb. 1807	Feb. 1807–Feb. 1809
11	283–300; Feb.–Aug. 10, 1807	Feb. 1807–Feb. 1817
12	301–327; Oct. 3, 1807–Feb. 1, 1808	Feb. 1808–Feb. 1810
13	328–355; Feb. 1, 1808–Feb. 1809	Feb. 1809–Feb. 1815
14	356–375; Jan.–Feb. 1809	Feb. 1809–Feb. 1819
15	376–405; Feb.–Aug. 5, 1809	Feb. 1809–Feb. 1815
16	406–426; Nov. 30, 1809–Feb. 5, 1810	Feb. 1810, Feb. 1812

Roll	Inclusive Case Nos. and Dates of Docketing	Terms
17	427–447; Feb. 5–16, 1810	Feb. 1810–Feb. 1813
18	448–468; Feb. 17, 1810–Jan. 28, 1811	Feb. 1810–Feb. 1817
19	469–490; Feb. 4–11, 1811	Feb. 1812–Feb. 1815
20	491–510; Feb. 13–Nov. 2, 1811	Feb. 1812–Feb. 1817
21	511–528; Nov. 2, 1811–Jan. 29, 1812	Feb. 1812–Feb. 1815
22	529–548; Jan. 30–Feb. 8, 1812	Feb. 1812–Feb. 1817
23	549–564; Feb. 8–Nov. 10, 1812	Feb. 1813–Feb. 1815
24	565–577; Nov. 17, 1812–Jan. 27, 1813	Feb. 1813–Feb. 1815
25	578–602; Jan. 27–Feb. 10, 1813	Feb. 1814–Feb. 1815
26	603–615; Feb. 19–July 30, 1813	Feb. 1814–Feb. 1819
27	616–634; Aug. 3, 1813–Jan. 31, 1814	Feb. 1814–Feb. 1824
28	635–644; Jan. 24–Feb. 17, 1814	Feb. 1814–Feb. 1817
29	645–657; Jan. 27–Feb. 7, 1814	Feb. 1814–Feb. 1816
30	658–662; Feb. 1814	Feb. 1814–Feb. 1818
31	663–666; Feb. 7 and Mar. 3, 1814	Feb. 1814 and Feb. 1816
32	667–703; Feb. 1814–Jan. 2, 1815	Feb. 1814–Feb. 1820
33	704–708; Jan. 2, 1815	Feb. 1815–Feb. 1818
34	709–728; Jan. 2–Feb. 9, 1815	Feb. 1816–Feb. 1824
35	729–746; Feb. 10–21, 1815	Feb. 1815–Feb. 1820
36	747–759; Feb. 21–Nov. 4, 1815	Feb. 1816–Feb. 1821
37	760–764; Nov. 1815	Feb. 1816–Feb. 1818
38	765–778; Dec. 1815–Jan. 27, 1816	Feb. 1816–Feb. 1823
39	779–796; Jan. 27–Feb. 6, 1816	Feb. 1816–Feb. 1818
40	797–808; Feb. 6–16, 1816	Feb. 1816–Feb. 1822
41	809–824; Feb. 16–Dec. 6, 1816	Feb. 1816–Feb. 1822
42	825–866; Dec. 6, 1816–Feb. 3, 1817	Feb. 1817–Feb. 1821
43	867–880; Feb. 5–June 10, 1817	Feb. 1817–Feb. 1820
44	881–887; Aug. 2–Oct. 11, 1817	Feb. 1818
45	888–895; Oct. 14, 1817–Jan. 5, 1818	Feb. 1818–Feb. 1820
46	896–900; Jan. 16–27, 1818	Feb. 1819 and Feb. 1821
47	901–919; Jan. 31–Feb. 12, 1818	Feb. 1818–Feb. 1824
48	920–937; Feb. 12–July 27, 1818	Feb. 1819–Feb. 1821
49	938–961; Sept. 18–Dec. 26, 1818	Feb. 1819–Jan. 1829
50	962–978; Dec. 31, 1818–Feb. 1, 1819	Feb. 1820–Feb. 1823
51	979–1002; Feb. 1–Mar. 1, 1819	Feb. 1821–Feb. 1823
52	1003–1027; Mar. 3, 1819–Feb. 26, 1820	Feb. 1820–Feb. 1826
53	1028–1056; Feb. 4–Mar. 20, 1820	Feb. 1820–Jan. 1827
54	1057–1079; May 6, 1820–Jan. 16, 1821	Feb. 1821–Feb. 1825
55	1080–1099; Jan. 16–Feb. 16, 1821	Feb. 1821–Feb. 1826
56	1100–1113; Feb. 16–Mar. 8, 1821	Feb. 1821–Feb. 1825
57	1114–1132; Mar. 8, 1821–Jan. 14, 1822	Feb. 1822–Feb. 1824
58	1133–1153; Jan. 21–Feb. 8, 1822	Feb. 1822–Feb. 1826
59	1154–1172; Feb. 11–Aug. 5, 1822	Feb. 1822–Jan. 1827
60	1173–1197; Aug. 5–Dec. 21, 1822	Feb. 1823–Jan. 1827
61	1198–1213; Dec. 21, 1822–Feb. 4, 1823	Feb. 1825–Jan. 1827
62	1214–1227; Feb. 4–6, 1823	Feb. 1823–Jan. 1827
63	1228–1245; Feb. 7–Mar. 8, 1823	Feb. 1823–Jan. 1827
64	1246–1250; Mar. 14–July 30, 1823	Feb. 1826–Feb. 1832
65	1251–1263; Oct. 4, 1823–Jan. 14, 1824	Feb. 1825–Jan. 1832
66	1264–1281; Jan. 21–Feb. 25, 1824	Feb. 1824–Jan. 1830
67	1282–1300; Feb. 4–Mar. 12, 1824	Feb. 1824–Jan. 1828
68	1301–1323; Mar. 13, 1824–Feb. 3, 1825	Feb. 1824–Jan. 1828
69	1324–1338; Feb. 3–7, 1825	Feb. 1826–Jan. 1829
70	1339–1353; Feb. 8–Mar. 8, 1825	Feb. 1825–Jan. 1828
71	1354–1367; Mar. 24–Dec. 9, 1825	Jan. 1827–Jan. 1831
72	1368–1386; Dec. 9, 1825–Feb. 8, 1826	Jan. 1826–Jan. 1828
73	1387–1401; Feb. 8–28, 1826	Feb. 1826–Jan. 1830
74	1402–1419; Mar. 1–Aug. 1, 1826	Feb. 1827–Jan. 1830
75	1420–1433; Aug. 24, 1826–Jan. 11, 1827	Jan. 1827–Jan. 1829
76	1434–1448; Jan. 13–Feb. 3, 1827	Jan. 1827–Jan. 1829
77	1449–1465; Feb. 17–Aug. 2, 1827	Jan. 1827–Jan. 1830
78	1466–1482; Sept. 3, 1827–Jan. 14, 1828	Jan. 1829–Jan. 1836
79	1483–1494; Jan. 14–19, 1828	Jan. 1828–Jan. 1831
80	1495–1507; Jan. 19–Feb. 26, 1828	Jan. 1829–Jan. 1836
81	1508–1516; Feb. 27–Mar. 7, 1828	Jan. 1828–Jan. 1830
82	1517–1530; Mar. 8–Oct. 11, 1828	Jan. 1830 and Jan. 1836
83	1531–1542; Oct. 29–Dec. 27, 1828	Jan. 1829–Jan. 1831

Roll	Inclusive Case Nos. and Dates of Docketing	Terms
84	1543–1553; Dec. 28, 1828–Jan. 5, 1829	Jan. 1829–Jan. 1831
85	1554–1566; Jan. 5–14, 1829	Jan. 1829–Jan. 1836
86	1567–1581; Jan. 15–Feb. 9, 1829	Jan. 1829–Jan. 1831
87	1582–1594; Feb. 12–June 15, 1829	Jan. 1829–Jan. 1833
88	1595–1605; July 11–Nov. 23, 1829	Jan. 1830–Jan. 1843
89	1606–1618; Dec. 5, 1829–Feb. 1, 1830	Jan. 1830–Jan. 1832
90	1619–1635; Feb. 3–May 27, 1830	Jan. 1831–Jan. 1837
91	1636–1652; May 27–Dec. 7, 1830	Jan. 1831–Jan. 1836
92	1653–1665; Dec. 7, 1830–Jan. 10, 1831	Jan. 1831–Jan. 1836
93	1666–1670; Jan. 11–29, 1831	Jan. 1832 and Jan. 1833
94	1671; Feb. 2, 1831	Jan. 1835
95	1672–1685; Feb. 2–Mar. 18, 1831	Jan. 1831–Jan. 1836
96	1686–1702; Mar. 18–Dec. 24, 1831	Jan. 1832–Jan. 1834

Minutes of the Supreme Court of the United States, 1790–1950. M215. 41 rolls. DP.

This microfilm publication reproduces the engrossed minutes of the Supreme Court of the United States. These minutes contain a complete report of the date, the names of members and officials of the Court who were present, the admission of attorneys to the bar of the Court, the swearing in of new members, rules adopted, the argument of cases by counsel, the submission of cases to the court, orders and decrees by the Court in individual cases, and other activities of the Court. The minutes are arranged chronologically by date of the meetings of the Court and are not indexed.

Roll	Volume Numbers	Dates
1	[A]–D	Feb. 1, 1790–Aug. 4, 1828
2	E–G	Jan. 12, 1829–Aug. 7, 1837
3	H–L	Jan. 8, 1838–Jan. 24, 1848
4	M–P	Jan. 25, 1848–Jan. 19, 1855
5	Q–S	Jan. 22, 1855–Feb. 7, 1860
6	T–V	Feb. 8, 1860–Feb. 24, 1864
7	W–Y	Feb. 25, 1864–Mar. 24, 1868
8	Z	Mar. 25, 1868–Apr. 15, 1869
9	26–28	Oct. 24, 1869–Feb. 15, 1872
10	29–31	Feb. 16, 1872–Apr. 10, 1874
11	32–34	Apr. 13, 1874–Apr. 10, 1876
12	35–37	Apr. 10, 1876–Apr. 22, 1878
13	38–40	Apr. 22, 1878–Oct. 20, 1880
14	41–43	Oct. 20, 1880–Nov. 14, 1882
15	44–46	Nov. 15, 1882–Oct. 27, 1884
16	47–50	Oct. 27, 1884–Apr. 25, 1887
17	51–53	Apr. 25, 1887–May 13, 1889
18	54–57	May 13, 1889–Mar. 7, 1892
19	58–61	Mar. 7, 1892–May 26, 1894
20		Oct. 8, 1894–May 25, 1896
21		Oct. 12, 1896–May 22, 1899
22		Oct. 9, 1899–June 2, 1902

Roll	Volume Numbers	Dates
23		Oct. 13, 1902–May 29, 1905
24		Oct. 9, 1905–June 1, 1908
25		Oct. 12, 1908–May 29, 1911
26		Oct. 9, 1911–June 22, 1914
27		Oct. 12, 1914–June 12, 1916
28		Oct. 9, 1916–June 9, 1919
29		Oct. 6, 1919–June 6, 1921
30		Oct. 3, 1921–June 9, 1924
31		Oct. 6, 1924–June 6, 1927
32		Oct. 3, 1927–June 3, 1929
33		Oct. 7, 1929–May 31, 1932
34		Oct. 3, 1932–June 4, 1934
35		Oct. 1, 1934–June 1, 1937
36		Oct. 4, 1937–June 5, 1939
37		Oct. 2, 1939–June 8, 1942
38		July 29, 1942–June 12, 1944
39		Oct. 2, 1944–June 10, 1946
40		Oct. 7, 1946–June 23, 1947
41		Oct. 6, 1947–June 5, 1950

Dockets of the Supreme Court of the United States, 1791–1950. M216. 27 rolls. DP.

For the period before May 31, 1905, there are two series of Supreme Court dockets. The engrossed, or smooth, dockets, 1791–1905, give the complete history of each case as compiled from the various docket books in which the case had been entered. The rough dockets, 1803–1905, include all unfinished and new cases that were entered for each term. The series of engrossed dockets contains entries for cases that came before the Court during the period covered, with the exception of cases in original jurisdiction, 1829–1905, which are recorded only in the rough dockets. Beginning May 31, 1905, the Court maintained only one series of dockets in which all cases that come before the Court, in both original and appellate jurisdictions, are recorded. All three series are reproduced in this publication.

Roll	Types of Cases Docketed and Actions Begun	Inclusive Dates for Docket Entries
1	Original Appellate	1791–1801 / 1792–1834
2	"	1834–60
3	"	1860–72
4	"	1872–76
5	"	1876–82
6	"	1882–85
7	"	1885–88
8	"	1888–94
9	"	1894–1900
10	"	1900–2
11	Appellate / Rough docket entries for original cases	1902–5 / 1829–1905
12	Original and appellate	1905–9
13	"	1909–12
14	"	1912–15
15	"	1915–18
16	"	1918–21
17	"	1921–24
18	"	1924–26
19	"	1926–29
20	"	1929–32

Roll	Types of Cases Docketed and Actions Begun	Inclusive Dates for Docket Entries
21	"	1932–35
22	"	1935–38
	Original actions	1937–38
23	Original cases	1940–41
	Appellate cases	1938–41
	Original actions	1938–41
24	Original cases	1941–43
	Appellate cases	1941–44
	Original actions	1941–44
25	Original cases	1944–45
	Appellate cases	1944–46
	Original actions	1944–45
	Miscellaneous actions	1945–46
26	Original cases continued from October terms	1945, 46
	Appellate cases	1946–48
	Miscellaneous actions	1946–48
27	Original cases	1949
	Appellate cases	1948–50
	Miscellaneous cases	1948–50

General Records of the Department of the Treasury (Record Group 56)

Correspondence of the Secretary of the Treasury re: the Administration of Trust Funds for the Chickasaw and Other Tribes ("S" Series), 1834–1872. M749. 1 roll. DP.

Under the terms of the treaties of October 20, 1832, and May 24, 1834, the Chickasaw ceded their land in the States of Mississippi and Alabama to the Federal Government. The Government agreed to sell the lands for the benefit of the Chickasaw, to assist them in their removal to new homes somewhere west of the Mississippi, and to establish a perpetual fund for the use of the Chickasaw Nation from proceeds of the sales. Under the direction of the President, with the advice and consent of the Senate, the proceeds were to be invested in interest-bearing stocks and bonds on behalf of the Chickasaw Nation. Although the greater part of the correspondence relates to the trust fund of the Chickasaw, the trust funds of other Indian tribes are also mentioned.

Records of the Office of the Secretary of the Interior (Record Group 48)

Letters Sent by the Lands and Railroads Division of the Office of the Secretary of the Interior. M620. 310 rolls.

This microfilm publication reproduces transcripts of communications sent by the Division of Land and Railroads of the Office of the Secretary of the Interior from March 10, 1849 to November 5, 1904, and accompanying indexes for 1881–1903. From 1849, when the Department of the Interior was established, the Secretary of the Interior has had general supervisory control over the administration of the public domain. The Division of Lands and Railroads was not formally established until 1870. It was concerned chiefly with the work of the General Land Office, but it also did work relating to activities of other bureaus, especially the Geological Survey and the Office of Indian Affairs.

Through 1885, the letters were copied for the most part in chronological order. Thereafter, the letters to the Commissioner of the General Land Office, which constituted decisions in cases appealed to the Secretary from the Commissioner, or reviews of such cases, were copied in volumes separate from other letters. The respective volumes were designated "Decisions" and "Miscellaneous." There are many letters relating to the cases in the miscellaneous volumes; only the decisions of the Secretary were copied in the decision book. Letters copied out of chronological order account for the occasional overlapping of dates between volumes.

The following rolls are for the indexes.

Roll	Description	Dates
305	Indexes	1881, 1882
306	"	1883–89
307	"	1890–94
308	"	1895–98
309	"	1899–1902
310	" (to decisions only)	1902–3

Records of the Geological Survey (Record Group 57)

The Geological Survey was established in 1879 in the Department of the Interior to classify public lands and to examine the geological structure, mineral resources, and other products of the national domain. It replaced four earlier surveys: the U.S. Geological and Geographic Survey of the Territories (Hayden Survey), 1867–79; the U.S. Geographical and Geological Survey of the Rocky Mountain Region (Powell Survey), 1869–79; the U.S. Geographical Surveys West of the One Hundredth Meridian (Wheeler Survey), 1872–79; and the Geological Exploration of the Fortieth Parallel (King Survey), 1867–79. The Hayden and Powell Surveys in particular included ethnological and archeological studies.

Letters Received by John Wesley Powell, Director of the Geographical and Geological Survey of the Rocky Mountain Region, 1869–1879. M156. 10 rolls. DP.

This microfilm publication reproduces the letters received by Major John Wesley Powell, 1869–79. It includes the letters from frontiersmen and Indian agents, including Jacob Hamblin, the "Mormon Leatherstocking." The letters are arranged systematically first by year and then alphabetically by the surname of the correspondent and, occasionally, by the name of the institution represented by the correspondent.

John Wesley Powell, director of the Rocky Mountain Survey, was especially concerned with Indian vocabularies and linguistics, and he published works about these interests. Most of the records relating to these works are with the Records of the Bureau of American Ethnology at the National Anthropological Archives, Smithsonian Institution, Washington, DC.

Roll	Description	Inclusive Dates
1		Jan. 1, 1869–Dec. 31, 1872
2		Jan. 1, 1873–Dec. 31, 1874
3		Jan. 1–Dec. 31, 1875
4		Jan. 1–Dec. 31, 1876
5	A–I	Jan. 1–Dec. 31, 1877
6	J–Z	Jan. 1–Dec. 31, 1877
7	A–I	Jan. 1–Dec. 31, 1878
8	J–Z	Jan. 1–Dec. 31, 1878
9	A–L	Jan. 1–Dec. 31, 1879
10	M–Z	Jan. 1–Dec. 31, 1879

Records of the Geological and Geographical Survey of the Territories ("Hayden Survey"), 1867–1879. M623. 21 rolls. DP.

Dr. Ferdinand Vandiver Hayden directed the Geological and Geographical Survey of the Territories, 1867–79. The Survey included ethnological and archeological studies in Nebraska, Wyoming, Idaho, Montana, New Mexico, and Colorado.

The records are arranged in part alphabetically by the name of the person or country and in part chronologically.

Roll	Description	Date
Letters received:		
1	Vol. 1	Jan. 4, 1866–Jan. 4, 1870
2	Vols. 3–5	Jan. 1870–Dec. 31, 1872
3	Vols. 6–7	Jan. 1–Dec. 29, 1873
4	Vol. 2	1873–Mar. 21, 1874
5	A–B	1871–79
6	C–D	1871–79
7	E–G	1871–79
8	H–Mc	1871–79
9	M–O	1871–79
10	Q–Z	1871–79
Personal letters received:		
11	A–L	1872–79
12	M–Y	1872–79
13	Personal letters received chiefly from Fielding Bradford Meek	1863–66, 1874–76
14	Letters received from Government agencies	1867–79
Letters received from persons in foreign countries:		
15	Australia–Denmark	
16	England	
17	Finland–Ireland	
18	Italy–Venezuela	
19	Letters of application for positions, recommendations, and requests for publication	1872–79

Roll	Description	Date
20	Fiscal records including:	
	Accounts of records	1872–80
	Record of the Treasurer of the United States in account with F. V. Hayden	
	Ledger of Dr. Albert C. Peale	
	Ledgers	Apr. 1878–Mar. 1880
21	Miscellaneous records relating to the Hayden Survey	1867–79

Registers of Letters Received by the United States Geological Survey, 1879–1901. M157. 16 rolls. DP.

This microfilm publication reproduces a series of 26 registers of letters received by the Office of the Director of the United States Geological Survey, 1879–1901. The entries in these volumes are arranged in chronological order by the date of receipt of the incoming communication with some exceptions. For each letter, the following information is entered in the register: the date of receipt and file number assigned to the incoming communication (document number), the name and address of the writer, the date of the letter, a brief abstract of the contents, and a reference date or notation indicating the action taken in regard to the communication. Occasional omissions and other errors occur.

Notations relating to action taken with regard to the incoming correspondence are of particular significance for 1895–1901, since copies of outgoing communications of the Survey are not available for those years.

Roll	Dates
1	Jan. 8, 1879–Dec. 31, 1880
2	Jan. 3, 1881–Dec. 30, 1882
3	Jan. 2, 1883–Dec. 31, 1884
4	Jan. 1, 1885–Dec. 31, 1886
5	Jan. 3, 1887–Dec. 31, 1888
6	Jan. 2–Dec. 31, 1889
7	Jan. 2, 1890–Dec. 31, 1891
8	Jan. 2, 1892–Dec. 30, 1893
9	Jan. 2–Dec. 31, 1894
10	Jan. 2–Dec. 31, 1895
11	Jan. 2–Dec. 30, 1896
12	Jan. 2–Dec. 31, 1897
13	Jan. 3–Dec. 31, 1898
14	Jan. 3–Dec. 30, 1899
15	Jan. 2–Dec. 31, 1900
16	Jan. 2–Nov. 12, 1901

Letters Received by the United States Geological Survey, 1879–1901. M590. 118 rolls. DP.

This microfilm publication reproduces the letters received by the United States Geological Survey, 1879–1901; a six-volume index to these letters for 1880–89; and eight volumes of monthly reports for 1882–90.

The records cover numerous subjects including a survey and investigation of irrigation on Indian reservations and disputes over the western boundary of the Yakima Reservation and the Seminole border.

Roll	Document Numbers	Dates
1	Indexes	1880–85
2	Indexes	1886–89
3	1–463	Jan. 13–Dec. 9, 1879
4	1–399	Jan. 1–May 28, 1880
5	401–868	May 28–Oct. 28, 1880
6	869–1070	Oct. 28–Dec. 31, 1880
7	1–450	Jan. 3–May 3, 1881
8	451–940	May 3–Aug. 23, 1881
9	941–1376	Aug. 23–Nov. 5, 1881
10	1377–1606	Nov. 8–Dec. 31, 1881
11	1–552	Jan. 3–May 11, 1882
12	553–1076	May 11–Sept. 2, 1882
13	1077–1532	Sept. 2–Nov. 3, 1882
14	1533–1784	Nov. 4–Dec. 30, 1882
15	1–500	Jan. 2–Mar. 17, 1883
16	501–950	Mar. 19–May 15, 1883
17	951–1332	May 15–June 26, 1883
18	1333–1965	June 26–Sept. 28, 1883
19	1965–2456	Sept. 28–Nov. 26, 1883
20	1–450	Jan. 2–Mar. 21, 1884
21	451–899	Mar. 22–June 10, 1884
22	900–1386	June 7–July 19, 1884
23	1387–1828	July 19–Aug. 28, 1884
24	1829–2176	Aug. 28–Oct. 21, 1884
25	2177–2594	Oct. 21–Dec. 31, 1884
26	1–550	Jan. 2–Apr. 1, 1885
27	551–999	Mar. 27–May 26, 1885
28	1000–1652	May 27–July 31, 1885
29	1653–2010	July 31–Sept. 19, 1885
30	2011–2678	Sept. 21–Dec. 29, 1885
31	1–450	Jan. 2–Feb. 23, 1886
32	451–850	Feb. 23–Apr. 15, 1886
33	851–1300	Apr. 15–June 26, 1886
34	1301–1959	June 28–Sept. 14, 1886
35	1964–2468	Sept. 15–Dec. 31, 1886
36	1–625	Jan. 3–Apr. 27, 1887
37	626–1499	Apr. 27–July 29, 1887
38	1500–2323	July 30–Dec. 31, 1887
39	1–700	Jan. 3–May 4, 1888
40	701–1399	May 4–July 31, 1888
41	1400–2200	Aug. 1–Oct. 26, 1888
42	2201–2722	Oct. 26–Dec. 29, 1888
43	1–800	Jan. 2–Apr. 11, 1889
44	801–1500	Apr. 11–June 17, 1889
45	1501–2300	June 17–Aug. 5, 1889
46	2301–3000	Aug. 5–Oct. 30, 1889
47	3001–3466	Oct. 31–Dec. 31, 1889

(Unbound letters)

Roll	Document Numbers	Dates
48	2–700	Jan.–Mar. 1890
49	780–2309	Mar.–Sept. 1890
50	2313–3205	Sept.–Dec. 1890
51	4–700	Jan.–Apr. 1891
52	703–1383	Apr.–June 1891
53	1386–2119	June–Oct. 1891
54	2120–2589	Oct.–Dec. 1891
55	6–451	Jan.–Mar. 1892
56	452–858	Mar.–Apr. 1892
57	861–1445	Apr.–July 1892
58	1446–2199	July–Dec. 1892
59	1–572	Jan.–Apr. 1893
60	574–1358	Apr.–July 1893

Roll	Document Numbers	Dates
61	1359–2279	July–Dec. 1893
62	2–772	Jan.–Apr. 1894
63	784–1528	May–July 1894
64	1529–2259	Aug.–Nov. 1894
65	2262–2828	Nov.–Dec. 1894
66	1–619	Jan.–Feb. 1895
67	620–1092	Mar.–Apr. 1895
68	1111–2028	Apr.–June 1895
69	2029–2466	June–Aug. 1895
70	2467–3073	Aug.–Nov. 1895
71	3074–3486	Nov.–Dec. 1895
72	2–606	Jan.–Feb. 1896
73	607–1255	Mar.–May 1896
74	1256–1750	May–June 1896
75	1752–2295	June–July 1896
76	2296–3147	Aug.–Oct. 1896
77	3149–3455	Nov.–Dec. 1896
78	3459–3821	Dec. 1896
79	1–430	Jan.–Feb. 1897
80	432–1014	Feb.–Mar. 1897
81	1015–1462	Mar.–Apr. 1897
82	1463–1955	May–June 1897
83	1956–2460	June 1897
84	2461–3152	June–Sept. 1897
85	3153–3838	Sept.–Nov. 1897
86	3839–4215	Nov.–Dec. 1897
87	1–608	Jan.–Feb. 1898
88	609–1108	Feb.–Mar. 1898
89	1109–1668	Mar.–May 1898
90	1669–2200	May–June 1898
91	2201–2777	June–Aug. 1898
92	2778–3374	Aug.–Oct. 1898
93	3375–4133	Oct.–Dec. 1898
94	5–564	Jan.–Feb. 1899
95	565–1128	Mar. 1899
96	1129–1764	Mar.–Apr. 1899
97	1765–2178	Apr.–May 1899
98	2179–2815	May–July 1899
99	2816–3489	July–Sept. 1899
100	3490–4115	Sept.–Oct. 1899
101	4116–4773	Nov.–Dec. 1899
102	1–630	Jan.–Feb. 1900
103	631–1161	Feb.–Mar. 1900
104	1163–1728	Mar.–Apr. 1900
105	1729–2319	Apr.–June 1900
106	2320–2958	June–July 1900
107	2959–3602	July–Sept. 1900
108	3603–4306	Sept.–Nov. 1900
109	4307–5090	Nov.–Dec. 1900
110	1–622	Jan. 1901
111	625–1173	Feb. 1901
112	1174–1776	Mar. 1901
113	1777–2424$^1/_2$	Apr. 1901
114	Monthly Reports	1882–83
115	"	1884
116	"	1885–86
117	"	1887–88
118	"	1889–90

Letters Sent by the United States Geological Survey, 1879–1895. M152. 29 rolls. DP.

This microfilm publication reproduces a series of 35 letterbooks containing transcripts of outgoing communications of the Office of Director of the United States Geological Survey, 1879–95, and a two-volume index to these communications for 1879–83.

Roll	Dates
1	July 7, 1879–Dec. 31, 1880
2	Jan. 3–Dec. 31, 1881
3	Jan. 3–Dec. 30, 1882
4	Jan. 2–Dec. 31, 1883
5	Jan. 2–Aug. 12, 1884
6	Aug. 12–Dec. 31, 1884
7	Jan. 2–Dec. 31, 1885
8	Jan. 2–July 20, 1886
9	July 20–Dec. 30, 1886
10	Jan. 3–June 30, 1887
11	July 1, 1887–Feb. 18, 1888
12	Feb. 18–Oct. 2, 1888
13	Oct. 2, 1888–Mar. 30, 1889
14	Mar. 30–July 15, 1889
15	July 15–Dec. 11, 1889
16	Dec. 10, 1889–Apr. 15, 1890
17	Apr. 14–Sept. 1, 1890
18	Sept. 1, 1890–Jan. 21, 1891
19	Jan. 20–May 8, 1891
20	May 8–Sept. 23, 1891
21	Sept. 25, 1891–Mar. 16, 1892
22	Mar. 16–Aug. 6, 1892
23	Aug. 6–Dec. 31, 1892
24	Jan. 3–June 16, 1893
25	June 15–Dec. 30, 1893
26	Jan. 2–Aug. 13, 1894
27	Aug. 13–Dec. 31, 1894
28	Jan. 2–May 21, 1895
29	May 21–Dec. 8, 1895

Records of the Fish and Wildlife Service (Record Group 22)

"Alaska File" of the Office of the Secretary of the Treasury, 1868–1903. M720. 25 rolls. DP.

This microfilm publication reproduces five series of records received by the Secretary of the Treasury and filed in the "Alaska File" on fur sealing and salmon fishing. The file includes letters from special agents for the protection of fur seals. The Secretary of the Treasury was responsible for the duties and records relating to Alaskan fur sealing and salmon fisheries until July 1, 1903, when the functions were transferred to the newly created Department of Commerce and Labor.

The agents supervised the activities of the Alaska Commercial Co. and the North American Commercial Co., which from 1870–90 and 1890–1910, respectively, had leases to exclusive fur seal hunting rights on the Pribilof Islands. The agents also oversaw the welfare of the Islands' Natives and enforced regulations on the traffic in firearms, ammunition, and liquor.

Letters received relative to salmon fishers, 1889–1903, include those relating to the problems of regulating the importation of liquor, ammunition, and firearms, and a few concerning the Metlakahtla Indians.

Roll	Description	Date
Index to letters received relating to fur sealing:		
1		1868–1903
Letters received relating to fur sealing:		
2		Apr. 13, 1868–Dec. 30, 1879
3		Jan. 5, 1871–Dec. 29, 1877
4		Jan. 2, 1878–Dec. 26, 1885
5		Jan. 23, 1886–Dec. 30, 1889
6		Jan. 7–Dec. 20, 1890
7		Jan. 2–Dec. 3, 1891
8		Jan. 9, 1892–Dec. 31, 1893
9		Jan. 9–Dec. 29, 1894
10		Jan. 4–June 29, 1895
11		July 1–Dec. 31, 1895
12		Jan. 2–June 24, 1896
13		July 3–Dec. 23, 1896
14		Jan. 2–Dec. 30, 1897
15		Jan. 3–Dec. 31, 1898
16		Jan. 9, 1899–Dec. 31, 1900
17		Jan. 2, 1901–June 30, 1902
18		July 4, 1902–June 24, 1903
Letters received relating to salmon fisheries:		
19		Apr. 20, 1889–Dec. 20, 1897
20		Feb. 7, 1898–Dec. 12, 1901
21		Jan. 4, 1902–July 3, 1903
Reports from Collectors of Customs:		
22	Alaska, California	1895–1902
23	New York, other ports	"
24	Oregon, Washington	"
Miscellaneous records:		
25	Printed documents, maps	Feb. 3, 1869–Dec. 20, 1897

MILITARY ESTABLISHMENT RECORDS

The Army's primary responsibility in the West was the protection of white settlers against hostile Indians. To do this, the Army frequently established camps and forts in hostile territory.

Army garrisons were often established close to Indian agencies. The respective areas of authority of the agents and the Army commanders were often in dispute, and their viewpoints sometimes conflicted. There was continual controversy over the respective merits of civilian and military control over the Indians, particularly during the 1870's, when there was a strong movement to transfer the *Office of Indian Affairs* back to the War Department.

Records of the Adjutant General's Office, 1780's–1917 (Record Group 94)

The Continental Congress on June 17, 1775, appointed an Adjutant General of the Continental Army. After 1783 no further provision was made for such an officer until an act of March 5, 1792, (1 Stat. 241) provided for an adjutant, who was also to do the work of inspector.

The Adjutant General is charged with matters relating to command, discipline, and administration of the Military Establishment, and has the duties of recording, authenticating, and communicating the Secretary's orders, instructions, and regulations to troops and individuals in the Army. He is also responsible for issuing commissions, compiling and issuing the Army Register and the Army List and Directory, consolidating the general returns of the Army and Militia, and recruiting.

The Adjutant General's Office chiefly handles Army orders, correspondence, and other records, and it receives final custody of virtually all records concerned with the Military Establishment, including personnel of the Army and discontinued commands, noncurrent holdings of bureaus of the War Department, and special collections.

Indexes to Letters Received, Adjutant General's Office (Main Series), 1846, 1861–1889. M725. 9 rolls. DP.

Roll	Contents
1	Name Index, 1846, with Supplement (Indexes to Reports of Engagements and Expeditions, 1846–48)
	Subject Indexes:
	1861–71
	Name Indexes:
2	1861–64
3	1865–67
4	1868–72
5	1873–76
6	1877–80
7	1881–83
8	1884–86
9	1887–89

Index to General Correspondence of the Adjutant General's Office, 1890–1917. M698. 1,269 rolls. DP. 16 mm.

Letters Received

The Letters Received by the Office of the Adjutant General, 1822–80, are available as microfilm publications M567, M619, and M666. Correspondence relating to Indian matters is interspersed thoughout these publications. The following rolls contain consolidated files relating to Indians that were identified during the preparation of the publications.

Letters Received by the Office of the Adjutant General (Main Series), 1822–1860. M567. 636 rolls.

Roll	File	Description
12	14 S 1824	Correspondence relating to Col. Henry Leavenworth's expedition against the Arikara Indians in 1823.
66	104 A 1832	Copies of orders and communications issued by Brig. Gen. Henry Atkinson to the Army of the Frontier in connection with the Black Hawk War. See also file 105 A 1832 on the same roll.
197	234 T 1839	Report of Gen. Zachary Taylor relating to operations in Florida, from the opening of the campaign in the fall of 1838 to May 1839, with enclosures.

Roll	File	Description
202	69 B 1840	Series of resolutions and related papers adopted by the General Assembly of the State of Missouri relating to the conduct of the Missouri Volunteers during the Florida campaign of 1837–38 against the Seminole Indians.
260	26 W 1842	Reports of Gen. W. J. Worth and other officers relating to the operations of the Army in Florida, Oct.–Dec. 1841.
483	478 H 1853	Reports relating to the Indians living on the West Coast, 1853.
546	216 R 1856	Correspondence relating to the massacre of Lt. John L. Grattan and 20 soldiers near Fort Laramie on August 19, 1854.
586	270 P 1858	Records relating to an Indian war in Washington Territory and to treaties of peace signed with the Indians, 1858.
603	83 I 1859	Copy of a communication from the Postmaster General and correspondence relating to attacks on the overland mail route to Santa Fe by the Kiowa Indians, 1859.

Letters Received by the Office of the Adjutant General (Main Series), 1861–1870. M619. 828 rolls. DP.

Roll	File	Description
283	87 N 1864	Communications relating to affairs in the Department of New Mexico, Aug. 1863–Jan. 1864.
285	255 N 1864	Report, with enclosures, by a board of officers appointed to investigate the complaints of Charles Poston, Superintendent of Indian Affairs for Arizona Territory, against certain Army officers in the District of Western Arizona, 1864.
286	280 N 1864	Papers relating to the procurement and issuance of commissary stores for captive Navajo Indians in the Department of New Mexico, 1864. For additional records, see file 2143 S 1865 on roll 417.
367	145 I 1865	Papers relating to the investigation of charges made against Maj. Gen. Alfred Sully and his administration of Indian affairs on the Upper Missouri River, 1865.
483	5 I 1866	Papers relating to the Sioux uprising in Minnesota, 1862–1916.

Roll	File	Description
484	91 I 1866	Papers relating to the confinement of the Navajo Indians on the Bosque Redondo Reservation, New Mexico Territory, and to the transfer of their custody from the War Department to the Department of the Interior, 1866–67.
560	102 M 1867	Papers relating to the Fetterman massacre near Fort Phil Kearny, Dakota Territory, on Dec. 21, 1866.
561	223 M 1867	Papers relating to the relocation of the Navajo Indians on a military reservation at the Bosque Redondo, New Mexico Territory, 1863–67. Some of the papers relate to the cost of feeding the Navajo Indians during this period.
563	590 M 1867	Reports of the campaigns of Gens. Winfield S. Hancock and George A. Custer against the Sioux and the Cheyenne Indians, Mar.–May 1867. For additional reports, see files 523 M 1867 and 1093 M 1867 on rolls 562 and 565, respectively.
573	625 P 1867	Correspondence relating to unratified treaties made with the Apache Indians by Lt. Col. Guido Ilges, 14th Infantry, 1866–67.
574	798 P 1867	Report of Lt. Col. Robert N. Scott concerning the Indian tribes living near the boundary between British Columbia and Alaska, November 12, 1867.
629	42 I 1868	Correspondence relating to the implementation of the Medicine Lodge treaties with the Kiowa, Kiowa-Apache, Comanche, Cheyenne, and Arapahoe Indians, July–Sept. 1868.
639	807 M 1868	Report of Lt. Gen. William T. Sherman stating the reasons for the removal of the Navajo Indians from the Bosque Redondo Reservation, New Mexico Territory, June 24, 1868.
642	1275 M 1868	Reports relating to Indian tribes (Kickapoo, Lipan, and Mescalero Apache) inhabiting the territory of Mexico adjacent to the United States, 1868–69.
	1285 M 1868	Papers relating to the engagement on the Arickaree Fork of the Republican River, Kansas, between scouts under Maj. George A. Forsyth and a band of Sioux and

Roll	File	Description
		Cheyenne Indians, Sept. 17–20, 1868.
650	523 P 1868	Reports of Capt. Charles A. Whittier and Lt. Wager Barnet concerning military posts, settlements, and Indians in Arizona Territory and conditions in Sonora, Mexico, June 1868.
656	504 R 1868	Reports of expenditures made by War Department bureaus and commands in suppressing Indian hostilities, 1866–68.
671	645 W 1868	Papers relating to the cost of providing subsistence stores for certain bands of Ute and Apache Indians in the Department of New Mexico, 1866–68.
711	106 I 1869	Papers relating to the military expedition against the Piegan Indians and to other matters concerning Indians in Montana Territory, 1869–70.
718	207 M 1869	Reports of minor clashes with Kiowa and Pawnee Indians in western Kansas, Jan.–Apr. 1869.
722	703 M 1869	Correspondence relating to policy in regard to Indians who refused to go on reservations, May–Aug. 1869.
724	942 M 1869	Reports by Maj. Alexander Moore, 38th Infantry, of an expedition against the Apache Indians, Apr.–May 1869.
737	925 P 1869	Report of Bvt. Col. Reuben F. Bernard relating to the engagement between troops of the 1st and 8th Regiments, Cavalry, and Chiricahua Apache at Chiricahua Pass, Arizona Territory, on October 20, 1869. For other reports of actions against the Apache at this time, see file 841 P 1869 on the same roll.
791	65 I 1870	Papers relating to the claim of Yankton Indians for services as scouts in 1864 under Gen. Alfred Sully, 1870–92.
792	120 I 1870	Papers relating to the removal of intruders from lands belonging to the Cherokee Nation in the Indian Territory, 1870–71.
792	186 I 1870	Papers relating to the removal of trespassers from the Miami Indian Reservation in Kansas, 1870.
799	488 M 1870	Papers relating to the return of the Kickapoo and the Seminole (Negro) Indians

Roll	File	Description
		from Mexico to the United States, 1870–85.
807	98 P 1870	Reports relating to a proposal to establish a reservation for the Apache Indians in the White Mountains area of Arizona Territory, Nov. 1869–Mar. 1870.
808	507 P 1870	Reports of operations against the Apache Indians in the Department of Arizona, Apr.–June 1870.
812	102 R 1870	Copies of report by Gens. Sheridan and Custer and by other officers relating to activities against the Indians in the Military Division of the Missouri, 1868–69. For 1870 reports of Indian matters in the division, see file 786 M 1870 on roll 802.

Letters Received by the Office of the Adjutant General (Main Series), 1871–80. M666. 593 rolls.

Roll	File	Description
2	113 AGO 1871	Correspondence relating to the provision of food and ammunition for hunting to nearly 3,000 starving Indians of the Arapahoe, Cheyenne, and Sioux tribes under Chief Red Cloud at Fort Laramie, Wyoming Territory, 1871–72.
4	557 AGO 1871	Report by Brig. Gen. John Pope, commanding the Department of the Missouri, of a possible war with the Cheyenne and Arapahoe Indians in the spring of 1871. Included is correspondence relating to conditions at the Cheyenne and Arapahoe Agency and to the agent's defense of his policies against charges by the military officers of inefficient administration.
10	1305 AGO 1871	Correspondence relating to the arrest of Kiowa Chiefs Satanta, Satank, and Big Tree, who were charged with attacking a corn train of 12 wagons. The arrest was made by troops under Gen. William T. Sherman at Fort Sill, Indian Territory, May–June 1871.
	1339 AGO 1871	Correspondence relating to the request of financier Jay Cooke that 800 to 1,000 troops be sent to Dakota and Montana Territories to protect the Northern Pacific Railroad engineer-surveying parties, 1871.
15	1839 AGO 1871	Correspondence relating to the massacre of 23 Apache Indians at Camp Grant,

Roll	File	Description
		Arizona Territory, on April 30, 1871, by a party of citizens from Tucson.
16	2019 AGO 1871	Correspondence relating to activities of the Santee, Yankton, and other Sioux Indians in 1871 and 1872 in various locations (including the settlement on the Milk River, Montana Territory), and to the attack on Gallatin Valley, Montana Territory, by Sioux tribes from the Big Horn area.
20–22	2418 AGO 1871	Papers relating to the war with the Modoc Indians in northern California, 1871–73.
24	2465 AGO 1871	Correspondence relating to the selection by Vincent Colyer of the Board of Indian Commissioners of sites for Apache Indian reservations at Tularosa Valley and White Mountain, New Mexico Territory, and at Camp Grant and Camp Verde, Arizona Territory, 1871–72. Included is the order by Gen. George Crook that the Apache move onto the reservations by Feb. 15, 1872, or be considered hostile.
25	2564 AGO 1871	Correspondence relating to recommendations that the military posts at Cheyenne River, Grand River, Lower Brule, and Whetstone Agencies in Dakota Territory be moved or discontinued, Apr. 1872.
32	3314 AGO 1871	Correspondence relating to requests for the establishment of a military post at Beaver City in southern Utah, 1871–72. Included is information relating to the Mormons and the Mountain Meadows massacre in 1857.
37	3971 AGO 1871	Correspondence relating to the successful removal of intruders from lands set aside for the Osage and Cherokee Indians in Kansas, Nov. 1871–May 1872.
	3996 AGO 1871	Correspondence pertaining to a letter from the Superintendent of Indian Affairs for Montana regarding illicit trading with the Indians, 1871–72.
55	1119 AGO 1872	Correspondence relating to the proposed establishment of temporary posts along the Texas frontier to protect U.S. citizens against raiders from Mexico, 1872–73 ("Mexican Border Papers").

Roll	File	Description
58	1388 AGO 1872	Correspondence relating to reports by William H. Miller, subagent of the Whetstone Agency, Sioux Indian Reservation, Dakota Territory, that the commander of the agency refused to provide a guard to protect property under the charge of the agent, 1872.
60	1582 AGO 1872	Correspondence relating to raids by Comanche and Kiowa Indians in Texas, 1872–73 (including the Kiowa demand for the release of Chiefs Satanta and Big Tree), and to the scouting expedition under Col. Ranald S. MacKenzie to the Brazos River, June–Sept. 1872.
61	1603 AGO 1872	Correspondence relating to the attack on a Miniconjou Sioux war party by Capt. Charles Meinhold's company of the 3d Cavalry on the South Fork of Loup River, Nebraska, and to the subsequent award of the Medal of Honor to three members of the company and to William F. ("Buffalo Bill") Cody, who accompanied the party as a guide, 1872.
73	2770 AGO 1872	Correspondence relating to Ute Indians who had left their agencies at Uintah, Utah Territory, and White River, Colorado Territory, and were congregating in the San Pete Valley. The correspondence also deals with the suspected influence of Brigham Young and the Mormons in inducing the Indians off the reservations and with military efforts towards securing their return.
80	3323 AGO 1872	Correspondence relating to the attack on the escort party of the surveyors of the Northern Pacific Railroad by Arapahoe, Cheyenne, and Sioux warriors on August 14, 1872, at the mouth of Pryor's River in the Yellowstone Valley. Included is a journal kept by Maj. John W. Barlow relating to the escort of the surveying party, July 27–Oct. 1, 1872.
81	3512 AGO 1872	Correspondence and reports of Col. David S. Stanley relating to his escort of Northern Pacific Railroad engineers surveying the

Roll	File	Description
		proposed railroad route from Heart River, Dakota Territory, to the mouth of Powder River, 1872. For additional reports by Col. Stanley, see file 3159 AGO 1873 on roll 120.
83	3699 AGO 1872	Correspondence relating to events at the Red Cloud Agency, including Chief Red Cloud's refusal to move to White River and the capture by troops from Fort Laramie of 450 Indian ponies grazing illegally on the south side of the Platte River on the Fort Laramie Military Reservation, 1872.
86	4148 AGO 1872	Papers relating to the attack by troops under Col. Ranald S. MacKenzie on a village of about 200 Comanche Indians near McClellan Creek, Texas, on Sept. 29, 1873.
95	5103 AGO 1872	Correspondence relating to the discovery of valuable mines on the Ute Reservation in Colorado, the extension of the deadline for the removal of intruders on the reservation, and a dispute over pasturage between ranchers and a band of Ute Indians near Spanish Peaks, 1872–73.
95	5147 AGO 1872	Correspondence relating to the issuance of rations to Ocheo, leader of a band of Paiute Indians, and to the refusal of the Paiute to return to Yainax, Oregon, 1872–73. For additional correspondence relating to the Paiute, see files 3313 AGO 1873 on roll 121 and 7111 AGO 1879 on roll 536.
96	5176 AGO 1872	Correspondence relating to the scouting expedition of Lt. Charles Morton in Arizona Territory, June 6–19, 1872, during which the troops fought four battles with a band of Tonto Apache, and to the subsequent recommendation of the men on the march for the Medal of Honor, 1872–76.
108	1433 AGO 1873	Correspondence pertaining to a communication from Col. J. Reynolds, 3d Cavalry, commanding at Fort McPherson, Nebraska, regarding a talk held with Chiefs No Flesh and Pawnee Killer, 1873.
110	1780 AGO 1873	Correspondence pertaining to Clarke and Bill, merchants at James River Crossing,

Roll	File	Description
		Minnesota, who were involved in the liquor trade with the Indians and complained against their arrest and the seizure of their stock, 1873.
118	2933 AGO 1873	Correspondence and a report of proceedings of a board of investigation relating to the murder of Lt. Jacob Almy by Indians in May 1873 at the San Carlos Agency.
122	3326 AGO 1873	Correspondence pertaining to supplies delivered to Army officers to issue to Indians at Camps Apache and Beale's Springs and at Mojave Reservation in Arizona Territory, 1873–76.
123	3383 AGO 1873	Correspondence relating to the agreement with Cochise, chief of the Chiricahua Apache, negotiated by Gen. Oliver O. Howard, and to Gen. George Crook's criticism of the agreement and his request to be allowed to subdue Cochise with force, 1873–74.
126	4028 AGO 1873	Correspondence relating to Cheyenne raids in the territory between the Kansas Pacific Railroad and the northern frontier of Texas, 1873.
130	4477 AGO 1873	Correspondence relating to plundering by the Mescalero Apache Indians in southern New Mexico and to the attack by Capt. George W. Chilson's troops on a party of Mescalero Apache at the western base of the Guadalupe Mountains, New Mexico Territory, 1873.
131	4603 AGO 1873	Correspondence relating to a Department of Justice opinion categorizing Alaska as Indian country and stating that spiritous liquor could not be introduced there without an authorizing order from the War Department, 1873–75.
132	4667 AGO 1873	Correspondence relating to the proposal by the licensed Indian trader at Fort Benton, Montana Territory, that Indians be permitted to trade there, 1873–74.
133	4746 AGO 1873	Correspondence relating to the removal of nearly 1,000 Winnebago Indians from Wisconsin to Nebraska, Dec. 1873–Jan. 1874.
142	554 AGO 1874	Papers relating to requests for military aid to quell riots and murders caused by cattle herders and Indians

Roll	File	Description	Roll	File	Description
		in Lincoln County, New Mexico Territory, 1874. For more information on the Lincoln County war, see file 1405 AGO 1878 on rolls 397–398.			Indians of that reservation, 1875.
143	563 AGO 1874	Correspondence relating to increased Sioux Indian activities in the Department of the Platte, 1874, including the murder of Lt. Levi H. Robinson near Laramie Peak, Wyoming Territory, and to the request for the establishment of a military post to protect the Red Cloud and Whetstone Agencies.	193	1452 AGO 1875	Correspondence relating to the appointment of the military commandant as the Indian agent for Alaska and to his imposition of restrictions on trade, 1875–76. Also included is Gen. Oliver O. Howard's report of a tour in Alaska, June 1875.
147	1224 AGO 1874	Correspondence relating to disturbances at the Standing Rock Indian Agency, Dakota Territory, including the arrest of Chief Rain-in-the-Face of the Hunkpapa band of Sioux for the murder of two men on Col. David S. Stanley's Yellowstone expedition, and to the request for troops to enforce the enrollment of Indians at the agency, 1874.	194	1504 AGO 1875	Correspondence relating to the ouster of James E. Roberts as Indian agent at Fort Apache, Arizona Territory, and the removal of the Apache Indians from there to the San Carlos Indian Agency by San Carlos Agent John P. Clum, 1875–76.
153	1848 AGO 1874	Correspondence relating to the Indian situation at Camp Gaston, California, and the Hoopa Valley Reservation, 1874.	195–211	1653 AGO 1875	Papers relating to raids into Texas made between 1875 and 1884 by parties of Indians and Mexicans from the Mexican side of the Rio Grande ("Mexican Border Troubles").
159–164	2815 AGO 1874	Papers relating to the 1874–75 campaign against Arapahoe, Cheyenne, Comanche, and Kiowa bands in Indian Territory (the Red River War).	221	3517 AGO 1875	Correspondence relating to requests for military protection of the Crow Indian Agency, Montana Territory, from Sioux attacks, 1875. Also included is a report by Capt. George L. Tyler of a fight between Crow, Grosventre, and Nez Perce Indians and the 1,200 to 1,500 Sioux Indians below the mouth of the Big Horn River in June 1875.
167	3198 AGO 1874	Correspondence pertaining to inspections by military officers of flour for the Indian Service at Milk River and Blackfeet Agencies, Montana Territory, Fort Berthold, Dakota Territory, 1874–75.			
181	5009 AGO 1874	Correspondence relating to reports that miners had been working in the Black Hills country of the Sioux Indian Reservation, 1874–75.	220	3538 AGO 1875	Correspondence relating to a letter of the Commissioner of Indian Affairs recommending that a small guard be furnished for duty at Cimarron Agency, New Mexico Territory, to prevent depredations by Indians in that vicinity, 1875.
185	56 AGO 1875	Correspondence relating to permission given by the Indian agent at Wichita Agency, Indian Territory, for his charges to go north to hunt and to the protest lodged by Lt. Col. T. H. Neill, the commanding officer at Cheyenne River Agency, Dakota Territory, 1875.	224	3945 AGO 1875	Correspondence relating to a communication from the agent for the Cherokee Nation, Indian Territory, stating that hostile feelings existed between the rival Indian factions, 1875.
187	546 AGO 1875	Correspondence pertaining to military operations at Fort Stanton, New Mexico Territory, and to the	225	4228 AGO 1875	Correspondence relating to charges against Capt. John S. Poland, commander of the U.S. Military Station at Standing Rock Indian Agency, Dakota Territory, of arbitrary action in assuming control of trading and other activities of the Indians and businessmen at the agency, 1875–76.

Roll	File	Description
226	4354 AGO 1875	Correspondence relating to the removal of agent William F. M. Arny of the Navajo Indian Agency, Fort Defiance, Arizona Territory, after a council of the principal chiefs of the Navajo Nation at Fort Wingate, New Mexico Territory, in July 1875, and to the appointment of Alexander G. Irvine as his successor, 1875–76.
227	4608 AGO 1875	Correspondence relating to telegrams from Col. Ranald MacKenzie, commander at Fort Sill, Indian Territory, accusing the Interior Department of failing to furnish supplies to the Indians, 1875.
228	4720 AGO 1875	Correspondence pertaining to a threatened general Indian outbreak in eastern Nevada and measures to prevent it, 1875.
233	5650 AGO 1875	Correspondence relating to the fight between Company H, 5th Cavalry, and a band of 60 warriors of the Northern Arapahoe south of the buffalo station on the Kansas Pacific Railway on October 28, 1875.
238	6160 AGO 1875	Papers relating to military expeditions against the Sioux Indians in the Big Horn, Powder and Yellowstone Rivers areas, November 1875–July 1876.
247	265 AGO 1876	Correspondence relating to proposals to sell liquor in the Cherokee Nation, Indian Territory, 1876–78.
259	1929 AGO 1876	Correspondence relating to the total number of Indian scouts authorized to be employed by the Army and to requests for permission to enlist scouts in various departments, 1876–78.
264	2440 AGO 1876	Papers relating to Gen. George Crook's charge that Col. Joseph J. Reynolds and Capt. Alexander Moore failed to carry out orders in an attack on the village of Chief Crazy Horse near Powder River, Montana Territory, in March 1876, and the subsequent general courts-martial of Reynolds and Moore.
265	2576 AGO 1876	Correspondence relating to the removal of the Chiricahua Apache Indians to the San Carlos Indian Agency, Arizona Territory, 1876–77.
271	3570 AGO 1876	Correspondence relating to Gen. George Crook's battle with the Sioux and Cheyenne Indians under Chief Crazy Horse at Rosebud Creek, Montana Territory, June 1876.
	3597 AGO 1876	Correspondence relating to the claim of Young Joseph and his band of Nez Perce Indians to the Wallowa Valley, Oregon; the appointment of a commission to negotiate with Young Joseph; and the removal of the Indians to the reservation at Boise, Idaho Territory, 1876–77.
273	3770 AGO 1876	Papers relating to the defeat of Gen. George A. Custer and his whole command by Sitting Bull's band of Sioux Indians in the battle on the Little Big Horn River, Montana Territory, June 25–26, 1876.
274	3820 AGO 1876	Correspondence pertaining to the offer of volunteer military service by Montana citizens in response to the Custer defeat, 1876.
277–292	4163 AGO 1876	Papers relating to military operations in the Departments of the Platte and Dakota against the Sioux Indians ("Sioux War Papers"), 1876–96.
294	4408 AGO 1876	Correspondence relating to the proposed prohibition of the sale of arms and ammunition to Indians by traders, 1876–78.
321	1281 AGO 1877	Correspondence pertaining to the message of the Governor of Arizona concerning Indian depredations and his request for the removal of the commanding general of the Department of Arizona, 1877.
322	1322 AGO 1877	Correspondence, reports of surveys, and maps of the three wagon roads through the Sioux Reservation in Dakota Territory provided for by the agreement in 1876 with the Sioux. The three routes were from Bismarck to Deadwood City, from Fort Pierre to Deadwood City, and from Fort Niobrara, Nebraska, to Custer City.
323	1469 AGO 1877	Correspondence relating to timber cutting by whites on the Sioux Reservations in Dakota Territory, 1877–80.

Roll	File	Description
326	1927 AGO 1877	Correspondence relating to the arrest and removal of Geronimo's band of renegade Chiricahua Apache Indians from Ojo Caliente, New Mexico Territory, to the San Carlos Indian Agency, Arizona Territory, 1877.
330	2526 AGO 1877	Correspondence relating to the appointment of military officers to witness deliveries by contractors at Indian agencies. Also included are reports of the appointed officers, 1877.
335	3369 AGO 1877	Correspondence pertaining to a report from the commanding officer at Fort Reno, Wyoming Territory, alleging a deficiency of Indian supplies at the Cheyenne and Arapahoe Agency and starvation among the Indians, 1876–78.
336–340	3464 AGO 1877	Correspondence relating to the war with the Nez Perce Indians in 1877, including the battle at Bear Paw Mountain, Montana Territory.
345	3897 AGO 1877	Correspondence relating to intruders on the Klamath Indian Reservation, Oregon, and the possible necessity of removing the Indians, 1877–86.
361	4966 AGO 1877	Correspondence pertaining to troop operations commanded by Lt. J. W. Summerhayes to recover stock from Pima Indians in Arizona and to charges by Gen. A. V. Kautz, commanding the Department of Arizona, that the agent for the Pima, Maricopa, and Papago tribes was inattentive to his responsibilities.
362	4976 AGO 1877	Correspondence relating to the Indians in the area of Fort Benton, Montana Territory, including such matters as the sustenance of a band of Assiniboin and a band of Grosventre Indians and the expulsion of a group of Canadian mixed-blood Indians who had settled on the Milk River, 1877–79.
366	5705 AGO 1877	Correspondence relating to military operations against the Warm Springs Indians who fled from the San Carlos Indian Agency, Arizona Territory, 1877–79.
377–379	7316 AGO 1877	Correspondence relating to the war with the Bannock Indians and associated tribes, the Paiute, Klamath, and Umatilla, 1877–79.
381	7441 AGO 1877	Correspondence relating to requests for a military post in the Black Hills to protect settlers and the subsequent selection of a site for a military reservation at Bear Butte, Dakota Territory, 1877–78.
389	125 AGO 1878	Correspondence and reports relating to the inspection of beef cattle at the Kiowa and Comanche Agency, Indian Territory, 1878.
392	710 AGO 1878	Correspondence pertaining to the detailing of Army officers as acting Indian Agents at the Yankton, Crow Creek, Lower Brule, and Cheyenne River Agencies, Dakota Territory, 1878–84.
394	1036 AGO 1878	Correspondence pertaining to affairs at Standing Rock Agency, Dakota Territory, including the butchering of hogs and the cutting of timber, 1878.
395	1089 AGO 1878	Correspondence relating to the Ute Indians of Colorado and to the November 1878 agreement under which they relinquished their rights to 12 million acres of land.
397–398	1405 AGO 1878	Papers relating to the use of U.S. troops to suppress lawlessness in Lincoln County, New Mexico Territory ("Lincoln County War"), 1878–81. For earlier correspondence, see file 554 AGO 1874 on roll 142.
400	1499 AGO 1878	Correspondence and claims for compensation, 1878–96, for losses sustained during the Nez Perce Indian War in Idaho in the summer of 1877.
401	1620 AGO 1878	Correspondence concerning the removal of Ute and Apache Indians from the Cimarron Agency, New Mexico Territory, to the Southern Ute Agency, Colorado, and the Mescalero Agency, New Mexico Territory, 1878.
406	3042 AGO 1878	Correspondence about Maj. Gen. Philip H. Sheridan's contention that Indian raids along the Rio Grande were committed by Indians from the Fort Stanton Reservation, New Mexico Territory, and his proposal

Roll	File	Description	Roll	File	Description
		to give the Army exclusive control over them, 1878.			Comanche Agency, Indian Territory, 1879.
414	3930 AGO 1878	Correspondence pertaining to a complaint by Col. Elias C. Boudinot, Cherokee Nation, Indian Territory, against the seizure of his hotel by the Fort Gibson post trader and his request for War Department intervention on his behalf, 1878–84.	471–488	2653 AGO 1879	Papers relating to the intrusion by unauthorized persons or "boomers" into Indian Territory, including Oklahoma, the Cherokee Outlet, and the part of the Territory known as Greer County, Texas, 1879–93.
419	4613 AGO 1878	Reports from division and department commanders to the Joint Congressional Committee on the Indian Bureau Transfer, showing the number of troops at Indian agencies in each division or department and the estimated cost for maintaining these troops, 1878.	493	3417 AGO 1879	Correspondence relating to a request by a U.S. marshal for military assistance in arresting white outlaws in the Choctaw Nation, Indian Territory, 1879.
423	5641 AGO 1878	Correspondence relating to the Sept. 1878 consolidation of the Kiowa and Comanche Indian Agency with the Wichita Agency, Indian Territory, and to subsequent reports of dissatisfaction and unrest, 1878, 1879, and 1881.	513–517	4278 AGO 1879	Papers relating to the Ute Indian uprising of 1879 at the White River Agency, Colorado, and the subsequent military operations and reprisals, 1879–83.
425	5900 AGO 1878	Correspondence relating to the request of the Commissioner of Indian Affairs for 15 to 20 cavalrymen to be stationed at Tularosa, New Mexico Territory, to deal with Indian stragglers and to stop the liquor traffic in the vicinity, 1878.	522	5141 AGO 1879	Correspondence relating to the 1879 war with the bands of Indians in central Idaho known as the Sheepeaters ("Sheepeaters' War").
			526–528	6058 AGO 1879	Papers relating to military operations against Chief Victorio's band of Mescalero Apache in southern New Mexico, 1879–81, and one letter dated Mar. 13, 1886.
427	6310 AGO 1878	Correspondence relating to the arrest of Chief Moses and the attempts to relocate his band of Indians on the Yakima Reservation, 1878–79.	535	7076 AGO 1879	Correspondence relating to charges of illegal trading with Indians against the post trader at Fort Yates, Dakota Territory, 1879–81.
428–430	6470 AGO 1878	Papers relating to military operations against the Northern Cheyenne, 1878–79. Included is a report by a board of officers on the arrest and confinement of a number of Cheyenne Indians in the vicinity of Fort Robinson, Nebraska.	536	7111 AGO 1879	Correspondence pertaining to complaints by citizens and miners of harassment by roving Paiute bands, 1878–80.
449	8705 AGO 1878	Correspondence relating to the confinement of nearly 150 Northern Cheyenne at Fort Robinson, Nebraska, their refusal to return to the Indian Territory, their escape from the fort, and the attack by Capt. Henry W. Wessell's Company, 1878–79.	560	2608 AGO 1880	Correspondence relating to dissatisfaction among Indians of the Navajo Agency, Arizona Territory, with their agent, Galen Eastman; the assumption of military control by Capt. Frank T. Bennett, 9th U.S. Cavalry, both there and at Moqui Pueblo Agency; and the eventual reassignment of both agencies to Eastman, 1880.
454	71 AGO 1879	Papers pertaining to the inspection of flour and beef cattle at the Kiowa and	565	3153 AGO 1880	Correspondence pertaining to complaints of the Sioux Indians at Standing Rock Agency, Dakota Territory, about the number of troops at the reservation, the amount of timber cut there, and the cattle still due them for the seizure of their ponies by the Army, 1880–83.

Roll	File	Description
568	3619 AGO 1880	Correspondence relating to unauthorized white settlement on the Sioux Reservation at Fort Pierre, Dakota Territory, 1880.

Letters Received by the Office of the Adjutant General (Main Series), 1881–1889. M689. 740 rolls. DP.

Roll	File	Description
9	1504 AGO 1881	Papers relating to the mortal wounding of a Navajo Indian in Farmington, New Mexico Territory, by Frank Meyers and the subsequent investigation by Army officers that disclosed an absence of law and order in the vicinity because of the outlaw bands, Jan.–May 1881.
	1528 AGO 1881	Correspondence pertaining to important mines discovered at Cataract Creek, Arizona Territory, on the Havasupai Indian Reservation and the difficulties occasioned by the invasion of white miners. Also included are papers pertaining to the survey of Havasupai lands.
36–39	4327 AGO 1881	Papers relating to the battle between the command of Col. Eugene A. Carr, 6th Cavalry, and Apache Indians at Cibecue Creek, Arizona Territory, in Aug. 1881 and a court of inquiry at Fort Grant, Arizona Territory, to investigate charges of negligence against Colonel Carr, 1881–83.
41	4414 AGO 1881	Papers relating to aid for destitute Walapai and Navajo Indians, July 1881–Aug. 1891.
44	4746 AGO 1881	Correspondence and reports mainly concerning efforts to capture hostile Apache Indians who were terrorizing the border region of the District of New Mexico, July–Dec. 1881.
48	5200 AGO 1881	Correspondence relating to a request from the Department of the Interior that the War Department help move Little Chief and certain members of his band of Northern Cheyenne from the Cheyenne and Arapahoe Agency, Indian Territory, to the Pine Ridge Agency, Dakota Territory, Aug. 1881–Aug. 1883.
51	5517 AGO 1881	Correspondence relating to the intrusion of miners and ranchers on Chief Moses' reservation in Washington Territory, Sept. 1881–Feb. 1884.
54	5957 AGO 1881	Papers relating to engagements against Indians in Texas and New Mexico from 1850 to 1856 compiled in reply to a pension claim filed by the widow of William R. Talbot, Company G, 2d Dragoons. Included are evaluations as to whether the fighting constituted a war and efforts to define the limits of the areas involved, Sept. 1881–Dec. 1898.
56	6067 AGO 1881	Correspondence pertaining to the Paiute Indians in California, Nevada, Oregon, and the Territory of Washington, including their migration from the Yakima Agency, Washington Territory, to reservations at Malheur River in Oregon and Fort McDermitt and Pyramid Lake in Nevada. A number of the documents deal with the destitute condition of Indians, 1881–88.
77	364 AGO 1882	Papers and a report of Mar. 4, 1882, from the Secretary of War relating to a statement of expenditures for Indian wars and for the observation and control of Indians from July 1, 1871–June 20, 1882.
78	442 AGO 1882	Report by the Secretary of War and other papers relating to the status of Indian prisoners held under War Department orders, Jan.–Feb. 1882.
81	663 AGO 1882	Papers relating to the Frelinghuysen-Romero Agreement of July 29, 1882, providing for reciprocal crossings of the international boundary by troops of the United States and Mexico in pursuit of hostile Indians, Feb. 1882–June 1887.
85	1076 AGO 1882	Papers pertaining to actions taken by the sheriff of Chouteau County, Montana Territory, and special deputy U.S. marshals in collecting taxes and fines from Indians and Canadian mixed-bloods and in driving the mixed-bloods back to Canada, 1882.
88	1280 AGO 1882	Correspondence relating to a planned reduction of beef rations for the Arapahoe and Cheyenne, Comanche, and Kiowa Agencies; the fears of Army officers,

Roll	File	Description
		particularly of Capt. G. M. Randall, commander at Fort Reno, Indian Territory, that such a reduction would lead to an outbreak of violence; and the subsequent efforts of some officers to obtain a satisfactory quantity of beef for the Indians to avoid endangering the entire frontier with an uprising, Mar.–Sept. 1882.
92	1513 AGO 1882	Correspondence and reports relating to unrest among the Indians of the Navajo Reservation, Arizona Territory, including the recommendation that Indian Agent Galen Eastman be replaced because of his inability to deal with the situation. The file also includes information about Navajo Indians who had gone to the San Juan River Valley, New Mexico Territory, and the efforts of the Army to return them to the reservation, Apr.–Nov. 1882.
96–97	1749 AGO 1882	Papers relating to outbreaks of violence, including several murders in New Mexico and Arizona by Chiricahua Apache who escaped from the San Carlos Reservation, Arizona Territory, and to their pacification.
101	2180 AGO 1882	Papers concerning the threatened starvation of Indians on the Mescalero Apache Reservation, New Mexico Territory, after Congress failed to appropriate funds for rations and the subsequent efforts by Army officers and the Department of the Interior to obtain rations, May 1882–Aug. 1884.
108	2809 AGO 1882	Papers and reports relating to surveys of the boundaries of the White Mountain Reservation in Arizona Territory and of the Mescalero Apache Reservation in New Mexico Territory and to an Executive Order reducing the area of the latter, June 1882–Dec. 1884.
123	3875 AGO 1882	Papers relating to a potential Piegan Indian outbreak at the Blackfeet Agency, Montana Territory, due to insufficient food rations, 1882–83.

Roll	File	Description
138	5171 AGO 1882	Correspondence relating to the illegal sale of liquor in Indian Territory, 1882–83.
147	5942 AGO 1882	Correspondence relating to disorders near Okmulgee, Indian Territory, among the Creek Indians who rebelled against their leaders and to efforts of the Army to restore order, Dec. 1882–Nov. 1883.
173–202	1066 AGO 1883	Papers relating to the uprising of the Chiricahua Apache under Geronimo, Chatto, and Natchez and to their subsequent surrender and imprisonment in the East, 1883–1906. Included are records pertaining to the disposition of surrendered Chiricahua, Sept. 19, 1885–Apr. 8, 1886; the movement of U.S. troops into Mexico; and the death of Capt. Emmet Crawford from wounds received from Mexican troops. For other papers relating to Capt. Crawford, see file 4061 AGO 1883 on roll 231.
204	1181 AGO 1883	Correspondence relating to Chief Moses' trip to Washington, D.C., to confer with the Secretary of War and other officials over a dispute between farmers and Colville, Moses, and Okinagan Indians in Washington Territory, May–Sept. 1883.
205	1233 AGO 1883	Papers pertaining to fighting between war parties of Cree Indians from Canada and herders in Montana Territory, 1883.
224	3111 AGO 1883	Correspondence relating to the plan to visit Indians in Montana and Dakota by members of the Senate Committee on Indian Affairs and to the request of Sen. H. L. Davis that the Army provide transportation and other necessary aid during their tour, July 1883–May 1885.
271	1759 AGO 1884	Papers relating to reports from post officers of attempts by white men to dispossess nonreservation Indians settled along the Columbia River and other places within the Military District of the Columbia and to an Interior Department order, May 31, 1884, to U.S. land offices, instructing land agents to refuse to file all entries by whites for lands then

Roll	File	Description
		settled by Indians, Apr. 1884–Mar. 1885.
273	1882 AGO 1884	Papers pertaining to Indian depredations near Mitchell's ranch, New Mexico Territory, and measures taken to suppress them, 1884.
275	2016 AGO 1884	Correspondence relating to the death of Running Buffalo, a Cheyenne Indian, killed by a herder named Horton near Fort Supply, Indian Territory, in May 1884; the resulting conflict with the Indians; and the propriety of granting leases to cattlemen to drive livestock herds through Indian lands, May 1884–Feb. 1885.
279	2487 AGO 1884	Correspondence relating to the May 1884 killing of Sioux Chief White Thunder by Thunder Hawk and Spotted Tail at the Rosebud Agency, Dakota Territory, as a result of an old feud, June–Oct. 1884. Includes correspondence relating to disturbances at the Pine Ridge Agency, Dakota Territory, resulting from the arrival of T. A. Bland, publisher of the magazine *Council Fire*.
331	127 AGO 1885	Report of Lt. H. T. Allen's reconnaissance voyage to Alaska Territory, Oct.–Dec. 1884, and papers relating to an expedition by Lt. Allen and his party to the district of the Copper and Tanana Rivers to investigate the character and disposition of the natives, Dec. 1884–May 1885. Included are copies of Lt. Allen's reports of March and April 1885.
336	722 AGO 1885	Papers pertaining to an investigation into the shooting of an Indian by a white at an Indian camp in Grant County, Oregon, 1885.
341	1153 AGO 1885	Correspondence and several reports relating to a suspected outbreak of intertribal warfare, reported by Joseph Terrill, who lived near Fort McKinney, Wyoming Territory, involving Arapahoe, Blackfeet, Cheyenne, Crow, Piegan, Shoshoni, and Sioux Indians in Wyoming and Montana, Feb.–May 1885.
362–363	3140 AGO 1885	Correspondence relating to disturbances caused by Indians of the Cheyenne and Arapahoe Agency, Indian Territory, June 1885–

Roll	File	Description
		Sept. 1886, and Lt. Gen. Philip H. Sheridan's report, July 24, 1885.
402	7125 AGO 1885	Papers relating to a recommendation by Gen. F. C. Armstrong, U.S. Indian Inspector, that troops be sent to preserve order among Northern Cheyenne Indians at Tongue River, Montana Territory, and papers relating to attacks by Rosebud Indians in the Tongue River area against their agency, Nov.–Dec. 1885.
446	2104 AGO 1886	Papers pertaining to the appointment of Capt. J. M. Bell as temporary Indian Agent at Pine Ridge Agency, Dakota Territory, 1886.
452	2458 AGO 1886	Correspondence and reports relating to the condition of the Chief Moses and Joseph Indians in the Department of the Columbia, including a request that the Department of the Interior supply agricultural implements to them, May 1886–May 1887.
466	3395 AGO 1886	Papers relating to Richard Fitzpatrick's claim for damages caused by Indian depredations during the Seminole War and for losses sustained because of U.S. troops quartered on his plantation in southern Florida from 1838–42. Included are copies of reports and correspondence concerning military operations in Florida in 1838 and military maps of Florida. The papers are dated July 1886–Feb. 1887.
483	5269 AGO 1886	Report by Lt. J. T. Haines, 5th Cavalry, and copies of correspondence from the Department of the Interior relating to efforts to bring back Indians who left the Sac and Fox Indian Agency, Indian Territory, Sept. 1886–Jan. 1887.
	5304 AGO 1886	Papers relating to intertribal hostilities among the Blood, Piegan, Grosventre, and Crow Indians in the border region of the Department of Dakota, Oct. 1886–Aug. 1887.
489	5939 AGO 1886	Reports, recommendations, and other papers relating to efforts by the Army and the Department of the Interior to return Jicarilla Apache Indians, camped near Española, New Mexico

Roll	File	Description
		Territory, to the Mescalero Reservation and to adjust their grievances, Oct. 1886–June 1888.
513	477 AGO 1887	Papers relating to the protection of the Klamath Indian Reservation, Oregon, against poachers, cattlemen, and settlers. Reports and correspondence from the Department of the Interior are included, Jan. 1887–Dec. 1888.
517	827 AGO 1887	Correspondence and reports relating to problems caused by white settlers in the San Juan River country on the Navajo Reservation in the District of New Mexico, Feb.–Nov. 1887.
526	880 AGO 1887	Reports from officers in the Department of California and from officials of the Interior Department relating to the encroachment of white settlers and cattlemen on the Round Valley Indian Reservation, California, Apr.–Dec. 1887.
533	2889 AGO 1887	Papers and copies of reports relating to white intruders on the Coeur d'Alene Reservation, Idaho. Included is a transcript of the field notes by Darius F. Baker, U.S. Deputy Surveyor, on the survey of the boundary lines of the reservation.
536	3264 AGO 1887	Reports of Gen. Nelson A. Miles and other persons concerning operations in Arizona against renegade Apache from the San Carlos Reservation and the condition of the tribes there, June 1887–May 1889. Included is a letter from Maj. Gen. George Crook giving his views on the management of the Mohave, Yuma, and Tonto Apache.
537	3324 AGO 1887	Papers relating to the removal of Pine Ridge Cheyenne from the Tongue River Agency in Montana, where they had traveled to hold a sun dance, June–Oct. 1887. For additional records on this subject, see file 2493 AGO 1889 on roll 683.
538	3470 AGO 1887	Papers pertaining to an anticipated visit of Sioux Indians at the Crow Agency, Montana Territory, and a request by the Commissioner of Indian Affairs that they be intercepted, 1887.
548	4668 AGO 1887	Papers pertaining to a party of Comanche Indians from Indian Territory who visited the Mescalero Reservation in New Mexico. Other documents deal with general policies of allowing Indians to leave their reservations for visits, 1887.
549	4686 AGO 1887	Report of 1st Lt. George R. Burnett, 9th Cavalry, Sept. 10, 1887, and other correspondence concerning trouble between the Colorado militia and Colorado ("Colorow"), chief of the Ute Indians, and efforts of U.S. troops to bring the Ute back to the Uintah and Ouray Reservation, Aug.–Sept. 1887.
554	5199 AGO 1887	Papers relating to the protection of the Indians who accepted allotments of land in severalty on the Yankton Reservation, Dakota Territory, and to the removal of intruders on the Pipestone Reservation, Minnesota, Sept.–Oct. 1887.
557	5681 AGO 1887	Papers relating to the Crow Indian outbreak led by Deaf Bull in the vicinity of the Crow Agency, Montana, and to the subsequent investigation and imprisonment of the Indians involved, Oct. 1887–June 1890.
567	6839 AGO 1887	Papers relating to the death of Mary Wagnor, allegedly killed by Indians in the Rogue River Valley, Oregon Territory, in 1856. Included are 42 reports and enclosures filed by Lt. Col. R. C. Buchanan concerning his operations in the area during the Rogue River Indian War, 1855–56.
569	7007 AGO 1887	Correspondence, Dec. 1887–Dec. 1889, relating to Senate resolutions of Dec. 20, 1887, and Jan. 29, 1889, directing the Secretary of War to supply all records pertaining to Capt. Lawrence Hall's Company of Oregon Volunteers, which participated in the Cayuse Indian War of 1848 in the Oregon Territory. The requested information was furnished Dec. 7, 1889, and published as *Letter From the Secretary of War Transmitting Report of Capt. W. E. Birkhimer,* Senate Executive Document 6, 51st Congress, 1st session.

Roll	File	Description
634	3089 AGO 1888	Papers pertaining to Indian problems in the Departments of the Platte and Dakota. Included are documents concerning citizens' protests against troop removals, Indians under Lost Bull who left the Tongue River Agency in Montana, and Sioux from Pine Ridge Agency, Dakota Territory, who left for Tongue River to participate in a sun dance, 1888.
636	3340 AGO 1888	Report of Lt. Col. Simon Snyder, 10th Infantry, July 30, 1888, and related correspondence and telegrams concerning disturbances caused by Indians in the vicinity of the San Carlos Reservation, Arizona Territory, July–Sept. 1888.
663	7 AGO 1889	Correspondence and a printed report of the Secretary of War relating to the service of volunteers from Washington and Idaho Territories in the Nez Perce War of 1877.
665	281 AGO 1889	Correspondence of the acting Indian agent of Hoopa Valley Agency regarding the Lower Klamath Indians and land speculators and the request of the Commissioner of Indian Affairs for the removal of intruders from Indian land, 1889.
	299 AGO 1889	Papers relating to attempts by the Army to remove the heirs of Henry Harris, a white settler and U.S. citizen, from the Cherokee Nation, Indian Territory, Jan.–Mar. 1889.
667	567 AGO 1889	Correspondence relating to the attempted removal of cattlemen and their herds from Indian Territory and the problem of opening Oklahoma for public settlement, Feb. 1889.
676	1253 AGO 1889	Correspondence relating to the encroachment of white settlers on the Sioux Reservation.
696	3551 AGO 1889	Papers pertaining to the Flathead Indians in Montana and their strained relations with local authorities and citizens. Documents also relate to the activities of the troops sent to investigate the problem. See also file 5435 AGO 1889 on roll 716.
701	4310 AGO 1889	Reports of Capt. Quinton Williams, Inspector of Indian Supplies, on the

destitute condition of Indians of the Shoshone (Wind River) Reservation, Wyoming Territory, and copies of correspondence from the Department of the Interior relating to this matter, July–Sept. 1889.

Letters Sent

Letters Sent by the Office of the Adjutant General (Main Series), 1800–1890. M565. 63 rolls. DP.

The letters sent by the Adjutant General describe the Army's pacification efforts. Arranged chronologically, they include letters of instruction, requests for information, and orders for the movement of troops.

Roll	Dates
1	Sept. 9, 1800–Dec. 6, 1803
2	Dec. 10, 1803–Sept. 4, 1809
3	Sept. 4, 1809–July 13, 1812
4	Mar. 28, 1812–May 30, 1814
5	May 30, 1814–May 29, 1818
6	May 29, 1818–July 28, 1824
7	July 29, 1824–Feb. 23, 1830
8	Feb. 24, 1830–May 19, 1834
9	May 19, 1834–July 23, 1836
10	July 23, 1836–Oct. 9, 1838
11	Oct. 10, 1838–Dec. 31, 1840
12	Jan. 2, 1841–Nov. 21, 1842
13	Nov. 22, 1842–Dec. 31, 1844
14	Jan. 2, 1845–Sept. 5, 1846
15	Sept. 7, 1846–Mar. 15, 1848
16	Mar. 16, 1848–Dec. 31, 1849
17	Jan. 2, 1850–Dec. 10, 1853
18	Dec. 12, 1853–July 29, 1857
19	July 29, 1857–Sept. 4, 1860
20	Sept. 4, 1860–Jan. 22, 1862
21	Jan. 23, 1862–Jan. 31, 1863
22	Feb. 1–Oct. 31, 1863
23	Nov. 2, 1863–Mar. 31, 1864
24	Apr. 1–Sept. 14, 1864
25	Sept. 15, 1864–Jan. 25, 1865
26	Jan. 26–May 20, 1865
27	May 22–Aug. 28, 1865
28	Aug. 29–Dec. 30, 1865
29	Jan. 2–May 30, 1866
30	May 31–Nov. 8, 1866
31	Nov. 9, 1866–Apr. 3, 1867
32	Apr. 3–Aug. 16, 1867
33	Aug. 16–Dec. 20, 1867
34	Dec. 20, 1867–June 19, 1868
35	June 19–Nov. 16, 1868
36	Nov. 17, 1868–Apr. 30, 1869
37	May 1–Oct. 13, 1869
38	Oct. 13, 1869–Apr. 2, 1870
39	Apr. 2–Sept. 9, 1870
40	Sept. 10, 1870–Apr. 17, 1871
41	Apr. 18, 1871–Mar. 14, 1872
42	Mar. 14, 1872–Feb. 4, 1873
43	Feb. 5, 1873–Feb. 14, 1874
44	Feb. 14, 1874–Feb. 26, 1875
45	Feb. 26, 1875–Feb. 5, 1876
46	Feb. 7–Nov. 21, 1876
47	Nov. 22, 1876–Aug. 29, 1877

Roll	Dates
48	Aug. 30, 1877–June 3, 1878
49	June 4, 1878–Mar. 7, 1879
50	Mar. 8–Nov. 18, 1879
51	Nov. 18, 1879–July 27, 1880
52	July 27, 1880–May 5, 1881
53	May 6–Dec. 10, 1881
54	Dec. 10, 1881–May 10, 1882
55	May 10, 1882–Mar. 12, 1883
56	Mar. 12, 1883–Mar. 31, 1884
57	Apr. 1–Dec. 23, 1884
58	Dec. 23, 1884–Aug. 18, 1885
59	Aug. 18, 1885–May 19, 1886
60	May 19, 1886–Feb. 18, 1887
61	Feb. 18–Nov. 9, 1887
62	Nov. 10, 1887–Feb. 7, 1889
63	Feb. 7, 1889–June 2, 1890

Reports and Correspondence Relating to the Army Investigations of the Battle at Wounded Knee and to the Sioux Campaign of 1890–1891. M983. 2 rolls. DP.

The Battle at Wounded Knee Creek, South Dakota, took place on Dec. 29, 1890. A band of Sioux Indians in the custody of the 7th U.S. Cavalry was being disarmed when a fight broke out, resulting in numerous white and Indian casualties. Many of the Sioux casualties were women and children. Beyond these basic facts, the course of events at Wounded Knee and the ultimate responsibility for them have always been subjects for debate. The investigative reports and accompanying papers included in this microfilm publication record much of the earliest phase of that debate. They represent efforts of the Army to determine the circumstances surrounding the events at Wounded Knee and any possible misconduct on the part of the 7th Cavalry.

Roll	Contents
1	Name and Subject Index
	"Sioux Campaign, 1890–91," pp. 1–650
	"Sioux Campaign, 1890–91," pp. 651–975
2	"Sioux Campaign, 1890–91," pp. 976–1793
	Headquarters, Department of California, Report of Operations Relative to the Sioux Indians in 1890 and 1891 in the Department of Dakota, pp. 1794–2006
	Senate Executive Document No. 9, 51st Congress, 2d session, pp. 2007–2057. Reports of Brig. Gen. James W. Forsyth to Secretary of War Daniel S. Lamont

War Department Collection of Post-Revolutionary War Manuscripts. M904. 4 rolls. DP.

This microfilm publication reproduces the War Department's collection of post-Revolutionary War manuscripts and the accompanying name card index. The documents primarily cover 1784–1811 when the Federal Government fought against the Indians and guarded arsenals and frontiers in the Old Northwest and Southwest. The microfilm contains some of the earliest Territorial material relating to American Indians held by NARS.

The manuscripts (arranged in 101 consecutively numbered envelopes, or manuscript files) consist of about 500 documents that relate primarily to the pay and supply of State militia organizations mustered into Federal service from the close of the American Revolution until the War of 1812.

Roll	Description
1	Name Card Index to Manuscript Files, A–J
2	Name Card Index to Manuscript Files, K–Z
3	Manuscript Files, 1–66:
	Delaware (1)
	District of Columbia (2)
	Georgia (3–8)
	Territory of Illinois (9)
	Territory of Indiana (10–13)
	Kentucky (14–21)
	Maryland (22–24)
	Territory of Mississippi (25)
	New Jersey (26–27)
	Territory Northwest of the Ohio River (28–31)
	Territory of Orleans (32)
	Pennsylvania (33–37)
	South Carolina (38–41)
	Virginia (42–66)
4	Manuscript Files, 67–101:
	Territory Southwest of the Ohio River (67–88)
	United States Troops and Levies (89–97)
	Miscellaneous (98–101)

Records Relating to Military Service (Record Groups 94 and 109)

Records of the Adjutant General's Office, 1780's–1917 (Record Group 94)

The Federal Government fought against the Indians throughout the nineteenth century. Record Group 94 includes the compiled military service records of volunteer soldiers who fought against the Indians and the indexes to those records. For a complete description of the available microfilm publications see *Military Service Records: A Select Catalog of National Archives Microfilm Publications*.

Registers of Enlistments in the United States Army, 1798–1914. M233. 72 rolls.

These registers contain the names of enlisted men in the Regular Army, showing for each man when, where, and by whom he was enlisted, the period of enlistment, place of birth, age, civilian occupation, personal description, organization assignment, and enlistment number, with pertinent remarks. The information in the registers was compiled from enlistment papers, muster rolls of the Regular Army, and other records.

Rolls other than those listed below may contain information about Indians who served as soldiers in the Regular Army or soldiers who served in the Indian wars or campaigns.

Roll	Contents
70	Indian Scouts, 1866–77
71	Indian Scouts, 1878–1914

Compiled Records Showing Service of Military Units in Volunteer Union Organizations. M594. 225 rolls. DP. 16mm.

Roll	Contents
225	First Independent Co. through Seventh Independent Co.,
	Unassigned Detachments
	Other U.S. Organizations
	Brigade Bands
	Departmental Corps, Department of the Monongahela
	First Indian Home Guards
	Second Indian Home Guards
	Third Indian Home Guards
	Fourth and Fifth Indian Home Guards
	First Battalion, Cavalry, Mississippi Marine Brigade
	Light Battery, Mississippi Marine Brigade
	First Infantry, Mississippi Marine Brigade
	Marine Regiment, U.S. Volunteers
	General and Staff, Mississippi Marine Brigade
	Signal Corps Detachment, Mississippi Marine Brigade
	Ram Fleet, Mississippi Marine Brigade
	Battalion, Pioneer Brigade (Army of the Cumberland)

Military Service Records in the War Department Collection of Confederate Records (Record Group 109)

The War Department Collection of Confederate Records consists of records of the Confederate States of America acquired by capture or surrender at the close of the Civil War and those later acquired by donation or purchase. On July 21, 1865, the Secretary of War established a unit in the Adjutant General's Office for the collection, safekeeping, and publication of the "rebel archives."

Compiled Service Records of Confederate Soldiers Who Served in Organizations Raised Directly by the Confederate Government. M258. 123 rolls. DP. 16mm.

Roll	Contents
77	First Cherokee Mounted Rifles (1st Arkansas Cherokee Mounted Rifles), A–L
78	M–Y
79	First Cherokee Mounted Volunteers (Watie's Regiment, Cherokee Mounted Volunteers; 2d Regiment, Cherokee Mounted Rifles, Arkansas; 1st Regiment, Cherokee Mounted Rifles or Riflemen), A–K
80	L–Y
	First Squadron, Cherokee Mounted Volunteers (Holt's Squadron, Cherokee Mounted Volunteers)
81	First Chickasaw Infantry (Hunter's Regiment, Indian Volunteers)
82	First Choctaw Mounted Rifles
83	First Choctaw and Chickasaw Mounted Rifles, A–G
84	H–N
85	O–Y

Roll	Contents
86	First Creek Mounted Volunteers (1st Regiment, Creek Mounted Rifles or Riflemen; Creek Regiment, Mounted Indian Volunteers; 2d Regiment, Arkansas Creeks), A–H
87	I–S
88	T–Z
	First Osage Battalion. C.S.A.
	First Seminole Mounted Volunteers, A–C
89	D–Y
90	Second Cherokee Mounted Volunteers (2nd Regiment, Cherokee Mounted Rifles or Riflemen)
91	Second Creek Mounted Volunteers
	Cherokee Regiment (Special Service)
	Deneale's Regiment, Choctaw Warriors (Deneale's Confederate Volunteers)
	Shecoe's Chickasaw Battalion, Mounted Volunteers
	Washington's Squadron of Indians, C.S.A. (Reserve Squadron of Cavalry)
	Capt. Wilkins' Co., Choctaw Infantry
	Miscellaneous Indian Records

Compiled Records Showing Service of Military Units in Confederate Organizations. M861. 74 rolls. DP. 16mm.

Roll	Contents
74	First Cherokee Mounted Rifles (First Arkansas Cherokee)
	First Cherokee Mounted Volunteers (Watie's Regiment, Cherokee Mounted Volunteers; Second Regiment, Cherokee Mounted Rifles, Arkansas; First Regiment, Cherokee Mounted Riflemen)
	First Squadron, Cherokee Mounted Volunteers (Holt's Squadron)
	First Chickasaw Infantry (Hunter's Regiment, Indian Volunteers)
	First Choctaw Mounted Rifles
	First Choctaw and Chickasaw Mounted Rifles
	First Creek Mounted Volunteers (First Regiment, Creek Mounted Rifles or Riflemen; Creek Regiment, Mounted Indian Volunteers; Second Regiment, Arkansas Creeks)
	First Osage Battalion, C.S.A.
	First Seminole Mounted Volunteers
	Second Cherokee Mounted Volunteers (Second Regiment, Cherokee Mounted Rifles or Riflemen)
	Second Creek Mounted Volunteers
	Cherokee Regiment (Special Service)
	Deneale's Regiment, Choctaw Warriors (Deneale's Confederate Volunteers)
	Shecoe's Chickasaw Battalion, Mounted Volunteers
	Washington's Squadron of Indians, C.S.A. (Reserve Squadron of Cavalry)
	Capt. Wilkins' Co., Choctaw Infantry
	Miscellaneous Indian Records

Records of United States Army Continental Commands, 1821–1920 (Record Group 393)

From 1813 to 1921, the U. S. Army, for purposes of administrative control, was organized into commands designed as geographical or territorial divisions and departments. These varied in name, jurisdiction, and number, as reorganizations occurred frequently over the years. At times departments reported to divisions, and at other times they reported directly to the War Department. The military divisions were established to handle problems requiring greater effort than one department could produce. From 1867 to 1891, the Military Division of the Missouri coordinated the efforts of three departments (Missouri, Dakota, and Platte) against the hostile Indians in the Middle West. The Department of Texas was added to the division in 1871. Each department and division had an organization of staff officers corresponding to the War Department bureaus, to which the staff officers were responsible for the technical aspects of their duties.

The records of the U. S. Army continental commands are of the same types as those of the Adjutant General's Office, but they are organized separately for each individual command that created them. Although the field commands were primarily concerned with Indian wars and campaigns, the Army was interested in peaceful solutions to problems with Indians and performed duties other than policing and fighting them. Consequently, the correspondence series contains much correspondence with Indian agents and superintendents, commissioners, Indian chiefs, Interior Department officials, State and Territorial governors, and other officials.

Military Departments and Districts

Florida

Letters Sent, Registers of Letters Received, and Letters Received by Headquarters, Troops in Florida, and Headquarters, Department of Florida, 1850–1858. M1084. 10 rolls.

Roll	Description	Dates
Letters sent by Headquarters, Troops in Florida:		
1	Vol. 1	June 14–Dec. 10, 1850
	Vol. 2	Dec. 10, 1850–Oct. 7, 1852
	Vol. 3	Oct. 7, 1852–Apr. 18, 1853
	Vol. 4	Apr. 21, 1853–Apr. 18, 1854
	Vol. 5	Apr. 19, 1854–Dec. 31, 1855
	Vol. 6 (74/242 DFla)	Jan. 2–Apr. 11, 1856
Letters sent by Headquarters, Department of Florida:		
	Vol. 7 (5 DFla)	Apr. 13, 1856–Aug. 6, 1858
Letters sent by Headquarters, Troops in Florida, relating to Florida Volunteers:		
	Vol. 8	Jan. 29–Apr. 12, 1856

Roll	Description	Dates
Registers of letters received by Headquarters, Troops in Florida:		
	Vol. 1	June 1850–Dec. 1854
	Vol. 2	Jan. 1855–June 1856
Registers of letters received by Headquarters, Department of Florida:		
	Vol. 3 (2/12 DFla)	Apr. 1856–Aug. 1858
Letters received by Headquarters, Troops in Florida:		
2	Registered and unregistered	June 1850–Dec. 1852
3	"	1853–54
4	"	Jan. 1855–Apr. 1856
Letters received by Headquarters, Department of Florida:		
5	Registered letters, A–H	Apr.–Dec. 1856
6	Registered letters, J–Y	"
	Unregistered letters	"
7	Registered letters, A–G	1857
8	Registered letters, H–P	"
9	Registered letters, R–W	"
	Unregistered letters	"
10	Registered and unregistered letters	Jan.–Aug. 1858

"Memoir of Reconnaissances with Maps During the Florida Campaign," April 1854–February 1858. M1090. 1 roll. DP.

This microfilm publication consists of summaries of reports and accompanying maps received by Headquarters, Troops in Florida (Apr. 1854–Apr. 1856) and Headquarters, Department of Florida (Apr. 1856–Feb. 1858). The maps, rendered by Army officers during the Third Seminole War, include maps of Indian villages.

New Mexico and the 9th Military Department

Register of Letters Received and Letters Received by Headquarters, 9th Military Department, 1848–1853. M1102. 7 rolls.

Roll	Description
1	Register, 1851–53
	Letters received, 1848–49
2	Letters received, 1850
3	Letters received, Jan.–July, 1851
4	Letters received, Aug.–Dec. 1851
	Letters received, 1852, A–C
5	Letters received, 1852, D–S
6	Letters received, 1852, T–W
	Letters received, 1853, A–H
7	Letters received, 1853, J–W

Registers of Letters Received and Letters Received, Department of New Mexico, 1854–1865. M1120. 30 rolls.

Roll	Description	Dates
1	Register, vol. 1	1854–57
	Register, vol. 2	1858–61
	Register, vol. 3	Jan.–Nov. 1862

2	Register, vol. 4	Nov. 1862–Apr. 1864
	Register, vol. 5	Apr.–Dec. 1864
	Register, vol. 6	Jan.–Sept. 1865
3	Letters received	1854
4	Letters received	1855
5	Letters received	1856
6	Letters received	1857
7	Letters received, A–M	1858
8	Letters received, N–Z	1858
9	Letters received, A–K	1859
10	Letters received, L–Z	1859
11	Letters received, A–M	1860
12	Letters received, N–Z	1860
13	Letters received, A–L	1861
14	Letters received, M–Z	1861
15	Letters received, A–D	1862
16	Letters received, E–L	1862
17	Letters received, M–Z	1862
18	Letters received, A–E	1863
19	Letters received, F–P	1863
20	Letters received, Q–V	1863
21	Letters received, W–Z	1863
22	Letters received, A–B	1864
23	Letters received, C–F	1864
24	Letters received, G–Q	1864
25	Letters received, R–Z	1864
26	Letters received, A–F	1865
27	Letters received, G–Z	1865
28	Unregistered letters received	1854–61
29	Unregistered letters received	1862–63
30	Unregistered letters received	1864–65

Letters Received by Headquarters, District of New Mexico, September 1865–August 1890. M1088. 65 rolls. DP.

Roll	Dates
1	Sept.–Dec. 1865
2	1866
3	1866
4	1866
5	1867
6	1867
7	1867
8	1867
9	1867
10	1868
11	1869–70
12	1871
13	1871
14	1871
15	1872
16	1872
17	1873
18	1873
19	1873
20	1873
21	1874
22	1874
23	1874

Roll	Dates
24	1875
25	1875
26	1875
27	1876
28	1876
29	1877
30	1877
31	1877
32	Jan.–Apr. 1878
33	May–June 1878
34	July–Aug. 1878
35	Sept.–Dec. 1878
36	Jan.–Mar. 1879
37	Apr.–June 1879
38	July–Sept. 1879
39	Oct.–Dec. 1879
40	Jan.–June 1880
41	July–Dec. 1880
42	Jan.–Apr. 1881
43	May–Oct. 1881
44	Nov.–Dec. 1881
45	Jan.–Feb. 1882
46	Mar.–Apr. 1882
47	May–Sept. 1882
48	Oct.–Dec. 1882
49	Jan.–Mar. 1883
50	Apr.–June 1883
51	July–Sept. 1883
52	Oct.–Dec. 1883
53	Jan.–Apr. 1884
54	May–July 1884
55	Aug.–Dec. 1884
56	Jan.–June 1885
57	July–Aug. 1885
58	Sept.–Oct. 1885
59	Nov.–Dec. 1885
60	Jan.–Mar. 1886
61	Apr.–Dec. 1886
62	Jan.–June 1887
63	July–Dec. 1887
64	Jan.–Dec. 1888
65	Jan.–Dec. 1889
	Jan.–Aug. 1890

Letters Sent by the 9th Military Department, the Department of New Mexico, and the District of New Mexico, 1849–1890. M1072. 7 rolls. DP.

Roll	Contents	Dates
1	Letters sent	Oct. 1849–Aug. 1856
	Name index	July 1851–May 1856
2	Letters sent	Aug. 1856–Sept. 1862
3	Letters sent	Aug. 1862–Oct. 1866
4	Letters sent	Nov. 1866–Oct. 1872
	Subject index	Sept. 1870–Oct. 1872
5	Name and subject indexes	1872–76
	Letters sent	Oct. 1872–Dec. 1877
6	Name and subject indexes	1878–1881
	Letters sent	Jan. 1878–Aug. 1881

Roll	Contents	Dates
7	Name and subject indexes	1881–1883
	Letters sent	Aug. 1881–Sept. 1890

Texas and the 5th Military District

Letters Sent by the Department of Texas, the District of Texas, and the 5th Military District, 1856–1858 and 1865–1870. M1165. 3 rolls.

Roll	Dates
1	May 6, 1856–Apr. 27, 1858
	June 19–July 29, 1865
	Aug. 12, 1865–Aug. 21, 1866
	Aug. 20, 1866–Feb. 29, 1868
2	Mar. 1–Aug. 5, 1868
	Aug. 10–Dec. 31, 1868
	Jan. 1–Apr. 17, 1869
3	Apr. 17–Aug. 3, 1869
	Aug. 2–Dec. 31, 1869
	Jan. 3–Apr. 16, 1870

Letters Sent by Headquarters, Department of Texas, 1870–1894 and 1897–1898. M1114. 10 rolls.

Roll	Dates
1	Apr. 18–Dec. 29, 1870
	Dec. 29–31, 1870
	Jan. 3, 1871–Dec. 31, 1872
2	Jan. 2, 1873–May 31, 1875
	June 1–Dec. 31, 1875
3	Jan. 1–Sept. 30, 1876
	Oct. 2–Dec. 30, 1876
	Jan. 2–Sept. 5, 1877
	Sept. 5–Dec. 31, 1877
4	Jan. 1–June 6, 1878
	June 6–Dec. 30, 1878
	Jan. 2–Sept. 15, 1879
	Sept. 15–Dec. 31, 1879
5	Jan. 1–July 24, 1880
	July 24–Dec. 31, 1880
6	Jan. 1–Nov. 5, 1881
	Nov. 5–Dec. 31, 1881
	Jan. 3–Sept. 9, 1882
	Sept. 10–Dec. 30, 1882
7	Jan. 2–Oct. 11, 1883
	Oct. 11–Dec. 26, 1883
	Jan. 2–Nov. 11, 1884
	Nov. 11–Dec. 31, 1884
8	Jan. 2–Dec. 31, 1885
	Jan. 2–Dec. 31, 1886
	Jan. 3–Dec. 31, 1887
9	Jan. 2–Dec. 31, 1888
	Jan. 2–Dec. 31, 1889
	Jan. 2, 1890–Dec. 31, 1891
10	Jan. 2–Dec. 31, 1892
	Jan. 2–Dec. 30, 1893
	Jan. 2–Dec. 31, 1894
	Jan. 2, 1897–Mar. 11, 1898

10th Military Department

Records of the Tenth Military Department, 1846–1851. M210. 7 rolls. DP.

Roll	Contents
1	Letters sent, Mar. 23, 1847–July 8, 1851 (7 vols.)
2	Register of letters received, Jan. 25, 1847–Mar. 30, 1849 (1 vol.); and letters received, May 12, 1846–Dec. 30, 1847
3	Letters received, Jan. 9, 1848–Mar. 28, 1849

Roll	Contents
4	Letters received, Jan. 15, 1849–Feb. 27, 1850
5	Letters received, Mar. 2, 1850–July 9, 1851; and miscellaneous papers, Mar. 15, 1846–Sept. 30, 1847
6	Miscellaneous papers, Oct. 1, 1847–Apr. 28, 1849
7	Miscellaneous papers, May 4, 1849–June 26, 1851; orders and special orders, Feb. 13, 1847–July 22, 1848 (2 vols.); orders, Jan. 22, 1849–July 8, 1851 (1 vol.); and special orders, Jan. 15, 1849–June 23, 1851 (1 vol.)

Military Posts

Headquarters Records of Fort Cummings, New Mexico, 1863–1873 and 1880–1884. M1081. 8 rolls. DP.

The Army established Fort Cummings, at Cook Springs, New Mexico, to control the Apache and protect the trail to California. Fort Cummings was garrisoned by Regular and Volunteer troops until Aug. 1873, when it was abandoned because many of the Apache had been restricted to the Ojo Caliente Reservation. Because of increased Indian unrest, the Army reoccupied the post from July 1880 until Aug. 1884.

Roll	Description	Dates
1	Name and title index to letters sent	1863–73
	"	1880–84

Letters sent:

	Vol. 1 (9)	Oct. 20, 1863–Feb. 17, 1865
	Vol. 2 (10)	Feb. 20, 1865–June 18, 1867
	Vol. 3 (11)	June 24, 1867–Jan. 20, 1869
	Vol. 4 (12)	Jan. 23–Oct. 2, 1869
	Vol. 5 (13)	Oct. 3, 1869–Aug. 21, 1871
	Vol. 6 (14)	Sept. 3, 1871–July 23, 1872
	Vol. 2 (4)	July 28, 1872–Nov. 30, 1873
	Vol. 7 (15)	Oct. 25, 1880–June 24, 1881
	Vol. 8 (16)	June 26, 1881–Apr. 2, 1882
	Vol. 9 (17)	Apr. 3, 1882–Nov. 15, 1883
	Vol. 10 (18)	Nov. 22, 1883–Aug. 21, 1884

Endorsements sent:

2	Vol. 1 (21)	Nov. 1, 1866–Jan. 11, 1870
	Vol. 2 (2)	Jan. 2–Nov. 9, 1870
	Vol. 3 (3)	Nov. 10, 1870–Jan. 1, 1872
	Vol. 4 (22)	Jan. 3, 1872–Oct. 6, 1873
	Vol. 5 (23)	Oct. 26, 1880–Jan. 4, 1881
	Vol. 6 (24)	Jan. 5–Apr. 7, 1881
3	Vol. 7 (25)	Apr. 7–Oct. 30, 1881
	Vol. 8 (29)	Oct. 30, 1881–Feb. 22, 1882
	Vol. 9 (26)	Feb. 25–Dec. 22, 1882
	Vol. 10 (27)	Dec. 23, 1882–Feb. 27, 1884
	Vol. 11 (28)	Feb. 29–Aug. 17, 1884

Registers of letters received:

	Vol. 1 (1)	Nov. 1, 1866–Oct. 1, 1869
	Vol. 2 (4)	Feb. 10–June 3, 1872
		Apr. 4–July 16, 1873
	Vol. 3 (5)	Jan. 3, 1881–Mar. 3, 1882
	Vol. 4 (6)	Mar. 1, 1882–Feb. 7, 1884
	Vol. 5 (8)	Feb. 8–Aug. 18, 1884

Letters received:

4		1864–73
5		1880–81
6		1882
7		1883–84

Roll	Description	Dates
Orders:		
8	General and special orders, Vol. 1 (33)	Oct. 19, 1863–Feb. 23, 1865
	Vol. 2 (30)	Feb. 23, 1865–Dec. 31, 1867
	Vol. 3 (32)	Jan. 1, 1868–Aug. 22, 1869
	Vol. 1 (31)	Aug. 23–Oct. 2, 1869
	General orders, Vol. 1 (31)	Oct. 2, 1869–Aug. 4, 1873
	Special orders, Vol. 1 (34)	Oct. 2, 1869–Dec. 27, 1871
	Vol. 2 (35)	Jan. 1, 1872–Nov. 30, 1873
	General field orders, Vol. 1 (37)	Oct. 26, 1880–Jan. 17, 1881
	Special field orders, Vol. 1 (37)	Oct. 26, 1880–Jan. 23, 1881
	General field orders, Vol. 1 (38)	Feb. 5–Nov. 13, 1881
	Special field orders, Vol. 1 (38)	Jan. 24–Mar. 19, 1881
	Field orders Vol. 1 (38)	Mar. 21–Nov. 23, 1881
	Vol. 1 (36)	Nov. 30, 1881–Jan. 18, 1882
	Orders Vol. 1 (36)	Jan. 19, 1882–Aug. 21, 1884
Other Records:		
	"Record of Events" at Fort Cummings, Vol. 1 (33)	Nov. 1, 1863–Nov. 9, 1864
	Reports of scouts Vol. 1 (48)	Nov. 2, 1880–Aug. 1, 1882
	Register of charges and specifications preferred in courts-martial Vol. 1 (n.n.)	Sept. 1870–May 1873
	Lists of guards and prisoners ("Guard Report Book") Vol. 1 (51)	Aug. 23, 1865–Mar. 1, 1866

Headquarters Records of Fort Dodge, Kansas, 1866–1882. M989. 25 rolls. DP.

This microfilm publication reproduces the headquarters records of Fort Dodge, Kansas. Fort Dodge was established as a result of the Plains campaigns of 1865. Although the Plains campaigns ended with the signing of the Treaty of the Little Arkansas on Oct. 17, 1865, Fort Dodge remained an important factor in the settlement of the West.

Roll 25 of this publication contains several small series relating to Indians in general and to scouts, marches, and expeditions against Indians in particular. It includes a bound volume of narrative reports, journals, and memorandums of scouts and marches; five tabular statements of campaigns, expeditions, and scouts made from Fort Dodge; two reports of detachments; and copies of four Indian treaties.

Roll	Description	Dates
Letters sent:		
1	Vol. 1(n.n.)	Feb. 13, 1866–Sept. 20, 1867
	Vol. 2(n.n.)	Sept. 27, 1867–Nov. 8, 1868
	Vol. 3(59)	Nov. 8, 1868–Oct. 16, 1871
	Vol. 4(60)	Oct. 17, 1871–July 7, 1874
	Vol. 5(61)	July 9, 1874–Apr. 3, 1875
2	Vol. 6(62)	Apr. 3, 1875–May 30, 1880
	Vol. 7(63)	June 1, 1880–Oct. 2, 1882
Endorsements:		
	Vol. 1(13)	Mar. 7, 1866–May 26, 1868
	Vol. 2(14)	May 26, 1868–May 17, 1869
3	Vol. 3(50)	May 22, 1869–Feb. 18, 1870
	Vol. 4(15)	Feb. 23, 1870–June 29, 1871
	Vol. 5(n.n.)	July 1, 1871–Mar. 27, 1875
	Vol. 6(17)	Mar. 28, 1875–July 10, 1877
	Vol. 7(18)	Nov. 22, 1880–Oct. 7, 1881
	Vol. 8(19)	Oct. 8, 1881–Sept. 27, 1882
Registers of letters received:		
4	Vol. 1(n.n)	July 1, 1871–Feb. 28, 1875
	Vol. 2(52)	Mar. 1, 1875–Dec. 26, 1878
	Vol. 3(54)	Dec. 27, 1878–Jan. 27, 1880
	Vol. 4(55)	Jan. 27, 1880–Nov. 15, 1880
	Vol. 5(56)	Nov. 16, 1880–Sept. 17, 1882
Letters, telegrams and orders received:		
5	Registered letters received	July 1871–Feb. 1875
6	"	Mar. 1875–Dec. 1876
7	"	1877–78
8	"	1879
9	"	1880 and Jan.–Sept. 1882
10	Unregistered letters received	Apr. 1865–Dec. 1866
11	"	1867
12	"	1868
13	"	1869
14	"	1870
15	"	1871–72
16	"	1873
17	"	1874
18	"	1875
19	"	1876–77
20	"	Jan. 1878–Sept. 1882
21	Orders and circulars received	Apr. 1865–Dec. 1867
22	"	1868–71
	Bound letters, telegrams, and orders received (94)	Jan. 1873–Sept. 1874
Orders and circulars:		
23	General orders and circulars Vol. 1(80)	Jan. 1, 1866–July 3, 1872
	Vol. 2(81)	July 8, 1872–Aug. 30, 1878
	Vol. 3(82)	Sept. 10, 1878–Mar. 5, 1881
	Special orders Vol. 1(n.n.)	Jan. 1, 1866–July 13, 1868
	Vol. 2(84)	July 16, 1868–Apr. 5, 1871
24	Vol. 3(85)	July 1, 1871–Apr. 25, 1873
	Vol. 4(86)	Apr. 28, 1873–Apr. 28, 1875
	Vol. 5(87)	Apr. 29, 1875–Dec. 26, 1879

Roll	Description	Dates
	Special orders and orders Vol. 6(88)	Jan. 1, 1880–Oct. 2, 1882

Records relating to Indians and to scouts and marches:

Roll	Description	Dates
25	Reports, journals, and memorandums of scouts and marches (93)	1873–79
	Tabular statements of campaigns, expeditions, and scouts	Dec. 1867–June 1869
	Reports of detachments	Aug. 20, 1868–Sept. 2, 1868
	Indian treaties	Oct. 14, 1865; Oct. 17, 1865; Oct. 18, 1865; July 19, 1866

Records relating to deserters and prisoners:

Roll	Description	Dates
	Monthly reports of persons in arrest or confinement	1870–73, 1875–82
	Returns of deserters undergoing sentence	July 1868–Dec. 1869
	Returns of deserters apprehended and received	Dec. 1868–Mar. 1869, July 1869, and Apr. 1870
	Lists of deserters in confinement	Mar.–June 1868
	Descriptive list of deserters from Company F, 10th U.S. Cavalry	Apr. 20–30, 1869

Reports and rolls:

Roll	Description	Dates
	Consolidated morning reports of troops (64)	Apr. 1866–Aug. 1867
	Muster rolls of field and staff	Jan.–Apr. and Oct.–Dec. 1868
	Consolidated tri-monthly report of troops	Mar. 10, 1866
	Report of officers and enlisted-men instructed in military signals	Apr. 1872
	Reports of schools	Mar.–Dec. 1879

Records of Fort Hays, Kansas (Army Post), 1866–1889. T713. 22 rolls.

Fort Hays, Kansas, was established on Oct. 18, 1865, to protect the employees of the Kansas Pacific Railroad Company from Indian attacks. First called Fort Fletcher, the War Department renamed the installation Fort Hays on Nov. 17, 1866, in honor of Brig. Gen. Alexander Hays. Fort Hays was abandoned on Nov. 8, 1889.

Roll	Date

Letters sent by post commander:

Roll	Date
1	Nov. 28, 1866–Dec. 27, 1873
2	Jan. 3, 1874–Feb. 18, 1883
3	Feb. 20, 1883–Dec. 13, 1886
4	Dec. 14, 1886–Nov. 4, 1889

Letters received at post headquarters:

Roll	Date
5	Jan. 1867–Sept. 1868
6	Oct. 1868–May 1870
7	June 1870–Aug. 1871
8	Sept. 1871–Dec. 1872
9	Jan. 1873–Dec. 1874
10	Jan. 1875–June 1876
11	July 1876–Sept. 1878
12	Oct. 1878–Oct. 1880
13	Nov. 1880–Jan. 1882
14	Feb. 1882–Feb. 1883
15	Mar. 1883–Dec. 1884
16	Jan.–Nov. 1885
17	Dec. 1885–June 1887
18	July 1887–Oct. 1888
19	Nov. 1888–Nov. 1889

Orders:

Roll	Date
20	Jan. 1, 1869–Dec. 30, 1873
21	Feb. 28, 1871–Mar. 8, 1889
22	Mar. 9, 1881–Nov. 8, 1889

Headquarters Records of Fort Scott, Kansas, 1869–1873. M1077. 2 rolls.

The Army set up and abandoned Fort Scott three times. The fort was first established in 1842 to guard the frontier against hostile Indians. The records in this microfilm publication, however, cover the third period, Sept. 1869–Apr. 1873. With troops already serving there in Sept. 1869, the post was reestablished in January 1870 as an independent post to provide military protection to the Missouri River, the Gulf Railroad, and the fort itself. Although headquartered at Fort Scott, the units making up the command were stationed in camps along the railroad's route. The military abandoned the fort for the third, and final, time on Apr. 16, 1873.

The records consist of letters sent, endorsements sent, a register of letters received, letters received, and general and special orders.

Roll	Description	Dates
1	Letters sent	
	Vol. 1 (1)	Sept. 30, 1869–Mar. 28, 1872
	Vol. 2 (2)	Apr. 6, 1872–Apr. 16, 1873
	Register of letters received	
	Vol. 1 (3)	Sept. 22, 1869–Feb. 20, 1871
	Letters received	Nov. 27, 1869–Apr. 14, 1873
	Endorsements sent	
2	Vol. 1 (4)	Sept. 23, 1869–Sept. 29, 1870
	Vol. 2 (5)	Sept. 30, 1870–Apr. 14, 1873
	General orders	
	Vol. 1 (8)	Sept. 9, 1869–Mar. 3, 1873
	Special orders	
	Vol. 1 (6)	Sept. 9, 1869–Dec. 30, 1871

Roll	Description	Dates
	Vol. 2 (7)	Jan. 2, 1872–Apr. 16, 1873

Headquarters Records of Fort Verde, Arizona Territory, 1869–1891. M1076. 11 rolls.

The establishment of Fort Verde was a direct result of an influx of settlers into the Verde River Valley in central Arizona during 1865. Originally called Camp Lincoln, the installation was renamed Camp Verde in Nov. 1868, the Fort Verde in Nov. 1878. During the 1870's, the camp served as an important base for operations against the Apache.

During 1881 and early 1882, the strength of the garrison was reduced in preparation for abandonment, but a renewal of Indian hostilities in southern Arizona during the summer of 1882 led to a restoration of the full garrison.

On July 28, 1884, the War Department transferred part of the military reservation to the Department of the Interior. Fort Verde was ordered abandoned on Apr. 10, 1890, and the last detachment left on Apr. 25, 1891. The military reservation was transferred to the Department of the Interior on Oct. 15, 1890, and opened to settlement by homesteaders in 1895.

Roll	Description	Dates
Letters and telegrams sent:		
1	Vol. 1 (7)	July 2, 1873–May 24, 1874
	Vol. 2 (8)	May 26, 1874–Aug. 3, 1875 (pt.)
	Vol. 3 (9)	Aug. 3, 1875 (pt.)–July 4, 1877
	Vol. 4 (n.n.)	July 6, 1877–July 9, 1879
	Vol. 5 (10)	July 11, 1879–Aug. 5, 1880
	Vol. 6 (11)	Aug. 1, 1880–Dec. 23, 1881
	Vol. 7 (12)	Dec. 30, 1881–Nov. 30, 1884
	Name index to Vol. 8 (n.n.)	June 8–Dec. 28, 1885
	Vol. 8 (n.n.)	Apr. 1–Dec. 28, 1885
	Name index to Vol. 9 (n.n.)	1886
	Name index to Vol. 10 (13)	1889
	Vol. 9 (n.n.)	Jan. 1, 1886–Apr. 29, 1888 (pt.)
	Vol. 10 (13)	Apr. 29, 1888 (pt.)–Dec. 31, 1889
	Name index to Vol. 11 (14)	Jan. 2–Apr. 15, 1890
	Vol. 11 (14)	Jan. 2, 1890–Mar. 18, 1891
Telegrams sent:		
	Vol. (38)	Feb. 5, 1879–May 28, 1881
Endorsements sent:		
2	Vol. 1 (264)	June 30, 1869–Nov. 14, 1872
	Vol. 2 (15)	Nov. 15, 1872–Nov. 26, 1873
	Vol. 3 (n.n.)	Jan. 1, 1875–Feb. 4, 1876
	Vol. 4 (16)	Jan. 29, 1876–Dec. 5, 1877 (pt.)
	Vol. 5 (17)	Dec. 5, 1877 (pt.)–Oct. 30, 1878
	Vol. 6 (18)	Nov. 1, 1878–Nov. 13, 1879 (pt.)
	Vol. 7 (19)	Nov. 13, 1879 (pt.)–Dec. 2, 1880
	Vol. 8 (20)	Dec. 3, 1880–Nov. 2, 1883
	Vol. 9 (21)	Nov. 6, 1883–Nov. 17, 1884
	Vol. 10 (22)	Nov. 11, 1884–Oct. 24, 1885
Registers of letters received:		
3	Vol. 1 (1)	Nov. 11, 1874–Jan. 11, 1877
	Vol. 2 (2)	Jan. 1, 1877–July 23, 1878
	Vol. 3 (3)	Nov. 26, 1878–May 3, 1882
	Vol. 4 (4)	Aug. 12, 1882–Sept. 26, 1883

Roll	Description	Dates
	Name index to Vol. 5 (n.n)	Apr. 1, 1885–Feb. 17, 1886
	Vol. 5 (n.n.)	Apr. 1, 1885–Feb. 17, 1886
	Name index to Vol. 6 (n.n.)	Jan. 4–Dec. 27, 1887, and Jan. 1–Nov. 15, 1888
	Vol. 6 (n.n.)	Jan. 1, 1886–Nov. 15, 1888
	Name index to Vol. 7 (5)	Nov. 17, 1888–Oct. 25, 1889 (pt.)
	Vol. 7 (5)	Nov. 17, 1888–Oct. 25, 1889 (pt.)
	Name index to Vol. 8 (6)	Oct. 25, 1889 (pt.)–Apr. 14, 1891
	Vol. 8 (6)	Oct. 25, 1889 (pt.)–Apr. 14, 1891
Letters and telegrams received:		
4		Dec. 1870–74
5		1875–76
6		1877–78
7		1879–80
8		1881–87 and Jan.–Feb. 1891
Issuances:		
9	Orders, general orders, post orders, and circulars	
	Vol. 1 (23)	Sept. 29, 1866–July 21, 1878, and July 30, 1884
	Special orders and orders	
	Vol. 2 (24)	Sept. 24, 1875–Nov. 6, 1877
	Vol. 3 (25)	Nov. 7, 1877–Feb. 10, 1879
	Vol. 4 (26)	Feb. 12–Dec. 20, 1879
	Vol. 5 (27)	Dec. 22, 1879–Dec. 13, 1880
	Vol. 6 (n.n.)	Dec. 18, 1880–Aug. 16, 1883
	Vol. 7 (28)	Aug. 17, 1883–Dec. 30, 1884
	Vol. 8 (29)	Jan. 1, 1886–Dec. 31, 1889
	Vol. 9 (30)	Jan. 1, 1890–Apr. 25, 1891
	Special orders and circulars	
	Vol. 1 (31)	Mar. 22, 1871–July 15, 1872
	Vol. 2 (32)	July 27, 1872–Nov. 22, 1873
	Special orders	
	Vol. 3 (n.n.)	Nov. 25, 1873–Sept. 1, 1875
10	Special orders received from Division of the Pacific	Oct. 1870–Mar. 1880
	Special orders received from Department of Arizona	Dec. 1868–Sept. 1883
	Orders received from miscellaneous commands	Aug. 1872–Aug. 1883
Miscellaneous records:		
11	Monthly returns of scouts made from Camp Verde	Jan. 1874–July 1878
	Monthly special reports of prisoners in confinement at the post	Jan. 1874–Apr. 1891

Roll	Description	Dates
	Monthly reports of civilian employees, means of transportation, rations, and arms and ammunition on hand	May 1885–Apr. 1890
	Monthly and bimonthly reports of schools at the post	Apr. 1879–May 1890
	Register of charges and specifications preferred in courts-martial	
	Vol. 1 (37)	Mar. 1873–Sept. 1874
	Vol. (38)	Mar. 1877–Nov. 1878
	Vol. 2 (39)	July–Nov. 1885
	Chronology of significant events occurring at Camp Verde	
	Vol. (40)	Aug. 27, 1869–Nov. 29, 1871

Records of Fort Stockton, Texas, 1867–1886. M1189. 8 rolls. DP.

The Army first occupied Fort Stockton, Texas, in Dec. 1858. The site was on the "Great Comanche War Trail," the path taken by Indians on their annual raid across Texas into Mexico. The fort was also next to a major watering spot, Comanche Springs, and was on the mail and stage route between El Paso and San Antonio. This road, vital to the settlement of west Texas, was an important mail route and was used heavily by stage lines and travelers to and from California. The Army abandoned the post in 1861 and the Confederacy briefly held the post during the Civil War.

This publication reproduces most of the surviving records of the post-Civil War years. The records include many reports concerning conflicts with the Indians, especially in the 1860's. Some reports concern skirmishes, and letters from detachment commanders describe expeditions across deserts and mountains in search of raiding parties and their place of refuge.

Roll	Description	Dates
	Letters and telegrams sent:	
1	Letters sent	
	Vol. 1	July 7, 1867–Oct. 30, 1869
	Vol. 2	Nov. 1, 1869–May 2, 1873
	Vol. 3	May 2, 1873–Mar. 12, 1876
	Letters and telegrams sent	
	Vol. 4	Mar. 13, 1876–Dec. 31, 1878
	Vol. 5	June 11–Dec. 29, 1880
	Letters sent	
	Vol. 6	Jan. 3, 1881–Oct. 11, 1882
	Vol. 7	Jan. 1, 1885–June 27, 1886
	Telegrams sent	
	Vol. 8,	Dec. 3, 1880–May 29, 1885

Roll	Description	Dates
	Letters and telegrams received:	
2		Feb. 24, 1867–Dec. 27, 1874
3		Jan. 13, 1875–June 30, 1879
4		July 1, 1879–Nov. 25, 1884
5	Unregistered telegrams received	Jan. 1, 1881–Dec. 29, 1884
	Index and register of letters and telegrams received	Jan. 1, 1885–June 16, 1886
	Letters and telegrams received	Jan. 20, 1885–June 23, 1886
	Endorsements sent:	
6	Vol. 1	July 31, 1867–June 22, 1870
	Vol. 2	June 25, 1870–Sept. 26, 1871
	Vol. 3	Oct. 3, 1871–Oct. 20, 1873
	Vol. 4	Oct. 20, 1873–Dec. 28, 1875
	Vol. 5	Dec. 28, 1875–June 28, 1877
7	Vol. 6	June 30, 1877–Dec. 31, 1878
	Vol. 7	Jan. 1, 1879–Dec. 24, 1879
	Vol. 8	Dec. 24, 1879–Sept. 9, 1880
	Vol. 9	Sept. 10, 1880–Apr. 11, 1881
	Vol. 10	Apr. 13, 1881–May 17, 1882
8	Vol. 11	May 18, 1882–Aug. 10, 1884
	Vol. 12	Aug. 11, 1884–June 16, 1886
	Issuances:	
	Circulars	Jan. 7, 1881–Aug. 30, 1882
	Orders	
	Vol. 1	Jan. 2, 1882–Aug. 22, 1883
	Vol. 2	Aug. 24, 1883–Sept. 30, 1885
	Vol. 3	Oct. 3, 1885–June 26, 1886
	Records of field operations	Apr. 1885–Mar. 1886
	Tabular statements of scouts and expeditions	July 1868–Mar. 1881
	Journal of marches, scouts, and expeditions	Sept. 1873–Dec. 1879

Records of the Office of the Secretary of War (Record Group 107)

The Department of War was created by an act of August 7, 1789, (1 Stat. 49) that made the Secretary of War responsible for all military and naval matters, including Indian affairs. By 1824, an Office of Indian Affairs was established within the Department, but in 1849 the Office was transferred to the Department of the Interior.

Registers of Letters Received by the Office of the Secretary of War, Main Series, 1800–1870. M22. 134 rolls.

According to the recordkeeping practices in the nineteenth century, registers were maintained as a permanent record of the receipt and disposition of letters. They also helped locate letters that were arranged to correspond with the entries in the registers.

The registers include cross-reference entries that show the date the letter was received, the name(s) of the person(s) or subject(s) of primary concern in the letter, and the file number under which the letter is entered. The early cross-references relate almost exclusively to names, but by the time of the Civil War numerous references to subjects appear, such as "Galveston, Recapture of," and "Creek File." Cross-reference entries are not numbered.

The rolls in this microfilm publication are organized chronologically. This publication serves as a finding aid to the records filmed in M221 below.

Letters Received by the Secretary of War, Main Series, 1801–1870. M221. 317 rolls. DP.

The letters and enclosures reproduced in this publication were received from officials of subordinate bureaus of the War Department, officials of other executive departments, Army officers and civilian agents in the field, governors of States and Territories, the President, Members of Congress, and private individuals. They relate to a variety of topics, including Indian affairs.

This microfilm publication reproduces unbound letters, with their enclosures, that were received by the Secretary of War, 1801–70. These letters are filed by date blocks, thereunder by the file number assigned when they were entered in the register.

Letters Received by the Secretary of War, Unregistered Series, 1789–1861. M222. 34 rolls. DP.

This microfilm publication reproduces unbound letters, with their enclosures, that were received by the Secretary of War, 1801–70. These letters are filed by date blocks, The letters are arranged by year and thereunder alphabetically, most by the initial letters of the surname or office of the writer, but a few by the initial letter of the subject.

The letters and enclosures reproduced in this publication were received from all sources, and relate to a variety of topics, including Indian affairs.

Letters Sent by the Secretary of War Relating to Military Affairs, 1800–1889. M6. 110 rolls.

This microfilm publication reproduces bound volumes of record copies of letters sent by the Secretary of War, 1800–1889. Although a separate series "Letters Sent, Indian Affairs, 1800–1824" (M15) of letters sent contains most of the letters sent regarding Indian affairs, many letters on that subject were recorded in this general series, not in the specialized series. After 1824, all letters relating to Indian affairs were recorded in this general series. The letters are arranged chronologically and deal with many topics in addition to Indian affairs.

Roll	Volume	Inclusive Dates
1	1	Nov. 12, 1800–June 21, 1803
2	2	June 21, 1803–Apr. 30, 1806
3	3	May 1, 1806–Dec. 31, 1808

Roll	Volume:	Inclusive Dates
4	4	Dec. 15, 1808–Nov. 12, 1810
5	5	Nov. 13, 1810–June 30, 1812
6	6	July 1, 1812–June 29, 1813
7	7	July 1, 1813–Dec. 20, 1814
8	8	Dec. 22, 1814–Apr. 29, 1816
9	9	May 2, 1816–Jan. 31, 1818
10	10	Feb. 2, 1818–Feb. 19, 1820
11	11	Feb. 21, 1820–Oct. 9, 1823
12	12	Oct. 13, 1823–Aug. 10, 1830
13	13	Aug. 7, 1830–Dec. 31, 1833
14	14	Jan. 2, 1834–Jan. 18, 1836
15	15	Jan. 19–May 25, 1836
16	16	May 25–Dec. 14, 1836
17	17	Dec. 15, 1836–Sept. 30, 1837
18	18	Oct. 2, 1837–Mar. 21, 1838
19	19	Mar. 20–Nov. 30, 1838
20	20	Dec. 1, 1838–May 31, 1839
21	21	June 1, 1839–Feb. 29, 1840
22	22	Mar. 2–Sept. 26, 1840
23	23	Sept. 28, 1840–June 30, 1841
24	24	July 1, 1841–Sept. 30, 1842
25	25	Oct. 3, 1842–Apr. 29, 1845
26	26	May 1, 1845–Oct. 7, 1846
27	27	Oct. 8, 1846–Aug. 13, 1847
28	28	Aug. 17, 1847–Dec. 29, 1848
29	29	Jan. 2–Dec. 31, 1849
30	30	Jan. 1–Dec. 31, 1850
31	31	Jan. 1–Sept. 29, 1851
32	32	Oct. 1, 1851–Apr. 30, 1852
33	33	May 1–Nov. 30, 1852
34	34	Dec. 1, 1852–Sept. 30, 1853
35	35	Oct. 1, 1853–June 30, 1854
36	36	July 1, 1854–Apr. 28, 1855
37	37	May 1, 1855–Mar. 31, 1856
38	38	Mar. 31, 1856–Feb. 28, 1857
39	39	Mar. 3–Dec. 30, 1857
40	40	Jan. 4–Oct. 30, 1858
41	41	Nov. 1, 1858–Sept. 30, 1859
42	42	Oct. 1, 1859–Oct. 30, 1860
43	43	Nov. 1, 1860–June 29, 1861
44	44	Apr. 10–June 30, 1861
45	45	July 1–Aug. 31, 1861
46	46	Sept. 2–Oct. 31, 1861
47	47–48	Nov. 1, 1861–Apr. 5, 1862
48	49A–49B	Apr. 3–June 22, 1862
49	50A–50B	June 23–Sept. 20, 1862
50	51A–51B	Sept. 20, 1862–Mar. 7, 1863
51	52–52A	Mar. 9–Aug. 17, 1863
52	53A–53B	Aug. 15, 1863–Jan. 14, 1864
53	54A–54B	Jan. 5–Mar. 12, 1864
54	55A–55B	Mar. 3–May 15, 1864
55	56A–56B	May 12–Aug. 20, 1864
56	57A–57B	Aug. 22–Dec. 15, 1864
57	58A–58B	Dec. 16, 1864–May 13, 1865
58	59–60	May 13, 1865–Apr. 25, 1867
59	61–62	Apr. 26, 1867–July 31, 1869
60	63–64	July 31, 1869–Dec. 16, 1870
61	65–66	Jan. 3–July 11, 1871
62	67	July 11–Dec. 30, 1871
63	68–69	Jan. 2–July 1, 1872
64	70–71	Apr. 29–Dec. 31, 1872
65	72	Jan. 2–Dec. 31, 1873
66	73	Jan. 2–Dec. 31, 1873
67	74	Jan. 2–Dec. 28, 1874

Roll	Volume	Inclusive Dates
68	75	Jan. 2–Oct. 20, 1874
69	76	Sept. 22–Dec. 31, 1874
70	77	Jan. 4–Dec. 31, 1875
71	78	Jan. 2–Dec. 31, 1875
72	79	Jan. 1–Dec. 30, 1876
73	80	Jan. 5–Dec. 30, 1876
74	81	Jan. 2–Dec. 31, 1877
75	82	Jan. 2–Dec. 31, 1877
76	83	Jan. 2–Dec. 31, 1878
77	84	Jan. 2–Dec. 31, 1878
78	85	Jan. 2–Dec. 31, 1879
79	86	Jan. 2–Dec. 31, 1879
80	87–88	Jan. 2–Dec. 31, 1880
81	89–90	Jan. 2–Dec. 31, 1880
82	91–92	Jan. 3–Sept. 7, 1881
83	93–94	Sept. 8–Dec. 31, 1881
84	95–96	Jan. 3–May 19, 1882
85	97–98	Apr. 21–Oct. 20, 1882
86	99–100	Sept. 27–Dec. 30, 1882
87	101–102	Jan. 2–May 26, 1883
88	103–104	May 14–Dec. 31, 1883
89	105	Jan. 2–May 31, 1884
90	106	Jan. 2–May 28, 1884
91	107 and 107(cont.)	May 28–Dec. 31, 1884
92	108	May 28–Dec. 30, 1884
93	109	Jan. 2–July 13, 1885
94	110	Jan. 2–July 15, 1885
95	111–112	July 13–Dec. 31, 1885
96	113	Jan. 2–June 2, 1886
97	114	Jan. 2–June 8, 1886
98	115	June 1–Dec. 31, 1886
99	116	June 3–Dec. 31, 1886
100	117	Jan. 3–July 9, 1887
101	118	Jan. 3–July 8, 1887
102	119	July 9–Dec. 31, 1887
103	120	July 8–Dec. 31, 1887
104	121	Jan. 3–May 3, 1888
105	122	Jan. 3–May 4, 1888
106	123	May 3–Dec. 31, 1888
107	124	May 5–Dec. 31, 1888
108	125	Jan. 2–Sept. 2, 1889
109	126	Jan. 2–Sept. 30, 1889
110	127–128	Sept. 16–Dec. 31, 1889

Correspondence of the War Department Relating to Indian Affairs, Military Pensions, and Fortifications, 1791–1797. M1062. 1 roll.

Records of Miscellaneous Military Establishments

Records of the Office of the Judge Advocate General (Army) (Record Group 153)

Registers of the Records of the Proceedings of the U.S. Army General Courts-Martial, 1809–1890. M1105. 8 rolls. DP.

This microfilm publication reproduces 17 volumes of the records of the proceedings of the U.S. Army general courts-martial, 1809–90.

A general court-martial is the highest military tribunal convened to try violations of military law. Also registered in these volumes are records of the proceedings of courts of inquiry and of military commissions. Courts of inquiry are investigative bodies without power to impose punishment. Military commissions are special courts established under martial law for the investigation and trial of private citizens.

Indians who served in the Volunteer or Regular Army of the United States were subject to trial by court-martial, as were all other soliders. Indians who did not serve in the Army were also, on occasion, tried in military courts. In addition, white soldiers accused of misconduct involving Indians were subject to trial by court-martial.

Occasionally, Army officers involved in the peacetime administration of Indian affairs found their policies subject to investigation by military courts and commissions. Subjects investigated included the issuance of cattle and other goods under the auspices of the Office of Indian Affairs, the trial of an Indian by a military court, the attitude of Indians toward the military officers, and the selection of Indian children to attend the school at Carlisle, Pennsylvania.

Roll	Dates
1	1809–27
	1828
	1829–31
	1831–34
	1834–40
	1841–44
	1844–47
	1848–49
	1849–50
2	1851–58
	1859–62
	1862–63
	1859–62
	1862–63
3	1862–65
4	1862–66
5	1862–65
6	1862–68

Index to Publication Numbers

Instructions for Ordering Microfilm Publications

Positive copies of microfilm may be purchased at prices shown in this catalog or quoted by the Publications Sales Branch. Single rolls may be purchased separately. Prices are subject to change without advance public notice. The price includes postage or shipping on orders sent to domestic addresses (within the continental United States) at the fourth-class library rate. If the customer requests that microfilm be sent to a foreign address (including Canada or Mexico), or requests a special service to a domestic address (United Parcel Service or air mail), the order is subject to a shipping fee in addition to the cost of the microfilm.

The following special shipping fees are computed as a percentage of the cost of the microfilm order:

	Surface	Airmail
Domestic (UPS)	2%	5%
Foreign	5%	15%

Parcel post insurance is available to many foreign countries for surface mail and airmail; however, the maximum amount varies from country to country. This service is available when requested by the customer and the following fees apply:

Liability	Fee
$ 0.01 to $20.00	$0.85
20.01 to 50.00	1.10
50.01 to 100.00	1.65
100.01 to 200.00	2.35
200.01 to 300.00	3.85
300.01 to 400.00	5.10

Orders should be submitted on NATF Form 36, Microfilm Order (copies of which appear at the end of this catalog), or on institutional or commercial purchase order forms. Orders can be handled more quickly when they include the correct microfilm publication number(s), roll number(s), and price(s). Titles and dates of publications are not needed. Additional order forms will be sent on request.

Payment must accompany each order and should be in the form of a check or money order; cash payments are discouraged. Orders may also be charged to VISA or MASTERCARD accounts. Payments from outside the United States should be made by international money order, payable in U.S. dollars, or a check drawn on a U.S. bank. Make checks or money orders payable to National Archives Trust Fund (NEPS) and mail to Cashier (NJC), National Archives Trust Fund Board, Washington, DC 20408.

State and local government agencies, educational institutions, and businesses may purchase microfilm on an accounts-receivable basis but must submit purchase orders with their order forms unless other arrangements are made.

The National Archives will replace any film that has been processed improperly in our laboratory. Purchasers are responsible for checking immediately upon receiving the microfilm order to see that there are no laboratory errors, that they have received the correct items, that the order is complete, and that there has been no damage in shipping. The purchasers must notify the Publications Sales Branch of any problems within 60 days. Purchasers may not return microfilm orders without written permission from the Publication Sales Branch.

ORDER BLANKS CORRECTLY FILLED IN HELP TO SPEED PROCESSING OF YOUR ORDER

Microfilm publication numbers (preceded by an "M" or "T") are assigned to each microfilm publication. Please enter microfilm publication number and roll number in the proper column. As we accept orders for individual rolls as well as for complete microfilm publications, we must know which rolls you wish to purchase.

The microfilm pricing policy is described on page ix of this catalog.

Sample of Correctly Completed Form

M, T, or A NUMBER	ROLL NUMBER	PRICE
T624	1138	$17
T1270	89	$17

Additional order forms are available upon request

MICROFILM ORDER (Prices subject to change)		M, T, or A NUMBER	ROLL NUMBER	PRICE
TO	Cashier National Archives Trust Fund Board Washington, DC 20408			
Please send me the microfilm listed in this order. Enclosed is ☐ CHECK ☐ MONEY ORDER for $_____ or charge my ☐ VISA ☐ MASTER CHARGE				
ACCOUNT NUMBER EXPIRATION DATE				
SIGNATURE				
FROM	Name			
	Address (Number and street)			
	City, State and ZIP Code		**TOTAL PRICE**	

NATIONAL ARCHIVES TRUST FUND BOARD

NATF Form 36 (8-79)

Due to increased printing and postage costs, the National Archives Trust Fund Board is charging individuals $2.00 for microfilm catalogs. The catalogs are not produced at taxpayer expense and the $2.00 will be used to defray costs so that we can publish more microfilm subject-area catalogs. Catalogs will continue to be issued free of charge to libraries, genealogical societies, and other organizations.

$2.00 Credit

Clip and enclose this coupon for **$2.00** toward the purchase of one or more rolls of microfilm.

(Offer applies only to individual purchasers, not organizations)

This coupon may not be duplicated

ORDER BLANKS CORRECTLY FILLED IN HELP TO SPEED PROCESSING OF YOUR ORDER

Microfilm publication numbers (preceded by an "M" or "T") are assigned to each microfilm publication. Please enter microfilm publication number and roll number in the proper column. As we accept orders for individual rolls as well as for complete microfilm publications, we must know which rolls you wish to purchase.

The microfilm pricing policy is described on page ix of this catalog.

Sample of Correctly Completed Form

M, T, or A NUMBER	ROLL NUMBER	PRICE
T624	1138	$17
T1270	89	$17

Additional order forms are available upon request

MICROFILM ORDER *(Prices subject to change)*		M, T, or A NUMBER	ROLL NUMBER	PRICE
TO	Cashier National Archives Trust Fund Board Washington, DC 20408			
Please send me the microfilm listed in this order. Enclosed is □ CHECK □ MONEY ORDER for $ _____ or charge my □ VISA □ MASTER CHARGE				
ACCOUNT NUMBER EXPIRATION DATE				
SIGNATURE				
FROM	Name			
	Address (Number and street)			
	City, State and ZIP Code		**TOTAL PRICE**	

NATIONAL ARCHIVES TRUST FUND BOARD   NATF Form 36 (8-79)

MICROFILM ORDER *(Prices subject to change)*		M, T, or A NUMBER	ROLL NUMBER	PRICE
TO	Cashier National Archives Trust Fund Board Washington, DC 20408			
Please send me the microfilm listed in this order. Enclosed is □ CHECK □ MONEY ORDER for $ _____ or charge my □ VISA □ MASTER CHARGE				
ACCOUNT NUMBER EXPIRATION DATE				
SIGNATURE				
FROM	Name			
	Address (Number and street)			
	City, State and ZIP Code		**TOTAL PRICE**	

NATIONAL ARCHIVES TRUST FUND BOARD   NATF Form 36 (8-79)

ORDER BLANKS CORRECTLY FILLED IN HELP TO SPEED PROCESSING OF YOUR ORDER

Microfilm publication numbers (preceded by an "M" or "T") are assigned to each microfilm publication. Please enter microfilm publication number and roll number in the proper column. As we accept orders for individual rolls as well as for complete microfilm publications, we must know which rolls you wish to purchase.

The microfilm pricing policy is described on page ix of this catalog.

Sample of Correctly Completed Form

M, T, or A NUMBER	ROLL NUMBER	PRICE
T624	1138	$17
T1270	89	$17

Additional order forms are available upon request

MICROFILM ORDER (Prices subject to change)		M, T, or A NUMBER	ROLL NUMBER	PRICE
TO	Cashier National Archives Trust Fund Board Washington, DC 20408			
Please send me the microfilm listed in this order. Enclosed is ☐ CHECK ☐ MONEY ORDER for $ _____ or charge my ☐ VISA ☐ MASTER CHARGE				
ACCOUNT NUMBER EXPIRATION DATE				
SIGNATURE				
FROM	Name			
	Address (Number and street)			
	City, State and ZIP Code		**TOTAL PRICE**	

NATIONAL ARCHIVES TRUST FUND BOARD

NATF Form 36 (8-79)

MICROFILM ORDER (Prices subject to change)		M, T, or A NUMBER	ROLL NUMBER	PRICE
TO	Cashier National Archives Trust Fund Board Washington, DC 20408			
Please send me the microfilm listed in this order. Enclosed is ☐ CHECK ☐ MONEY ORDER for $ _____ or charge my ☐ VISA ☐ MASTER CHARGE				
ACCOUNT NUMBER EXPIRATION DATE				
SIGNATURE				
FROM	Name			
	Address (Number and street)			
	City, State and ZIP Code		**TOTAL PRICE**	

NATIONAL ARCHIVES TRUST FUND BOARD

NATF Form 36 (8-79)

ORDER BLANKS CORRECTLY FILLED IN HELP TO SPEED PROCESSING OF YOUR ORDER

Microfilm publication numbers (preceded by an "M" or "T") are assigned to each microfilm publication. Please enter microfilm publication number and roll number in the proper column. As we accept orders for individual rolls as well as for complete microfilm publications, we must know which rolls you wish to purchase.

The microfilm pricing policy is described on page ix of this catalog.

Sample of Correctly Completed Form

M, T, or A NUMBER	ROLL NUMBER	PRICE
T624	1138	$17
T1270	89	$17

Additional order forms are available upon request

MICROFILM ORDER *(Prices subject to change)*		M, T, or A NUMBER	ROLL NUMBER	PRICE
TO	Cashier National Archives Trust Fund Board Washington, DC 20408			
Please send me the microfilm listed in this order. Enclosed is ☐ CHECK ☐ MONEY ORDER for $ _____ or charge my ☐ VISA ☐ MASTER CHARGE				
ACCOUNT NUMBER EXPIRATION DATE				
SIGNATURE				
FROM	Name			
	Address (Number and street)			
	City, State and ZIP Code		**TOTAL PRICE**	

NATIONAL ARCHIVES TRUST FUND BOARD   NATF Form 36 (8-79)

MICROFILM ORDER *(Prices subject to change)*		M, T, or A NUMBER	ROLL NUMBER	PRICE
TO	Cashier National Archives Trust Fund Board Washington, DC 20408			
Please send me the microfilm listed in this order. Enclosed is ☐ CHECK ☐ MONEY ORDER for $ _____ or charge my ☐ VISA ☐ MASTER CHARGE				
ACCOUNT NUMBER EXPIRATION DATE				
SIGNATURE				
FROM	Name			
	Address (Number and street)			
	City, State and ZIP Code		**TOTAL PRICE**	

NATIONAL ARCHIVES TRUST FUND BOARD   NATF Form 36 (8-79)